Black and Indigenous

Black and Indigenous

*Garifuna Activism and Consumer Culture
in Honduras*

Mark Anderson

University of Minnesota Press

Minneapolis

London

Published by the University of Minnesota Press
111 Third Avenue South, Suite 290
Minneapolis, MN 55401-2520
http://www.upress.umn.edu

Library of Congress Cataloging-in-Publication Data

Anderson, Mark David.
 Black and indigenous : Garifuna activism and consumer culture in Honduras / Mark Anderson.
   p. cm.
 Includes bibliographical references and index.
 ISBN 978-0-8166-6101-5 (hc : alk. paper) — ISBN 978-0-8166-6102-2 (pb : alk. paper)
  1. Garifuna (Caribbean people)—Honduras—Ethnic identity.   2. Garifuna (Caribbean people)—Honduras—Social conditions.   3. Honduras—Race relations.
 I. Title.
 F1505.2.C3A53 2009
 305.89'979207283—dc22

                                                                    2009034190

Printed in the United States of America on acid-free paper

The University of Minnesota is an equal-opportunity educator and employer.

16 15 14 13 12   10 9 8 7 6 5 4 3

Contents

Acronyms

CABO	Central American Black Organization
CADEAH	Consejo Asesor Hondureño para el Desarrollo de las Etnias Autóctonas de Honduras (Honduran Advisory Council for the Development of Autochthonous Ethnic Groups)
CAFTA	Central American Free Trade Agreement
CCARC	Caribbean Central American Research Council
CNOH	Coordinadora de Organizaciones Negras de Honduras (National Coordinator of Black Organizations)
COHPI	Consejo Hondureño de Pueblos Indígenas (Honduran Council of Indigenous Promotion)
CONPAH	Confederación de Pueblos Autóctonos de Honduras (Confederation of Autochthonous Peoples of Honduras)
COPINH	Consejo Cívico de Organizaciones Populares e Indígenas de Honduras (Civil Council of Popular and Indigenous Organizations of Honduras)
FETRIXY	Federación de Tribus Xicaques de Yoro (Federation of the Xicaque Tribes of Yoro)
FTA	Free Trade Agreement
IDB	Inter-American Development Bank
IHAH	Instituto Hondureño de Antropología e Historia (Honduran Institute of Anthropology and History)
IIH	Instituto Indigenista Hondureño (Honduran Indigenous Institute)
ILO	International Labor Organization
IMF	International Monetary Fund
INA	Instituto Nacional Agraria (National Agrarian Institute)
MASTA	Moskitia Asla Takanka
NAFTA	North American Free Trade Agreement
NGO	Nongovernmental organization
ODECO	Organización de Desarrollo Étnico Comunitario (Organization for Ethnic Communitarian Development)

OFRANEH	Organizacíon Fraternal Negra Hondureña (Black Fraternal Organization of Honduras)
ONILH	Organización Nacional Indígena Lenca de Honduras (The National Organization of Indigenous Lencas of Honduras)
PAPIN	Programa de Apoya a los Pueblos Indígenas y Negros de Honduras (Program to Support Indigenous and Black Communities of Honduras)
PATH	Proyecto de of Honduras Administración de Tierras de Honduras (Land Administration Project of Honduras)
PDRH	Partido Democrático Revolucionario de Honduras (Honduran Revolutionary Democratic Party)
PUD	Partido Unificación Democrática (Democratic Unification Party)
SAVE	Scientific, Academic, Volunteer, and Educational Tourism
SECPLAN	Secretaría de Planificación, Coordinación y Presupuesto (Secretary of Planning)
SFCO	The Standard Fruit Company
UAPIN	Unidad de Apoyo a los Pueblos Indígenas y Negros (Indigenous and Black Peoples Support Unit)
UFCO	The United Fruit Company
UNIA	Universal Negro Improvement Association
USAID	United States Agency for International Development

Introduction

The earliest reference to the word "indigenous" recorded in the *Oxford English Dictionary* juxtaposes indigeneity with blackness. In the seventeenth century, Sir Thomas Browne asserted, "Although in many parts thereof there be at present swarms of Negroes serving under the Spaniard, yet were they all transported from Africa, since the discovery of Columbus; and are not indigenous or proper natives of America."

The statement comes from a chapter called "Of the Blackness of Negroes," where Browne attempts to refute the idea that the skin color of Negroes resulted from equatorial geographies (Browne, 370–78). His assertion that Negroes were not indigenous to the Americas was designed to demonstrate that peoples born at similar latitudes did not share the same physical features and thus it was not the sun but ancestry that explained the "blackness of Negroes." Perhaps it is no small irony that an early use of "indigenous" in English marked a clear distinction between proper natives and enslaved Africans in the Americas. Although Browne did not name the indigenous natives of the Americas as Indians, he assumed that the arrival of Columbus marked the moment of difference between proper natives (who Columbus infamously named *indios*) and other subjects. But what if we question that assumption and look anew at the categories of Negro and Indian, blackness and indigeneity? What investments go into the making and marking of these distinctions as oppositions, such that New World Blacks can never be indigenous? Or can they?

On the occasion of the 500th anniversary of the European "encounter" with the Americas, anthropologist Michael Taussig suggests that the colonial opposition between the figures of the Black and the Indian endures:

> For while the Indian has been recruited to the task of carrying
> the originary America and thus the seed of the great American
> story (perhaps no time more than now, when there are burgeoning
> Indian movements and worldwide concern for the rain forest), the
> *Negro* has been recruited as the carrier of disturbance and frag-

mentation in that great American story, even threatening it with destruction. (1996, 323–34)

For Taussig, the figure of the Black sits uneasily within a white–Indian contrast, disrupting the great American story of discovery as a subject out of place, out of culture, and out of history. Lest we take his words to imply that Indians occupy a privileged position, we should remember that the conceptual location of Indians as original Americans has never implied either full inclusion within structures of power or genuine autonomy from them. Those rendered as Blacks, Indians, and related categories (e.g., *mulato, zambo*) have been subject to similar forms of discrimination and exploitation.

In the period since Taussig gave his address, Latin America has witnessed a marked increase in Black activism, articulated in complex ways with indigenous movements. Black activists insisted that they be included in the transnational protest movements surrounding the quincentennial commemoration of 1492, eventually named the "Continental Campaign for Indian, Black and Popular Resistance" (Hale 1994). In Honduras, the Organización de Desarrollo Étnico Comunitario (ODECO, the Garifuna Organization for Ethnic Communitarian Development) used that slogan in demonstrations held on the Honduran equivalent of Columbus Day (known as the "Day of the Race"), protesting the invisibility and marginalization of Afro-Hondurans. Another key Garifuna organization, the Organización Fraternal Negra Hondureña (OFRANEH, the Black Fraternal Organization of Honduras) had already helped create an unprecedented confederation of organizations representing indigenous and Black peoples within a single paradigm of struggle. But by the end of the decade, that confederation and the interethnic, interracial unity it represented developed serious rifts (Anderson 2007). Meanwhile, ODECO increasingly distanced itself from indigenous struggle in favor of highlighting the particular problems of Afro-descendants. As elsewhere in Latin America, blackness was no longer invisible, but what relation would it bear with indigeneity and Indians?

Garifuna are a group of people who were deported from the Caribbean island of St. Vincent to Central America in 1797. During the nineteenth century, they established coastal settlements in areas that came under control of the present nation-states of Belize, Guatemala, Nicaragua, and Honduras, where the largest population resides. They played a crucial role in regional economies, combining subsistence production (agriculture and fishing) with wage labor while carving out spheres of limited cultural autonomy based in beachfront communities. Since their arrival in Honduras, Garifuna have been interpellated by others as racially Black and subject to forms of oppression based on their perceived racial and cultural difference from whites and the majority population, today known as *mestizos*. The position of Garifuna within Honduras has changed over time. In the early twentieth century, Garifuna became incorporated into the fruit-based enclave economy dominated by North American banana companies. In the 1940s, Garifuna began to migrate to the United States, establishing the basis for transnational networks that are constitutive features of Garifuna society and identity formation today (Gonzalez 1988; England 2006). At the end of the century, they were engaged in a variety of forms of struggle that creatively engaged the opposition between indigeneity and blackness.

That Garifuna, and this study, would dwell over questions of indigeneity and blackness and Indian and Black relations has multiple origins, from contemporary political economies of difference to the history of the group on St. Vincent. The outlines of that history are well known.[1] During the sixteenth and seventeenth centuries, St. Vincent was one of the last strongholds of the people the Spanish called "*caribes*" (a corruption of the indigenous word *Callínago*),[2] the source of the English terms Carib, Caribbean, and cannibal. African slaves came to the island via shipwrecks, maroonage, and Carib raids on European settlements. Out of the relations between Caribs and Africans emerged a people who the British called Black Caribs, today known as Garifuna. Garifuna retained a high degree of independence from colonial control until the British acquired formal treaty rights (in European eyes) to St. Vincent from the French in 1763. French planters, traders, and missionaries had become established on part of the island in the early 1700s, but Garifuna managed to retain considerable political and territorial autonomy while interacting extensively with the French and the wider Caribbean world. British planters sought to expand sugar production on St. Vincent, and the contest for land and authority that ensued led to a series of conflicts between the British and Garifuna. In 1773, Garifuna were forced to acknowledge British rule, but a French–Garifuna alliance gained control of the island between 1779 and 1783, when the British reacquired sovereignty. Garifuna rose once more in the mid-1790s, again allying with the French. The British defeated the resistance after a bloody conflict. Colonial officials and planters successfully lobbied the British imperial government to remove the "Black Caribs," portraying them as Africans who had usurped the customs and identity of "pure" Indians, labeled "Red Caribs" or "Yellow Caribs." They thus used blackness as a weapon to deny Garifuna native status on the island, deporting them to Spanish territory (Hulme 1986; Anderson 1997). Of the 4,338 Garifuna captured in 1796, only 2,026 survived their internment and journey to arrive in Central America in 1797.[3]

The British classified Caribs according to color, removing those identified as "Black" and leaving behind those deemed "Yellow" (Gonzalez 1988, 23). This action exemplifies how racial distinctions can divide people into sojourners and natives, such that even subjects who disrupt the binaries of African and native and Black and Indian would suffer their dualisms. However, it is not my intention to tell the Garifuna story today as a simple reflection of what happened on St. Vincent. Scholars, in fact, know little about the initial conditions under which the "mixture" of diverse peoples occurred, and, even if we did, it would tell us little about how Garifuna conceptualize, annunciate, and perform a sense of identity via categories such as "Black," "indigenous," or "Indian" in the present. This work strives to produce an account of how Garifuna (from activists involved in projects of ethnic mobilization to people unaffiliated with organizations within a community where I conducted research) produce representations of self and other and race and culture.

The histories told of Garifuna on St. Vincent require interpretation oriented by present modes of attention and attachment. An encounter between a young man nicknamed Chino and an outsider offering an authoritative interpretation of Garifuna history and culture is instructive. One night in 1997, during a stint of my fieldwork in the community of Sambo Creek, Chino and I went to the local hotel to drink a beer. Then in his midtwenties, Chino worked a variety of jobs. He had recently returned from the city of San Pedro Sula, where he had reupholstered a bus interior for a cousin. As we sat down, Danny, an unkempt, expatriate Cuban American and more or less permanent occupant of the hotel, sauntered over and ruined any possibility of peaceful conversation. Whenever he saw me, Danny accused me of working for the Central Intelligence Agency, but tonight he wanted my advice on securing benefits from the U.S. government for his military service. Perhaps to show good faith in my claims of being an anthropologist, he went to his room to find a book he said "told everything about the Garifuna." Danny returned with a photocopy of the first major monograph on the Garifuna, Douglas Taylor's *The Black Caribs of British Honduras* (1951).

I had read the ethnography and was familiar with the author's contention that despite their "Negro" phenotype, the Black Caribs were bearers of a predominately "Amerindian" culture.

> The Black Carib are, in the main, descendants of African Negroes brought to the West Indies as slaves, but who escaped from their

European masters and took refuge among the Island Carib in Saint Vincent, subsequently adopting the latter's language and, to a considerable extent, culture. There they emerged as a distinct society at the beginning of the eighteenth century; largely supplanted the native Indians, their erstwhile hosts, during its course. (15)

Taylor traces most Garifuna cultural practices, particularly language and religion, to Amerindian (Carib or Arawakan) roots. Although he asserts that Garifuna retain African personality traits, he attributes the substance of Garifuna culture to Indian origins such that "it is in the imponderable aspects that the culture of the Black Carib differs most from that of their Indian forebears in the Lesser Antilles, so as to constitute, as it were, a Negro cake composed of Amerindian ingredients" (138).

Danny, avoiding such strained metaphors, said that the book proved that the ancestors of Garifuna were Indians. "They all say 'We're African, we're African,' but it's not true." Chino scoffed and Danny responded by flipping to the back of the book and pointing to a photo of a St. Vincent Carib: "This is what your grandfather looked like. Why do you think they call you Chino?" Chino, somewhere between angry and amused, shot back: "Did you ever see my grandfather, did you ever know my grandfather?" And so it went for a minute or two, Danny trying to turn Garifuna into Indians while Chino insisting that they were Blacks. Walking away with Chino, I said, "You know it's true there was a mixture in St. Vincent" and he said: "Yeah, but these people want us to think we're backward." Reflecting later, I began to ponder why he associated indianness rather than blackness with the idea of "backward," a stereotype long associated with Garifuna, who others typically identify as Black.

Like Chino, most Garifuna I know call themselves Black (*negro*), taking possession of a racial label invoked by others as an epithet. This racial identity was displayed with such quotidian regularity that it took on the quality of the obvious, if not the mundane. Friends and relatives greeted each other by saying "hola negra." On the concrete podium used for the town fair's coronation ceremony, someone spray painted "*Soy negro y que pedo*" ("I'm Black and what of it"), and an eighteen-year-old nicknamed "Africa" had written "*Soy Africa. Tócame y sientes mi poder*" ("I'm Africa. Touch me and feel my power"). Stereos blasted reggae, hip-hop, and soul. Even one of the buses running from Sambo Creek to La Ceiba was painted red, black, green, and yellow, known locally as "the colors of Africa."

Young women arranged their hair back into cornrows, up with extension-aided braids, flat in a fashion known as "scrunch," and, in countless other ways, borrowed styles from Blacks elsewhere. Young men accentuated their blackness by dressing in baggy pants with brand names like Boss and Tommy Hilfiger, high-top Nike basketball shoes, and T-shirts depicting personalities ranging from Martin Luther King to Mike Tyson and Boyz II Men to Bob Marley. Those who sported the hottest brand-name gear visibly belied the notion that Garifuna were "backward."

These practices signal participation in the Black diaspora and membership in the racial category Black. What then of the Indian and indigenous aspect of Garifuna heritage and identity? Although Chino, in the context of a discussion with two foreigners, insisted on his blackness, others, in different contexts, represent themselves in ways that articulate similarities between Garifuna and indigenous peoples. This is most striking among OFRANEH, a Garifuna organization that struggles to secure recognition and rights for Garifuna as a *pueblo* (people). OFRANEH has provided crucial support for land struggles in Sambo Creek and other Garifuna communities and employs a discourse of territoriality borrowed from indigenous movements. It is the "Black Fraternal Organization of Honduras" yet often refers to Garifuna as a *"pueblo indígena"* (indigenous people). A draft proposal for a "Garifuna Territorial Law" offers the following definitions:

> Garifuna Community: The entirety of families of Afrocaribbean ancestry (*ascendencia afrocaribe*) who share sentiments of identification bound to their aboriginal past and who maintain traits and values of their own traditional culture, as well as their own forms of autonomous social organization and control.
>
> Pueblo Indígena: The entirety of Garifuna communities which maintain a historical continuity and are determined to preserve, develop and transmit to future generations their traditional territories in accordance with their own cultural values, social organizations and legal systems. (OFRANEH 1999, 2–3)

Notice that Garifuna communities are characterized as "Afrocaribbean," which can be understood as Afro-Caribbean or Afro-Carib Indian, even as the collection of Garifuna communities is defined as an indigenous people. In addition, notice that the proposal represents Garifuna as possessing characteristics typically associated with indigenous peoples: as having an "aboriginal past"; maintaining a traditional culture and forms of social organization; and occupying territories. This discourse of indigeneity functions as a crucial component of Garifuna political claims to cultural and territorial rights within the Honduran nation-state.

We see, then, that the differentiation between the concepts "Black," "Indian," and "indigenous" is more complicated than we might otherwise assume and that multiple forms of self-representation exist with respect to these categories. This book inquires into the contradictions and convergences produced between the figures of the Black and the Indian and the concepts of blackness and indigeneity through an analysis of the politics of race and culture among Garifuna in Honduras. How can we interpret and explain the variety of discourses and practices of race and culture among Garifuna, who produce various meanings of blackness with variable emphasis on the indigenous? What are the different implications of bearing and affirming Black and/or indigenous identities? Are these forms of identification contradictory or compatible? How can we explain the seeming paradox between nativist assertions and diasporic affiliations and between affirmations of tradition and modernity, rootedness and cosmopolitanism, blackness and indigeneity?

In attempting to answer these questions, this book moves through a number of forms of inquiry: histories of racial formation, nationalism, and representations of culture and difference in Honduras; the politics of Garifuna movements and their variable modes of struggle and representation; and everyday practices of race and culture among people, particularly young men, in a Garifuna community. Each sphere of analysis involves a problem of scale, informed by power relationships that cut across national borders. For example, Honduran nationalism in the first half of the twentieth century involved racialized responses to U.S. imperialism. Contemporary ethnic mobilization in Honduras cannot be understood without attention to pan-American currents of identity politics, from civil rights struggles to Black nationalisms to indigenous movements. Likewise, state responses to such mobilization are deeply informed by, among other actors, multilateral institutions such as the World Bank and Inter-American Development Bank (IDB). Finally, everyday practices of self in a Garifuna community are shaped by the circulation of ideas, goods, people, images, styles, and symbols engendered by transnational migration networks that intimately matter even in the lives of those who never leave.

The research for this book is based on twenty-four months of ethnographic fieldwork conducted between 1994 and 2004, with the longest visit occurring in 1996–1997. I lived in Sambo Creek, where I studied everyday discourses and practices of Garifuna identity formation, particularly among the young men with whom I established closest relations. I also investigated historical dimensions of the community, particularly issues of interethnic relations, racism, and land tenure. As a complement to this research, I studied the politics of Garifuna organizations. Some of the activists were wary of having a *gringo* anthropologist in their midst, but they generously allowed me to attend events and shared their perspectives on Black and indigenous mobilization in Honduras, often referred to simply as "*la lucha*"—the struggle.

The Argument, in a Nutshell

This book explores the multiple ways in which Garifuna maneuver within racialized structures of inclusion and exclusion and possibility and exploitation. As a number of scholars have observed, during the past two decades Latin American states have embraced policies of "multiculturalism," granting cultural recognition and rights to ethnic groups historically marginalized within the nation.[4] This multicultural turn has been fueled by ethnic activism and transformations in the policies of state agencies and multilateral institutions such as the World Bank and IDB. Peoples understood to be indigenous are the principal subjects of such reforms, though in several countries certain groups identified as "Afrodescendants" have also been able to participate in collective cultural rights regimes (Hooker 2005a). One major component of this book tracks the formation and politics of the multicultural paradigm in Honduras, in which activists positioned Garifuna as a people of African descent with the juridical status of indigenous. Their claims, I argue, are not simply based on representations of Garifuna as a group of mixed African and Indian ancestry but on a configuration of indigeneity as marking a particular cultural status or condition, a mode of being more than a matter of blood. Exploring the formation of Garifuna activism and Honduran multiculturalism allows us to open a window on to emerging, contested meanings of blackness and indigeneity as overlapping rather than exclusive categories of identification even as it demonstrates the differences and tensions between them.

If blackness can take on the symbolic meanings typically associated with indigeneity—associations with tradition, rootedness in territory, a special relationship to nature—it also becomes filled with the signs of subaltern, cosmopolitan modernity. In the Garifuna community where I conducted research, high levels of migration to the United States help fuel an intense interest in symbols and commodities associated with "Black Americans" (as local residents refer to U.S. African Americans).

I investigate the local meanings of "Black America" and the ways in which Garifuna, especially young men, appropriate styles and brands from elsewhere to fashion public identities as assertively Black and cosmopolitan in everyday struggles for status and respect. I analyze these practices and discourses as forms of diasporic affiliation that attempt to reconfigure the position of Garifuna in ethnoracial hierarchies through asserting participation in modernity, as Blacks. These practices reach across power differentials between the United States and Honduras to tap into forms of blackness that, from a location in Honduras, are associated both with racial resistance and U.S. dominance. Modes of identity formation that draw on the symbolic power of Black America thus coexist in tension with activist and local discourses of (Black) indigeneity that emphasize the particularity of Garifuna identity, cultural traditions, and ancestral presence in place, sometimes directed against neoliberal dominance and U.S. imperialism. I argue that the tensions between different modes of identification (between indigenous assertions and cosmopolitan affiliations) reflect the difficulties in navigating contemporary structures of power and difference, where Garifuna are both recognized as an "ethnic subject" with collective rights and cultural value and stigmatized as a Black, racial–cultural other still at the margins of modernity and the nation.

Negro or Indian? Debating Cultural Origins

The themes of blackness and indigeneity central to this work revisit some of the core fascinations of early scholarship on the Garifuna. In the 1950s, the authors of the first two full-length monographs on "Black Caribs" debated whether Garifuna should be considered, in cultural terms, as bearing a predominately African or Amerindian heritage. As noted previously, Taylor argued in 1951 that while Black Caribs might physically and even psychically be understood as a "Negro cake," their cultural heritage or "ingredients" derived primarily from Indians. His contemporary, Ruy Coelho (1955), argued to the contrary that in cooking, family structure, cooperative labor, and

religion, Black Carib culture demonstrated the "survival" and "reinterpreta-
tion" of African cultural elements.

Both Taylor and Coelho studied under Melville Herskovits, a student
of Franz Boas and leading figure in the anthropology of Afro-America.
Herskovits sought to produce a science of acculturation and the survival
of African culture in the Americas to counter assumptions that the African
past had been lost in slavery. As David Scott argues:

The New World Negro had been ideologically constituted by
dominant and racist nineteenth century discourse as a figure with
neither a determinant past nor, its supposed corollary, a distinctive culture. And by the mid 1920s, black counterdiscourses were,
in the articulation of racial identity-politics, making impressive
and unignorable claims for an active African heritage. Therefore,
on the conceptual terrain established by the categories of Boasian
culture, the task presented to the new anthropology was to show
in as scientifically conclusive a way as possible that the New World
Negro did in fact have both a determinate past and a distinctive
culture. (1991, 277)

That task operated in the shadow of the figure of the Indian, the principle
object of investigation within Boasian anthropology. Black Caribs proved
a particular source of fascination as a group of mixed heritage with a distinctive language and culture of indeterminate origins. In his 1941 classic
The Myth of the Negro Past, Herskovits asserted: "this unstudied people
constitutes one of the strategic points for future attack on New World
Negro acculturation, since they represent an Indian–African amalgam
that should establish a further control in the historical laboratory where
this problem is to be studied." (1990, 93)[5]

If his students Taylor and Coelho ultimately disagreed on the relative
predominance of African and Amerindian features within Black Carib
culture, another line of analysis argued that contemporary Black Carib societies represented processes of adaptation to Western civilization rather
than the endurance of tradition. Nancie Gonzalez is the foremost propo-
nent of this perspective. The most important ethnographer and ethnohis-
torian of Garifuna, Gonzalez has produced a remarkable scholarly opus
that spans five decades and demonstrates several theoretical and meth-
odological shifts as well as a consistent interest in Garifuna adaptations to

modernization (1959, 1969, 1970, 1983, 1988, 1997). I draw attention to her contention that Black Caribs are a "neoteric society," understood as:

> societies whose traditional culture has been forcibly changed or dissolved through the intervention of forces from the Western world, or to societies of mixed-bloods who have found themselves occupying a position between the two cultures from which they derived. Such groups have characteristics different from those of the larger society within which they are living, yet they cannot be termed primitive, peasant, folk or any other such designation which implies a traditional basis for society. The mere fact of miscegenation does not bring this about, of course. Rather, a society must also be placed in the position of having to adopt to an economy dependent upon industrialization through the mechanisms of migrant wage labor, while being denied full admission to the industrial society as a whole, both as a class and as individuals. (1969, 9–10)

Within this paradigm, the debate concerning the Indian versus the African origins of Garifuna cultural practices appears beside the point because the society lacks a basis in tradition resulting from economic dependency, especially migrant labor. Nonetheless, Gonzalez portrays Garifuna as an Afro-American people.[6] Critical of the Herskovitsian effort to identify African cultural survivals, she interprets Afro-American cultures as products of recent adaptations to modernity and its exclusions rather than as enduring traditions.[7]

In contrast, Mary Helms (1981), a scholar working outside of the debates surrounding New World Black cultures, argued for the endurance of the Amerindian heritage of Garifuna practices. Tracing contemporary patterns of domestic organization to the "Island Caribs," Helms attempts to refute Gonzalez's argument that those patterns are recent products of migration. She also attacks the claim that "contemporary Black Carib society reflects 'shallow' and 'traditionless' (Neoteric) cultures" (85) and "the trend at the present . . . to regard the Black Carib, or Garifuna as they now call themselves, as an Afro-American people" (78). She thus suggests that Garifuna have deep cultural roots and should be considered an Amerindian people. Although Gonzalez and Helms offer conflicting accounts, they implicitly employ similar figures of the Indian (Island Carib) and Black (Afro-American) as signifiers for, respectively, the living presence of the

cultural past and cultural adaptation to the present. Whereas the figure of
the Indian signifies deep cultural roots, the figure of the Black is understood in the opposite terms, as a being torn from native time and space
and caught in the netherworld between tradition and modernity.

While various anthropologists disputed the Indian and African origins
of Garifuna culture and disagreed on whether Garifuna represented a traditional or adaptive society, none of them connected present-day adaptations to Amerindian features of Garifuna society. Garifuna culture becomes
identified with the figure of the Indian solely as the endurance of deep
traditions, reflecting wider constructions of the contemporary Indian as
relevant only as a being bearing remnants of a native past. Garifuna representations of themselves, and Indians, sometimes echo these ideas.

Although the Herskovitsian paradigm fell out of favor in much Afro-
American anthropology, the effort to identify African roots of Garifuna
culture persisted in some U.S.-based scholarship (Franzone 1994), in the
work of some Garifuna scholars (see chapter 3) and in popular, public
discourse about and among Garifuna.[8] For now, one example will suf-
fice. One evening I met a transmigrant who had returned to inaugurate
the construction of a secondary school funded by the Committee for the
Betterment of Sambo Creek in New York City. Most people in the community located me as a gringo doing research and giving English classes,
but this man placed me in the related slot of tourist. He enthusiastically
proclaimed the virtues of Garifuna culture, relating how Garifuna were
Africans who went to St. Vincent and later came to Honduras: "Garifuna
have the best culture of Honduras. We have the dance, African. We have
the autochthonous Garifuna food, African. We have the language, autochthonous Garifuna, African." Noting that Garifuna culture attracted attention from foreigners, he queried rhetorically "What does Honduras have
of culture? Nothing."

The veracity of such accounts interests me less than the spaces of difference they assert and occupy. Marking certain cultural practices to exemplify enduring African traditions constitutes one mode of affirming
blackness, reverberating with Herskovitsian anthropology, the Negritude
movement that emerged in the first half of the twentieth century, Afrocen-
trisms of the late twentieth century, and the cultural work of some Garifuna intellectuals over the past three decades. The transmigrant's use of the
term "autochthonous" adds another dimension, linking ideas of African
origins to notions of native culture typically associated with indigenous

peoples. As discussed in chapter 3, in the late 1980s Garifuna, Lenca, Miskito, and activists from other peoples employed the term *"pueblos autóctonos"* (autochthonous peoples) to signify the similar cultural status of groups otherwise differentiated as negro (Black) and indígena (indigenous). In this discourse, to be autochthonous is to bear a deep, rooted difference from dominant national culture as well as the West. These observations reveal how representations of difference can simultaneously involve claims of belonging to the nation ("Garifuna have the best culture of Honduras") and distancing from the nation ("What does Honduras have of culture? Nothing"). They also suggest that self-representations can include nativist and diasporic dimensions. Finally, they remind us that claims to native identity also have a history and that invoking "autochthony" or its conceptual relative "indigeneity" involves drawing on models of culture and identity that have their own past and, like the transmigrant, travel. In order to pursue such lines of inquiry, I turn from questions of cultural origins to the conceptual terrain of blackness and indigeneity.

On Blackness and Indigeneity (in the Americas)

Following the surge of indigenous and Black activism and the emergence of Latin America multiculturalisms in the 1980s and 1990s, a number of authors have advocated studying indigenous and Black peoples and movements within the same conceptual framework.[9] Peter Wade (1997) identifies and critiques a tendency in Latin Americanist scholarship to study Blacks in terms of race (with a focus on slavery and race relations, with the assumption that Black is a phenotypical category) and Indians in terms of ethnicity (with a focus on cultural otherness and the assumption that Indian is a cultural category). Wade argues that this reflects colonial and Republican "structures of alterity" that institutionalized Black and indigenous identities in different ways. The recent turn toward multiculturalism has reconfigured, and reproduced, distinctions between these categories. A collection of articles on "Afro-Indigenous Multiculturalisms," edited by Shane Greene (2007a), examines the ways in which indigenous and Black peoples are positioned in different ways in different juridical regimes of recognition, from radically distinct identities (the case of Peru) to virtual equivalents (the case of Honduras). Indeed, I argue that the Honduran case pushes the Black–indigenous distinction to the point where we can speak of a Black indigeneity or indigenous blackness (Anderson 2007).

In this section, I offer a conceptual orientation toward rethinking an indigenous–Black dichotomy, engaging associated categories and concepts, especially "Indian," native, and diaspora. I analyze the racial categories Black and Indian, noting how they are not simply categories based on presumed differences in phenotype, descent, or culture but, with their connotations of African and American origins, also presume geographic significance. This obvious but oft-neglected feature of the categories helps bring to light the common equation between Indian and indigenous in the Americas. Disrupting that equivalence, I turn to a discussion of the concept of diaspora, arguing that blackness should not be simply equated with a diasporic condition of displacement. Engaging literature that focuses on diaspora as a process, I highlight how identifications with a Black diaspora can coexist with the production of blackness as native, grounded in place, with the sentiments and politics of indigeneity. Finally, I suggest that while structures of recognition often deny Blacks full belonging in the nation, or the native status of indigenous, indigenous as a legal category involves ambiguities and openings that render it compatible with blackness in the New World.

I begin with a bit of word play, quoting definitions from the *Oxford English Dictionary* (1971 edition):

Negro: An individual belonging to the African race of mankind, which is distinguished by a black skin, black wooly hair, flat nose and thick protruding lips.
Indian (2): Belonging or relating to the race of original inhabitants of America and the West Indians.
Indigenous: Born or produced naturally in a land or region; native or belonging naturally to (the soil, region, etc.) (Used primarily of aboriginal inhabitants or natural products).

Notice how Negro and Indian are both identified as "races," defined in terms of geographic origins. The Negro race is attributed phenotypical features and characterized as African. The Indian race is understood as the original (pre-Colombian) inhabitants of the New World. In this sense, the Indian race is conceptualized as "indigenous" to the New World. Notice, however, that the definition of indigenous provides multiple inflections of being "native." It can simply mean being born in a particular place, bear the more complicated connotations of "belonging naturally," or contain the deepest sense of nativity—aboriginality.

The English terms "Negro" (which precedes "Black" as an identity category) and "Indian" derive from Spanish meanings. Whitten notes that the term negro was used in the Kingdom of Castile "as a replacement for other names for African peoples, or African descended peoples" as early as the fourteenth century (2007, 357). "Indio," as a term of reference to the native inhabitants of the Americas, first came into use by Columbus. Geographic origins mattered more than phenotype in determining how blackness, more than indianness, became associated with slavery in the New World. The Spanish Crown had no preoccupations with enslaving Africans because Spain had no territorial jurisdiction in Africa. In contrast, whether the Indian could be enslaved represented a political conundrum; the Crown had obligations to protect and convert Indians precisely because they were natives of regions where Spain asserted authority. These obligations, though continuously violated in Indian enslavement, were taken seriously by the Crown and justified its dominion in the New World (Pagden, 33–34).

It is beyond the scope of this discussion to even outline the position of (free and enslaved) "negros" and "indios" in the colonial order in relation to Spanish *peninsulares* and *criollos* and the *castas*—mestizo, mulato, and so forth—that proliferated as a result of intermixture.[10] I simply want to reiterate the deep geographic associations with the categories "Indian" and "Black" emergent from colonialism, associations that still resonate in the production of race, ethnicity, and indigeneity in the Americas.[11] I make this generalization aware of the enormous variation in classification schemes and dynamics across regions and nations. The number and type of identity categories, the meanings attached to them, and the relative importance of the various principles through which individuals become classified in categories (e.g., phenotypical features, perception of ancestry, cultural characteristics, class status) differ between Brazil and the United States or between Brazil and Honduras. Moreover, the extent to which blackness and indianness have been incorporated as part of national culture and identity also differs significantly across nation-states. Recognizing the importance of such differences, however, should not blind us to the ways in which Negro and Indian became transimperial and later transnational categories shaped by the geographies of power that produced them (see Wade 1997, 21).

Given my central concern with Garifuna engagements with blackness, I want to reflect for a moment on the category Black/Negro in relation to the dynamic interplay between interpellation (identity ascription from without) and self-identification. Scott notes:

> We do not simply choose our selves. One is not black simply by choice; one's identity is always in part constituted—sometimes against one's will—within a structure of recognition, identification, and subjectification. On my view, the black diasporic subject is a subject whose 'historical fate' has been produced as black in and through raced social relations, ideological apparatuses, and political regimes. (1999, 125)

Garifuna, historically and contemporarily interpellated as Black, have had to confront a series of negative associations with that category that resonate far beyond Honduras. These include attributions of biological inferiority crystallized in the scientific racisms of the nineteenth and twentieth centuries; attributions of collective personality characteristics such as hypersexuality; associations between blackness and cultural deficiencies (e.g., lack of civilization, witchcraft, backwardness); associations with menial work and the stigmas of inferior social position, themselves produced by racial hierarchies; and exclusion from consideration as true nationals. In many respects, these stigma overlap with those applied to the Indian. Dominant associations between Garifuna, blackness, and African origins have been employed both to position Garifuna (like Indians) as outside of civilization and modernity *and* as not truly native. Although the national, indeed indigenous, status of Garifuna has been reworked in an era of multiculturalism, attributions of African origins can still be leveraged to cast doubt on Garifuna indigeneity and their status as "real" Hondurans. As Garifuna must by necessity confront racialization as Blacks, they have engaged blackness in a variety of different fashions within particular conditions of possibility.

It is important to note that New World Black subjects are often framed by a third term, diaspora. In the traditional use of the term, diaspora refers to the "condition" of a people displaced from a homeland, scattered from an original place of belonging. Scott, in the quote above, mentions the "black diasporic subject," whose historical fate was to be racialized as black. We might reverse the order of the words to note that in the Americas, part of the historic fate of the Black subject was to be constructed as diasporic, as dwelling in displacement, out of place, and in loss of home.

The semantic field associated with the traditional notion of a diaspora as a condition (uprooted, dispersed, separated, and so forth) appears antithetical to the notion of indigenous, with its semantic field of native, at home, belonging, integrated, and so on (Harvey and Thompson 2005). Given this distinction, we should resist equating New World Blacks, or blackness, with a diasporic condition. Black subjects are, of course, not simply members of a diaspora but native citizens of particular nations, regions, places, and communities, who belong in place and make claims to place. They have been positioned as out of place subjects by histories of displacement and ongoing processes of racialization and marginalization.

If the last reflections inch us closer toward recognizing the possibility of black indigeneity in the New World, to further that proposition I engage recent scholarship on blackness and diaspora that moves beyond the traditional understanding of diaspora as a condition of displacement to analyze the relationship between diaspora, nationalism, and nativism.[12] A concern with multiple relations and attachments within and beyond particular nation-states lies at the heart of much diaspora theory (Braziel and Mannur, 2003). The cultural studies work of Paul Gilroy (e.g., 1991, 1992) and Stuart Hall (e.g., 1991, 2003), emerging from an analysis of the politics of race and nation in the United Kingdom, has provided a key source of inspiration—and critical departure—in the field. Gilroy asserts:

Black Britain defines itself crucially as part of a diaspora. Its unique cultures draw inspiration from those developed by black populations elsewhere. In particular, the culture and politics of black America and the Caribbean have become the raw materials for creative processes which redefine what it means to be black, adapting it to distinctively British experiences and meanings. (1991, 154)

He suggests an approach that combines analysis of diasporic affiliations across nation-states with analysis of social relations and identity formations within nation-states.

An intricate web of cultural and political connections bind blacks here to blacks elsewhere. At the same time, they are linked into the social relations of this country. Both dimensions have to be examined and the contradictions and continuities which exist between them must be brought out. (1991, 156)

This approach is tied to a critique of the racial exclusions of British nationalism and a critique of essentialism (ethnic absolutism) produced by Blacks. It theorizes Black British culture and identity as produced both in relation to the nation-state and in relation to Black populations "elsewhere." The approach also decenters Africa—as a homeland of displacement, imagined return, and cultural roots—to highlight the importance of lateral routes of exchange between Europe, the Caribbean, and the United States, what Gilroy calls the "Black Atlantic."

This work helped open avenues to consider "diaspora" not simply in terms of a condition of displacement but in terms of processes (Thomas and Clark, 12–13), conceived as practice (Edwards 2003), relation (Brown 2005), identification (Gordon 1998; Gordon and Anderson 1999), and dialogue (Matory 2005), grounded in particular locations, networks, and/or communities. Rather than presume a shared condition, these approaches analyze the complex conversations, antagonisms, solidarities, political projects, and identity formations that occur when Black subjects engage in diasporic processes across national borders. Owing a debt to cultural studies approaches, they developed in part as a critical response to a tendency in some diaspora theory to celebrate diasporic subjectivities or consciousness.[13] While Gilroy and Hall wrestle with the complex relations of Black subjects to nation-states and diaspora and call attention to the dynamic interplay between "roots" and "routes" in identity formation, their critiques of nationalism and essentialism—from "above" or "below"—tend to juxtapose and privilege diaspora as an outernational, hybrid orientation over assertions of ethnic particularism and, by extension, nativism.[14] Gilroy writes: "the Black Atlantic can be defined . . . through the desire to transcend both the structures of the nation state and the constraints of ethnic and national particularity. . . . These desires have always sat uneasily alongside the strategic choices forced on Black movements and individuals embedded in political cultures and nation states" (1992, 19). Gilroy privileges purported desires for transcendence offered by diaspora against strategic comprises associated with the "constraints" of national and ethnic particularity. However, close historical and ethnographic analysis of the disparate cultural and political work associated with diasporic processes (drawing on disparate Black cultures, dialoguing across the Black Atlantic, identifying with particular Blacks elsewhere, etc.) complicates uniform evaluations of the relationships between diaspora, nation, and ethnic particularity.

Jacqueline Brown's ethnography of "Black Liverpool" (2005) is especially instructive. Brown analyzes the production of resolutely local, em-
placed Black community—self-identified as Liverpool-born Black—as
a product of simultaneously local, national, and cosmopolitan histories,
informed by British notions of place, race, and nation. The production
of a grounded, localized particularity has emerged, in part, via diasporic
encounters, which Brown insists must be understood in terms of antagonisms and unequal power relations across the African Diaspora. Diasporic
resources drawn from the United States become mobilized in struggles
against white racism and in the politics of gender among Liverpool's
Blacks. Liverpool-born Blacks simultaneously render themselves as part
of the African Diaspora and distinguish themselves from other Blacks,
including Africans and Afro-Caribbean groups in Liverpool, precisely in
terms of their distinct relation to place. In the process, blackness becomes
entangled with assertions of a kind of native presence. Brown takes seriously both the cultural and political work of diasporic affinities and the
work of differentiating, particularistic assertions.

This perspective travels well to the Garifuna case in Honduras, where
the power asymmetries between the United States are dramatic and where
Garifuna engage in forms of nativism based on notions of cultural difference, community formation, territorial presence, and indigeneity. Garifuna
identifications with blackness take on numerous forms. Some of these
have diasporic dimensions; that is, they posit relations to particular com-
ponents of the African Diaspora. On the one hand, identifications with
Africa, particularly as a source of racial and cultural roots, have become
increasingly common over the past several decades (Johnson 2007). On
the other hand, Garifuna also position themselves as part of an African
Diaspora via transnational routes of affinity and difference across other
Black spaces and populations. Black America is particularly significant
here. In addition to these diasporic identifications, Garifuna, collectively
and individually, can simultaneously assert themselves as Blacks, Hondurans, Afro-Hondurans, and Garifuna and insist on their rooted, native
presence and indigenous status. Rather than privilege one mode of (Black)
identity formation from the outset, I strive to take them all seriously and
to understand the relations between them.

Having unsettled the relationship between blackness and diaspora and
advocated an open-ended analysis of the relationship between diasporic
processes and place-based, particularistic identity formations and politics,

we can return to the concept of indigenous. In the broadest sense, "indigenous" refers to a condition of native presence. The amount of time something must be present to "count" as indigenous is subject to debate and disagreement. In this sense, calling something indigenous involves an *assertion* of presence before the arrival of something, or someone, else. The term "indigenous peoples" has gained currency with the development of indigenous movements that, in the past several decades, have become important actors in national and international political forums (Niezen 2003). The term is characterized by an absence of definitional closure, in part because those who speak in its name insist on the principle of self-definition. Niezen identifies three areas of common agreement in international law, tied to notions of ancestry, space, culture, and power: (1) "descent from original inhabitants of a region prior to the arrival of settlers who have since become the dominant population; (2) maintenance of cultural differences, distinct from a dominant population; (3) political marginality resulting in poverty, limited access to services, and absences of protections against unwanted 'development'" (19). Even these criteria are not universal. For example, an important international convention on indigenous rights ratified by the Honduran government, Convention 169 of the International Labor Organization, glosses indigenous peoples as:

> Peoples in independent countries who are regarded as indigenous on account of their descent from the populations which inhabited the country, or a geographical region to which the country belongs, at the time of conquest or colonization or the establishment of present State boundaries and who, irrespective of their legal status, retain some or all of their own social, economic, cultural and political institutions.[15]

Garifuna, as a people who inhabited the coast of Honduras before the formation of independent states and who can claim their own distinctive institutions, qualify as indigenous. Under this criterion, you do not need to be Indian to bear indigenous rights in the Americas.

If the category "indigenous people" represents a particular type of subject position, we can analyze indigeneity as a form of political practice, as a bundle of concepts, associations, assertions, and/or rights mobilized in acts of self-representation by marginalized social subjects. Indigeneity, in this sense, involves discursive frames or models through which subjects voice claims in the world (Tsing 2007). These frames are neither singular nor static, temporally or spatially. They travel and change in relation to how they are mobilized and translated by particular movements within regional and national political contexts. In later chapters, we look closely at how Garifuna activisms engage with Latin American indigenous movements and key concepts such as autonomy and territoriality. We also consider more local, everyday expressions of attachment to place, "ancestral" land, and cultural traditions. In both cases, indigeneity is a mode of identity representation that involves assertions of native presence, cultural distinctiveness, and attachments to territory.

The politics of such claims should not be dismissed as parochial nativism. Indigeneity has provided a crucial frame through which members of rural communities defend themselves against a variety of forms of oppression, particularly land and resource appropriation. As Tsing argues for another context, "the claim that rural communities might have rights based in their traditional cultures is one of the few interruptions of a deadly business as usual" (2007, 36). Of course, recognizing the importance of indigenous politics should not lead us to ignore the exclusions and essentialisms they may enact.[16] However, to consider indigeneity solely in terms of essentialism is to miss the diversity, dynamism, and possibilities of the movements articulated in its name. As I argue in reference to a key strand of Garifuna activism, indigenous politics can help produce cross-ethnic alliances that articulate with left critiques of dominant political and economic models as neoliberal imperialism.

In this section, I have provided a conceptual orientation toward blackness and indigeneity not as mutually exclusive categories but as modalities of identity formation that can overlap with each other. This can appear counterintuitive because: (a) in the Americas indigeneity is intimately associated with the category Indian/indio, such that the terms "indigenous peoples" and "indígena" can function as a synonym for "Indian"; (b) New World blackness, associated with African origins, is often rendered in terms of displacement rather than emplacement. Nonetheless, the Garifuna case illustrates that subjects interpellated as Black and who identify as Black can assert indigenous status, and not merely because they can claim Indian descent. Indigenous status here refers both to the broadest sense of being native born and the legal sense of bearing an indigenous condition as a culturally distinct people. This case thus suggests that assertions of Indian heritage may not be necessary for the production of indigeneity. Garifuna produce forms of Black indigeneity that partially disrupt a conceptual–political grid that links indigeneity with Indians and Blacks with displacement. At the same time, Garifuna engage in diasporic processes that reinscribe the meanings of what it means to be Garifuna and Black; in this sense too, we can analyze their significance to help disrupt an opposition between indigeneity and diaspora commonly found in scholarship.[17]

"Questioning an essential opposition does not eliminate the historical differences or tensions expressed by the contrast" (Clifford 2007, 199), either in scholarship or the worlds it strives to apprehend. In a review essay on diaspora, Clifford notes that "the claims of diaspora" are often "caught up and defined against: (1) the norms of nation-states; (2) indigenous, and especially autochthonous claims by tribal peoples" (1994, 307). He carefully delineates these oppositions as zones of relational contrast, as mutually entangled rather than diametrically opposed. The Black, diasporic, and indigenous modes of identity formation I analyze in this book coexist but in uneasy tension and occasional conflict. For example, a Black–indigenous dichotomy continues to structure the ways in which racialized subjects navigate nativist attachments and diasporic affiliations. I argue in some depth that oppositions between cosmopolitanism and indigeneity also inform Garifuna identity formations and the tensions between them. These modes of identification are, or course, shaped by their past and, just as importantly, previous constructions of their past and identity, by themselves and others. They also respond to current structures of power and possibility. The final sections of the introduction provide an orientation to contemporary structures of difference and the position of Garifuna within them.

Locating Garifuna in Official Multiculturalism: A Beginning

Today, people known as Garifuna reside in four Central American countries as well as in the United States, concentrated in cities such as New York, Miami, New Orleans, Houston, and Los Angeles. Within Honduras, they are most commonly associated with coastal "Garifuna communities,"[18] many of which are occupied not just by Garifuna but also by members of the majority population of Honduras, typically identified in formal circles as mestizos or *ladinos*.

Garifuna also form significant populations in cities such as La Ceiba, San Pedro Sula, and Tegucigalpa. The most recent (contested and problematic) government census calculates that there are 49,952 Garifuna in Honduras.[19]

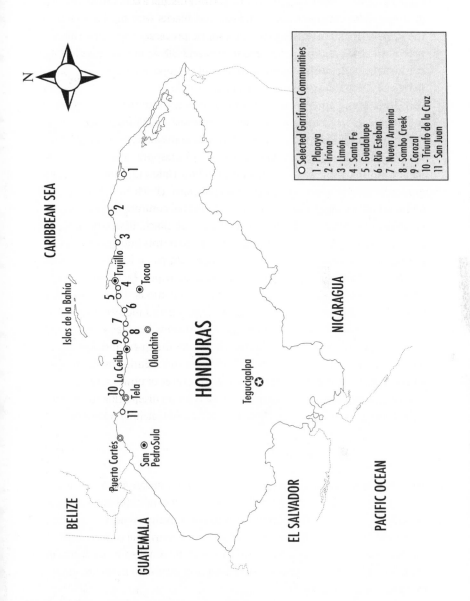

Honduras, with selected Garifuna communities. Map by Juan Mejia.

CARIBBEAN SEA

Selected Garifuna Communities
1 - Plapaya
2 - Iriona
3 - Limón
4 - Santa Fe
5 - Guadalupe
6 - Río Esteban
7 - Nueva Armenia
8 - Sambo Creek
9 - Corozal
10 - Triunfo de la Cruz
11 - San Juan

Islas de la Bahía

Trujillo

Tocoa

HONDURAS

Olanchito

La Ceiba

Tela

Puerto Cortés

San PedroSula

Tegucigalpa

NICARAGUA

EL SALVADOR

PACIFIC OCEAN

BELIZE

GUATEMALA

N

Garifuna are officially counted as one of nine "ethnic groups" (also known as *grupos poblacionales* or *etnías autóctonas*). The others are Negro inglés (Creoles) (13,303), Tolupán (10,343), Pech (4,138), Misquito [Miskito] (55,500), Lenca (300,594), Tawahka (2,649), and Chortí (37,052) (República de Honduras 2001).[20] The Negro inglés/Creole population consists of descendants of Creole and English-speaking people of African descent who migrated to Honduras from various parts of the Caribbean in the nineteenth and early twentieth centuries. As an official ethnic category, Creoles are mostly identified with the Bay Islands, though they also reside on the mainland. Like Garifuna, they are considered Black or Afro-Honduran in racial terms. The other groups are considered Indian and indigenous, although the Miskito have a history of intermixture involving peoples of African descent. The ethnic groups constitute 7.2 percent of the Honduran population and are juxtaposed with the category "Other," which leaves the majority designation, 92.8 percent of the population, racially and ethnically unmarked and unnamed.

The counting and naming of groups have changed in accordance with particular historical and political conjunctures. In the first half of the twentieth century, the census recorded the ancestors of current Garifuna as negros without differentiating them from other Blacks. From 1945 until 1988, the census did not differentiate groups on the basis of race or ethnicity. By the 1990s, Garifuna were officially represented as an *etnia* (ethnic group) with a distinctive culture now claimed as part of the national patrimony. In fact, Garifuna acquired an international reputation as bearers of a traditional culture that merits protection such that, in 2001, the United Nations Educational, Scientific and Cultural Organization (UNESCO) declared Garifuna language, dance, and music "Masterpieces of Oral and Intangible Heritage of Humanity." By the end of the twentieth century, Honduras itself had been officially defined as a multiethnic nation.

The increased visibility of Garifuna as part of the nation could be seen at the quintessential moment of national celebration—Independence Day. According to media coverage of the official 1997 celebration, the performance that received the loudest applause was led by a group of mestiza high school students who, dressed in revealing, two-piece outfits with a generic Indian motif, danced the famous Garifuna *punta*. As if to underscore the connection between punta as a form of erotic, heteronormative otherness integral to the nation, the news report I watched shifted immediately to a dancing Black woman dressed in flowing skirts of yellow, red, and green. Punta, once associated primarily with Garifuna wakes, has become a popular, commercialized cultural form that has achieved a kind of unofficial status as the national dance and music. In the first half of the twentieth century, self-ascribed patriots identified the presence of Blacks as a problem for the purity of the "Honduran race," understood as the product of Indian–Spanish interrelations. At the end of the century, mestizas dressed like Indians and dancing like Blacks could stand for the nation.

In later chapters, I analyze this shift from mestizaje to multiculturalism within projects of Honduran nationalism but a cautionary note is in order from the start. The official recognition of ethnic groups and the popularization of Garifuna cultural elements such as food, dance, and music should not be interpreted within simple narratives of progress from exclusion to inclusion. Rather, what I hope to communicate is the proliferation of multiple discourses of race, culture, ethnicity, and nation; the ambivalence of multicultural rhetoric; and the contested character of indigeneity and blackness. Ann Stoler, drawing on Foucault, argues that ruptures in racial formations often involve recuperations of earlier racial discourses:

> Discourses about race and how it is known—that is, the popular and erudite theories that inform knowledge of it—are plural not singular, are sedimentary not linear. It is within these sedimented folds that new planes and surfaces re-emerge. These preserved possibilities account for why racial discourses so often appear as new and renewed at the same time. (160)

The relatively new discourses of ethnicity and multiculturalism have not replaced previous understandings of difference that rendered Garifuna as racially negro and culturally backward. Moreover, official rhetorics of diversity and tolerance often belie lived oppressions and encode their own forms of exclusion, even when they assert inclusion.

Listen to the injunction of a school textbook that affirms ethnic diversity yet equates the ladino (mestizo) with Honduran: "The ladino youth, that is you, the Honduran student, should respect these ethnic groups, love them and accept them because they are part of our racial heritage. You should not discriminate against them or offend them because you would be offending yourselves" (Medina Bardales, 150). This multicultural tolerance still renders ethnic groups distinct from the Honduran student, as others not to be offended. For the celebration marking 200 years since Garifuna arrived to

Honduras, the stage agency charged with the legal defense of ethnic groups ended its commemoration statement with the contradictory message: "*El Pueblo Negro Garifuna*, a vigorous culture. They like us are also Hondurans!" The official multiculturalism that became codified in the 1990s represents a space of ongoing struggles around the meanings of nation, culture, and race, haunted by the legacies of mestizo nationalism and informed by the structural dynamics of power within and across Honduras.

Post–Banana Republic?

Any account of ethnic relations in Honduras must come to terms with the subordinate position of the country within the global order of nation-states. For over a century, Honduras has been derided as the quintessential "banana republic." As interpreted from the political left, that derogatory label indexes the development of a North Coast enclave economy dominated by U.S.-based fruit companies, which dates to the early twentieth century. It also points to the political subordination of the Honduran state to the U.S. government, represented most notoriously by the Reagan administration's use of Honduras as a regional lynchpin against revolutionary movements (in Guatemala and El Salvador) and states (Nicaragua) in the 1980s. However, the image of Honduras as a banana republic ignores the complex histories of political, cultural, and economic relations and elite formation within Honduras (Euraque 1996a). Moreover, by the turn of the twenty-first century the country would better be described, in economic terms, as a "remittance republic," "tourist republic," or "*maquiladora* republic" as the importance of fruit production has subsided relative to other sectors of economic activity. In 2005, remittances sent from Hondurans living abroad (mostly in the United States) accounted for 22 percent of the Gross Domestic Product (GDP), exceeding foreign direct investment (Bamrud 2006). Since the early 1990s, maquiladora production in low-paying work (particularly textile manufacturing) grew dramatically while tourism increased steadily. Nonetheless, Honduras remains one of the poorest countries in the Western hemisphere, ranking only ahead of Guatemala and Haiti in the United Nations Development Program (2005) index of human development.

Structural transformations in the Honduran economy are often linked to the full implementation of neoliberal policies initiated during the presidency of Rafael Callejas (1990–1994) and continued by subsequent governments.

In the 1980s, factions of the Honduran elite and military used the strategic political position of Honduras in U.S. counterrevolutionary objectives to stave off most structural adjustment reforms promoted by the U.S. State Department, the International Monetary Fund (IMF), and the IDB. With the electoral defeat of the Sandinistas in Nicaragua, factions of the elite that saw economic prosperity through the embrace of transnational capital and diversified production were able to influence the direction of both major political parties in supporting "reforms" that devalued national currency, favored external over internal markets, reduced agricultural subsidies, promoted privatization of state industries, and opened limited spaces of social protest and participation in governance (Robinson, 118–32). As elsewhere in Latin America, these initiatives worsened economic conditions for the majority of Hondurans.

Neoliberal policies and structural transformations inform the dynamics of struggle around race and culture among Garifuna. They contribute to pressures on lands and resources claimed by Garifuna communities and provoke nativist politics defending culture and territory. Garifuna communities have long experienced pressures on communal lands that, until very recently, were not recognized by the state as collective property. In fact, as I argue in chapter 3, Garifuna activists took up a struggle grounded in a discourse of indigenous rights in the 1980s in part to pursue land claims. Neoliberal reforms initiated in the 1990s encouraged the diversification of resource extraction and land speculation on the North Coast. Tourist projects, agribusiness, peasant encroachment, ecological reserves, and property transfers have spawned a series of conflicts in and around Garifuna communities. Land and territorial rights remain the most hotly contested arena of struggle, and a recent property-titling initiative, funded by the World Bank, has been opposed by OFRANEH for its faulty incorporation of the collective rights of indigenous and Black peoples. Garifuna organizations themselves come into conflict over how to confront the development initiatives promoted by the state and multilateral institutions. State and international recognition of multiculturalism and ethnic rights incites a variety of responses, from the proliferation of NGOs promoting ethnic inclusion in development projects to direct confrontations with visions of prosperity promoted under a free market paradigm. They also create expectations that Garifuna can cash in on their culture. Under these conditions, discourses of indigeneity, ancestral rights, and cultural preservation take on multiple forms and resonate broadly with many Garifuna, including those living and working abroad.

At the same time, economic pressures and transnational relations intensify desires for migration, particularly to the United States. Migration to the United States began in the 1940s and accelerated in the three decades before the implementation of neoliberal reforms (Gonzalez 1988). The economic transformations of the 1990s nonetheless increased dependence on migration as a strategy of survival and betterment. Many younger people I met portrayed moving to the United States as the only viable route toward economic and social mobility. An older resident of Sambo Creek who made a living as a musician and artisan once told me that the youth of today had two vocations: to study in school or to go to the United States. The reliance of most households on remittances, the class divisions produced on the heels of transmigration, the validation of knowing places beyond one's home, and the dreams of social mobility associated with working abroad contribute to a stark sense of disparity between the United States and Honduras (England 2006). Although such migration-inspired sentiments are common throughout Central America and Mexico, the intense interest in the signs and symbols of Black America among Honduran Garifuna marks a noteworthy difference.

If the modes of governance that Hale calls "neoliberal multiculturalism" (2005) have shaped the contours of organized ethnic politics in Latin America, the dynamics of consumerism within racialized capitalism incite forms of desire and affiliation that have received less attention from scholars. In an era characterized by the intense use of racial and ethnic differences as a marketing strategy, by the global proliferation of hip-hop as a commodity and symbol of (typically masculine) resistance, by the "planetary stardom" (Gilroy 2000, 78) of athletes such as Michael Jordan, U.S.-based blackness becomes a resource for navigating everyday racial dynamics in Honduras. Practices of Black cosmopolitanism jostle together with practices of Black indigeneity as divergent responses to oppression in contemporary structures of power.

Notes on Terminology

Throughout the book, I analyze identity terms (e.g., negro, *moreno*, indio) as they are used in Honduras and include a glossary of these terms for easy reference. Here, I need to say a few words concerning my use of meta-identity terms (e.g., race, ethnic group, people) that circulate in political discourse and everyday life. I take for granted that race (categorizing groups and individuals based on physical appearance and/or perceived biological descent) is a social construction that nonetheless remains crucial to identity formations and power relations (Harrison 1995; Winant 2001). I use "racial" to refer to categories based on perceptions of common descent from people of a particular geographic, continental point of reference and the resultant combinations derived from "mixing." Thus, I consider white, Asian, Black, Indian and mestizo to be racial categories, even though ascription to a particular category may rely on perceptions of cultural characteristics as much as (or more than) perception of physical characteristics.

The term "ethnicity" typically references group identities based on shared cultural characteristics, sometimes as a substitute for the biological fallacies of racial discourse. Ethnicity also tends to reference more particular group identities (e.g., African American, Irish American, Garifuna) than "races" (e.g., Black, white). In this sense, Garifuna can be understood as an "ethnic group" commonly associated with the broader racial category Black. My interest lies in how people who identify as Garifuna understand themselves in relation to categories such as Black and Indian (and indigenous). In order to understand the production of Garifuna identities, we must also understand how Garifuna engage with racial classifications. Ultimately, I hope to show that the distinctions between race and ethnicity, and between biological and cultural modes of making difference, become deeply interwoven within identity discourses, whether produced by the state, "ethnic" activists, or ordinary citizens. I sometimes use the modifier "ethnoracial" to highlight how identity categories often entangle notions of biological and cultural differences and associate ethnic particularity with racial classifications. Nonetheless, to develop these arguments I find it necessary to use the language of ethnicity when referring to the cultural and historical particularity of Garifuna and the language of race when referring to their association (imposed and/or affirmed) with broader categories based on perceived descent from a common continental origin, particularly "Black" and "Indian." Indigenous, I suggest, is a category with a complex relation to the metacategories of race and ethnicity.[21]

Another complication bears addressing. My use of the terms "ethnic" and "ethnic group" in reference to Garifuna contradicts the argument by many Garifuna activists that they should be considered a "people" or "nation." Indeed, the term "ethnic group," often the state's label of choice, implies a subnational identity and minority status (Williams 1989) that those claiming the status of people seek to subvert. Recognizing the distinction, I prefer to reference Garifuna as a people, though I also refer to Garifuna as an ethnic group when discussing their positioning within state discourse. I do, however, also use the term "ethnic" as a modifier to signal the common position of Garifuna in relation to other "peoples" (Miskito, Lenca, etc.), to describe, for example, the "ethnic politics" that developed in the 1980s. I know of no suitable adjectival form of the term "people" and I consider the most likely alternative, "indigenous," as too much a subject of analytical attention and political contestation to play the role. Garifuna are an indigenous people; but in order to understand how they came to occupy that status, we must analyze the meanings of identity terms and struggles over them.

Chapter Overviews

The first two chapters provide ethnographic and historical grounding for the sections that follow while developing their own arguments and interventions. Chapter 1 provides an account of the community where I conducted research, introducing some key, recurrent themes: the idea and practice of "community"; transmigration; class differentiation; land displacement; and local discourses on modernity, tradition, and racism. The chapter explores local uses and meanings of racial and ethnic categories, analyzing how Garifuna identify with the racial category Black, identify racism as a crucial feature in their lives, and produce ambivalent accounts of their relationship to tradition and modernity.

Chapter 2 analyzes the historical position of Garifuna and constructions of blackness within Honduras in the first half of the twentieth century, while also exploring transformations in Garifuna self-representations in the public sphere. In this period, dominant constructions of the Honduran nation positioned Garifuna in the ambiguous position of what I call "native Blacks." On the one hand, they were compared with Indians and culturally positioned as primitive others within the nation. On the other hand, they were racially positioned as Black, a category that represented a foreign threat to the nation. These representations emerged, in part, out of struggles over ethnoracial hierarchies and labor competition on the North Coast. The chapter also examines how Garifuna negotiated their difficult position vis-à-vis mestizo nationalisms. I identify a shift from self-representations that emphasized Garifuna cultural particularity and differences from other groups identified as Blacks to affirmations of a Black identity in antiracist struggles that emerged in the 1950s. The chapter shows how racial and ethnic identities change over time as a result of conjunctions between transnational processes and struggles for inclusion within nations.

The subsequent two chapters focus on Garifuna organizations and institutional power, tracing the formation of a panracial ethnic movement in the 1980s, the consolidation of official multiculturalism in the 1990s, and the paradoxes of racial–cultural politics in the new millennium. Honduras is perhaps the only country in Latin America where peoples identified as Black and indigenous occupy the same juridical position as ethnic subjects with collective rights. Chapter 3 offers an interpretation of how the multicultural paradigm in Honduras took on this character. I discuss transformations in state discourses of ethnicity and examine transformations of Garifuna activism in the 1980s, when OFRANEH took up indigeneity as a frame of struggle and self-representation. I trace the complex negotiations between blackness and indigeneity resulting in a paradigm of "ethnic autochthonous" politics that informed state programs and legislation in the 1990s. The chapter follows key developments in ethnic politics in that decade, paying particular attention to conflicts over the meaning and scope of ethnic recognition and rights, particularly with regard to land, resources, and territory.

Chapter 4 continues this discussion, analyzing how state institutions attempt to diffuse the oppositional potential of ethnic movements through defining the limits of ethnic rights and managing structures of "participation." I show that while activists do not always accept these limits, the politics of participation contribute to conflicts not just between activists and the state but also between activists themselves. I proceed to examine differences between the two principal Garifuna organizations, ODECO and OFRANEH, in terms of their political projects, engagements with blackness and indigeneity, and relations to neoliberalism. Whereas OFRANEH continued working within a model of indigenous rights, linking collective cultural rights to critiques of neoliberalism and U.S. imperialism, ODECO increasingly placed Garifuna within an emergent, hemispheric politics designed to heighten the visibility of Afro-descendants and combat racial discrimination through legislation. I ultimately highlight surprising conjunctures between these different modes of "identity politics" and anti-imperialist projects that cut across racial and ethnic lines.

The final chapters return to the politics of race and culture in everyday life, examining daily discourses and practices of blackness and indigeneity. Chapter 5 draws on a scandal involving U.S. hip-hop entrepreneur Sean

Combs and Honduran factories to introduce an analysis of how young men embrace the fashions and styles they associate with "Black America". Working off their own interpretations, I analyze these practices as forms of Black diasporic cosmopolitanism that remake the Garifuna image. In these practices, assertions of ethnic particularity and indigeneity give way to assertions of participation in the broader category Black and associations with the resistance, status, and masculinity of a stereotyped Black America. In developing this account, I resist both romantic accounts of cultural resistance and cynical accounts of cultural imperialism, arguing that the symbolic power of Black America relies both on subaltern resistance and on U.S. hegemony.

Practices of Black cosmopolitanism produce representations of a Garifuna subject that differ from the images of deep cultural traditions and rooted ethnic difference central to official multiculturalisms and Garifuna activisms. In many ways, they represent efforts to escape the limits of being rendered a traditional subject. Nonetheless, most Garifuna I know also engage in everyday discourses and practices of indigeneity. Chapter 6 examines everyday engagements with indigeneity in Sambo Creek, ranging from positive assertions of the value of custom, critical evaluations of tradition, and local efforts to recuperate ancestral land. The chapter analyzes the relationships between different modes of Garifuna identity formation discussed in previous chapters, focusing on the tensions between them to explore what they reveal about the paradoxes of ethnic recognition and dilemmas of subject formation in an era of multicultural neoliberalism.

Ultimately, I hope this book manages to capture something of the complexity of the politics of race and culture among Garifuna in Honduras as a window into contemporary modes of dominance and efforts by social subjects to chart a course within and against them. It does so by examining what Garifuna make of themselves under the constraints they face and by exploring how their practices of self-making dwell upon, and expose, ideological oppositions between blackness and indigeneity and diasporas and nativisms, which are the product of colonialism, nationalism, and imperialism in the Americas.

I also hope that this book will be of use to Garifuna struggles. Activists sometimes call *antrópologos* (anthropologists) *antropófagos* (cannibals). If Garifuna have historically been labeled "savage," they reverse the evaluation, casting anthropologists as cannibals that feed off the natives to make their careers. Rather than treat Garifuna as a remnant of cultural exotica, my project analyzes power relations (Honduran nationalisms, everyday racisms, and official multiculturalisms) shaping Garifuna lives. As I became more involved in studying Garifuna activisms, several activists wondered to what use it might be put. Would a study of organizations expose their strategies to their enemies? Would a study of powerful institutions, such as the World Bank, be more useful? I have tried to take these questions to heart, drawing primarily on publicly available discourses produced by organizations and identifying institutional strategies for mitigating the progressive potential of ethnic politics.

Still, I have no doubt learned more from Garifuna activists than they will learn from me about the dynamics of political struggle and institutional power. I hope that analysis of Garifuna activisms illuminates the importance of their struggles and encourages further dialogue about where Garifuna politics has been and where it may go. A more significant contribution may lie in the book's analysis of the tensions between different aspects of Garifuna identity formation, especially between consumer practices that engage Black America and affirmations of Garifuna ancestrality. By shedding light on the tensions between blackness, indigeneity, and cosmopolitanism as products of the difficult position that Garifuna occupy in relations of power, I hope this study provides resources for activists to creatively engage everyday forms of identity struggle that respond, in part, to the limitations of multicultural recognition and the endurance of racial discrimination.

1

Race, Modernity, and Tradition in a Garifuna Community

In 1994, I came to Honduras to conduct preliminary fieldwork. Before arriving I had arranged to meet officers of the Black Fraternal Organization of Honduras (OFRANEH), an organization that promotes the cultural, political, and territorial rights of the Garifuna people. I approached OFRANEH with a project on the education of Garifuna as a window into interethnic relations and racial–cultural discrimination in Honduras. Leaders of the organization voiced support for the project, but tensions immediately surfaced. One problem concerned where myself and my partner at the time should reside. I hoped that we could live in the city of La Ceiba—where OFRANEH had its headquarters—because high schools were located in the city and because almost all previous studies had neglected Garifuna living in cities.[1] But the president of OFRANEH was skeptical. He told me it would be difficult to find a host family in La Ceiba and added that if I wanted to study Garifuna culture I needed to live in a Garifuna community.

Influenced by critiques of the culture concept and village studies, I was confronted with a perspective on community as the quintessential locus of culture and identity. As Sahlins quips, anthropologists began to panic about the notion of culture around the same time the peoples they typically studied were "talking up their culture" (20). The same could be said of place; as anthropologists began to critique reifications of community and emphasize transnational relations and multisited ethnographies, a politics of territoriality emphasizing integral relations between place and culture gained traction. Whether I liked it or not, my research could not avoid the Garifuna community. The president of OFRANEH and I soon reached a pragmatic compromise that my partner and I would live in Sambo Creek, a Garifuna community located within close reach of La Ceiba. A member of OFRANEH accompanied us on the bus and ran into a distant relative named Miriam. He asked Miriam if she knew of anyone who could rent us a room, and, upon arrival, she directed us to the house of her aunt Luz who occasionally accommodated foreign boarders. After negotiating room and board with Doña Luz and Miriam's brother Tyson, we saw Miriam again, and she asked us where we were from. I said "Texas" and she asked, "What's racism like in Texas?" Surprised by the question, I responded that where we lived (Austin) racism was not as open as in the past, when different groups were segregated and Blacks and Latinos were treated with contempt. Nonetheless, groups tended to live in their own neighborhoods and racism still existed. Miriam nodded and said: "Sounds like here."

In this chapter, I locate key themes of this book in everyday discourses of place, race, culture, tradition, and modernity within the "Garifuna community" of Sambo Creek. If racial-cultural identities are always made through social relations, places are made through interconnection rather than isolation (Tsing 2002, 456). As Gupta and Ferguson argue, "the identity of a place emerges by the intersection of its specific involvement in a system of hierarchically organized spaces with its cultural construction as a community or locality" (8). This approach draws attention to the historical production of place, locality, and community within uneven sets of power relations. However, social agents engaged in the making of community may partially elide the connections that constitute place, producing locality in terms of bound space coeval with a particular culture and identity. Such constructions are not simply characteristic of activist projects in defense of the Garifuna as a people but of everyday Garifuna practices and discourses of community, a lived reality involving extensive connections to other places and attachments to locality.

Garifuna evince deep relations to place as community, even when they do not live there. Many transmigrants who live and work abroad return when they can and, in absence, maintain ongoing connections through letters, gifts, videos, remittances, and phone calls to family and by participating in hometown associations (Gonzalez 1988; England 2006). Sambo Creek, like many other communities, has a transmigrant organization in New York City that funds projects such as the restoration of a church or the construction of a school. Community connotes a home of origin, dwelling, and return. It is also conceived as a privileged locus of Garifuna identity, language, and culture. However, if Garifuna affirm community as the site for the reproduction of tradition, they do so with considerable ambivalence, juxtaposing the desire to remain traditional with a desire to be modern.

This chapter introduces my fieldwork in a Garifuna community and explores a series of interrelated dynamics and discourses: the opposition between modernity and tradition; transmigration; land displacement; identity categories; and racism. Anticipating arguments central to the book as a whole, I suggest that the conflicts between the ideologically loaded notions of tradition and modernity do not find ready resolution in harmonious cultural hybridity but reflect deep tensions of everyday identity formation under conditions of racial-cultural hierarchy. We see such tensions reflected in local accounts of land displacement, one of the key threats to "community" in Sambo Creek; Garifuna discourses on land loss also highlight mestizo encroachment and racism. I then provide an analysis of Honduran ethnoracial terminology and Garifuna perceptions of racism. Much of the literature on anti-Black racism in Latin America suggests that its victims fail to fully recognize, and thus combat, forms of racial discrimination that oppress them.[2] In contrast, Garifuna I know voiced an acute awareness of racism within and beyond their community, despite the absence of overt racial conflict and official denials that racism is a problem in Honduras. Nonetheless, Garifuna discourses of modernity and tradition, intersecting in complex ways with discourses of blackness and indigeneity, reflect struggles to assert multiple forms of belonging within enduring racial-cultural hierarchies. The discourse of modernity continues to cast a shadow over Garifuna, even as they directly confront racism and affirm their cultural heritage.

Locating Fieldwork in Sambo Creek

Sambo Creek is located on the North Coast of Honduras, approximately twenty kilometers West of the port city of La Ceiba. According to the 2000 census, Sambo Creek has a population of 2,720 people, practically evenly divided between Garifuna (47.87 percent) and "otros" (mostly mestizos) (51.03 percent).[3] The historic center consists of a cluster of densely packed houses and other buildings (e.g., churches, a general store, a pool hall, a salon for meetings and dances) near the beach. A main road runs from the center to the La Ceiba-Trujillo highway, with residential areas and substantial unused private land lying on either side. Sambo Creek is a difficult place for me to characterize because of changes over the time that I have known it and because any descriptive angle I take could be countered by another, rendering appellations such as rural, urban, traditional, modern, thriving, declining, and so forth, a matter of perspective.

Based on observations from fieldwork conducted in 1979–1980, Carolyn McCommon described Sambo Creek as a "traditional, rural, Black Carib village," equating tradition and rurality with the lack of amenities such as electricity, sanitation, and water systems (60–61). She noted that the majority of houses were made of "wattle and daub" (with mud walls and palm-thatched roofs, known as *manaca*) or, if the owner had the means, were constructed clapboard style with the bark of the royal palm tree. Her understanding of tradition as the absence of the signs of modernity (problematic in itself) could not describe Sambo Creek in the mid-1990s, if for no other reason than that such signs proliferated, albeit unequally, within the community. By then the town had electricity, running water, and a septic system; most houses were constructed of cinderblock, and amenities such as refrigerators and electric stoves were increasingly common in the homes of relatively better-off families, most of which had transnational connections.

Graffiti drawn on a wall in Sambo Creek, 1999. Photograph by the author.

From an optic that focuses on the transnational dimensions of life and landscape, Sambo Creek no longer appears a "rural, traditional community," particularly if we pay attention to signs like the graffiti spread around town or the hip-hop clothes worn by many young men. Yet Garifuna (and mestizos) I know often described the place in such terms, pointing out "here we live close to nature" as we would bathe in the river or walk by the beach. The cultivation of crops such as yucca and plantains has diminished over the years, but some individuals, especially older women, continue to farm and the place has enough chickens, pigs, smells, and views to make it quite rural. Then again, Garifuna said that things have changed a lot since the road to La Ceiba was paved in the early 1980s, electricity arrived a few years later, and mestizos began to arrive in greater numbers. Several residents joked that Sambo Creek had practically become a neighborhood of La Ceiba.

My own perspectives on the community have been informed by my location within the household headed by Doña Luz, who was raising four grandsons while her daughter Emily lived and worked in New York. Emily had left Honduras in the early 1980s, shortly after the birth of her fourth son, Jason. Due to her undocumented status, she had never been able to return, though she kept in close contact and helped run family affairs from afar. Luz depended almost entirely on money sent by her daughter. Luz's husband lived in Miami but rarely sent support, and her only other child, a son, had been murdered in New York while trying to recover a debt. Forever grieving the loss of her son, Luz had persevered, supplementing remittance income by baking *casabe* bread (a traditional food and marker of Garifuna identity) and other goods for sale. In the mid-1980s, she managed to save enough money to build the modest cinder block house where I came to live during fieldwork.

Luz presided over a "matrifocal" household (Gonzalez 1969) with a composition of extended family members that varied over time. Luz and her grandsons (Marcos, Milton, Antonio, and Jason) formed the core members of the household. During the time I lived there, always in the ambiguous status between paying tenant and honorary kin, numerous other people lived in the house. Luz's nephew and one of my closest friends Tyson stayed for a while, avoiding family problems at home. A young family—wife, husband, and young child—embroiled in a property dispute in another community stayed for a couple of months. Jeni, a young woman from a community east of Trujillo, studied in La Ceiba and contributed domestic labor to the household, particularly cooking and washing (the youngest grandsons did much of the cleaning). Several other young women and men, always related to Luz, however distantly, stayed in the house for short periods of time. Although Luz was born and raised in Sambo Creek and her three sisters continued to live there, her kinship networks extended beyond the community to other Garifuna settlements, key cities like Tegucigalpa and La Ceiba, and the United States.

My social networks in Sambo Creek, and thus my fieldwork, were shaped by my affiliation with Doña Luz and her extended family. I developed relations of familiar sociality most readily with friends and relatives of Luz's extended family, particularly with young Garifuna men. I did establish relations with Garifuna and mestizo individuals independently from my familial affiliations. I taught an English class two nights a week and became friends with several of the young men and women who attended regularly. Playing basketball in the nearby community of Corozal gave me another entry point into the lives of young Garifuna men. My interest in Garifuna activism also led me to establish relations with a number of different Garifuna men in La Ceiba and various communities.

In the course of my fieldwork, I came to know a handful of Garifuna who were evangelical Christians. Although Evangelicals were strongly represented in the community, most people I knew identified as Catholic and critiqued what they saw as the hypocrisies of the *"Cristianos."* At the same time, most Garifuna I knew did not reveal to me any deep involvement in spirit possession and other rituals associated with the particularity of Garifuna religion and spirituality, in contrast to individuals and families studied by Johnson (2007) in the same region. My perspectives and knowledge of everyday life in the community were shaped by the contingencies of my familial connections, gender dynamics facilitating closer relations with men than women, and my research interests in the politics of race and culture.

Having qualified the capacity of my research to represent the diversity of Garifuna (not to mention mestizos) in Sambo Creek, I draw on two of my closest friends and key informants, the siblings Tyson and Miriam, to locate the importance of transnationalism and local perspectives on racism in Sambo Creek. Miriam, the eldest, liked to mock the flamboyance and laziness of her slightly younger brother. She often commented on how Tyson didn't like to fish, a staple of traditional male Garifuna subsistence practices now relegated by many younger Garifuna as an economically marginal activity. "He just fishes for women," she would say. By the time of my first fieldwork in the mid-1990s, Miriam had begun to set up an independent household with her husband, a man originally from another community, who worked much of the year on cruise ships. They first rented a house from an aunt of Miriam's living in New York and later bought a house from another relative living in the United States. Although Miriam had managed to find a measure of economic stability, only a few years prior she had been a domestic worker for an elite mestizo family in La Ceiba. She recounted the discrimination and humiliation she endured:

> I didn't sit with them to eat at the table. They shouldn't have treated their employ that way; they had to love their employee. I didn't share the same bathroom with them. Understand? Although I was serving them they always had a low opinion. I don't know. It was like that there. They gave me my own glass so that I wouldn't drink water from the same glass as them. For that I left them there because I was serving them and so they practically had to treat me like another one of the family. But I didn't share anything with them.

In Miriam's account, the moral imperatives of domestic work required that her patron treat her as an honorary member of the family. Instead, the mestizo family shattered the "mirage of care" (Scheper-Hughes, 108) by engaging in forms of discrimination that set her apart from the family and rendered her a threat to its purity. Class and racial differences became magnified in the social intimacies and distance characteristic of domestic work, resulting in strict boundaries of contact.

Tyson also had strong opinions concerning racism, linking it to the lack of Black economic power. He saw his own destiny determined by whether or not he would get to go abroad, studying English from the dictionary and movies, particularly movies depicting inner city African Americans. He shrugged off critiques by Miriam and others who suggested he was lazy, arguing that work paid so little in Honduras that to break your back made no sense. Walking with me around town, Tyson would point out how practically all the "good houses" in town were "built with dollars," from money earned at sea or in the United States. Honduran money, lempiras, held little value, and the currency devaluation prompted by neoliberal reforms made things worse. In the mid-1990s, Tyson lived in the house of his mother (and father; like others, he referred to the home as his mother's possession), a simple cinder-block structure built in the early

1980s that was wearing badly. He blamed his father for the lack of economic opportunities for himself and his siblings, expressing resentment that his father never took advantage of working on cargo ships to land in the United States. Tyson managed to migrate in 1998 with the passport of a U.S. African American soldier he bought from a friend of a cousin who bought it from someone else. He quickly established himself in New York as an air conditioning and heating mechanic, working long hours and earning good pay. When I visited Sambo Creek in 2004, his mother's house still needed repairs but had a new stove and refrigerator purchased by the wages Tyson earned in New York. By my last visit in 2008, the house was completely remodeled.

Economic Conditions and the Importance of Transmigration

As the stories of Miriam and Tyson suggest, the fortunes of most households rested heavily on money and goods sent from abroad. People I know identified only a handful of local mestizo and Garifuna residents as *pudientes*, wealthy individuals whose power and income based on land and business ownership were perceived as deriving largely from ill-gotten means. Nonetheless, status and class distinctions mark the landscape, by the size and quality of homes and possessions. Once or twice a year, one of the wealthier, documented transmigrants drove a bus loaded with goods from New York to Honduras. One day I saw the bus arrive and watched residents cart off appliances, bicycles, furniture, clothing, tools, and videos sent by relatives, who typically worked low-wage service sectors jobs such as home attendant and janitor. Large-scale transmigration from Sambo Creek to the United States began in the late 1960s, a decade later than in some communities (McCommon, 77). In that period, the Standard Fruit Company, where many Garifuna men from the community worked, scaled back operations in La Ceiba. Although the initial migration wave consisted primarily of men, residents estimate that now approximately equal numbers of women from the community live in the United States and joked that half the town lives in the United States, mostly in major cities such as Miami, Houston, New Orleans, and especially New York.

Economic opportunities in Sambo Creek were limited. A shrinking group of mostly older men fished in the Cayos Cochinos, a group of cays off the coast, as their primary source of subsistence and income. Fishing, however, is difficult work with variable returns on the labor. Many youth

Garifuna men returning from fishing, Sambo Creek, 2004. This "traditional" source of livelihood is on the decline. Photograph by the author.

preferred to hire themselves out as divers on international fishing boats, receiving good pay by local standards; but this work was irregular and lasted only several months in the year. A few men found construction work in Sambo Creek, whereas others worked in La Ceiba as tailors, butchers, shop assistants, and so forth, typically earning little more than the minimum salary, between 2.50 and 5.00 dollars (U.S.) a day. Others worked as waiters and bellhops in the Bay Islands where they earned better pay but had to pay for housing. Finally, work on cruise ships provided one of the most desirable job opportunities for "sons of the community" who did not reside in the United States.

Garifuna women faced even more limited opportunities in the local economy. A number of older women sold fruits and coconuts in La Ceiba or the banana plantations of Coyoles, located two hours away by bus. Although on good days vendors could earn above the minimum wage, the money they earned was often the primary source of household income, and vending was considered an occupation of the poor (see Khan 1987, 187). After a disease killed most of the coconut trees in the late 1990s, and with decreased access to land, vending possibilities became more restricted. Like Luz, many women engaged in small-scale vending of various goods (bread and sweets, ice, drinks, eggs, fruit) from their homes. Several women raffled items such as gold necklaces or sold the lottery, turning a small profit of a few dollars a week. Beyond the community, women lacking educational credentials worked in the maquiladora factories of San Pedro Sula, earning around 35 dollars a week. A few others worked as domestics for elite families in La Ceiba. After 2001, a number of young men and women found jobs at a new tourist complex located a few kilometers away as maids, waiters, bartenders, and porters (see chapter 6).

A small but growing number of women and men with high school and university education worked as nurses, teachers, office workers, or managers in cities such as La Ceiba and Tegucigalpa. During my research between 1994 and 2004, the handful of Garifuna nurses and teachers in Sambo Creek came mostly from outside the community and lived in La Ceiba. Although the opening of the first local high school in the late 1990s made it easier for *Sambenōs* to acquire a secondary education than when students had to travel to La Ceiba, residents' ability to stay in school and pursue university training hinged on family income and thus typically on transmigrant labor. On the whole, most younger Garifuna without transnational income earned only enough to support themselves and contribute small amounts to their households, rarely enough to save capital to establish a business or construct a new home. Most local businesses run by Garifuna men and women (for example, small snack and soda stores, drinking establishments) were funded by capital from relatives abroad. Overall, wealth and status differences between households in the community reflected the earning capacity of family members elsewhere.

Class Status and the Ambivalence of Tradition

Class and status differentiation do not simply reflect differences between Garifuna residents but suffuse local perceptions of what it means to be modern and traditional. Rather than attempt to evaluate whether Sambo Creek today is best understood as "traditional" or "modern," I examine how Garifuna residents represent their community, and themselves, through the dichotomy. Here, I find it helpful to draw from James Ferguson's approach to modernity in terms of "a global status and political economic condition: the condition of being 'first class'" (187). Ferguson argues that the modernization narrative of postcolonial progress has lost credibility in many places in the world, particularly Africa. He refers not just to scholarly critiques of development but to an everyday lack of faith that "third world" national societies and economies are "developing" along the temporal telos where the rest could catch up to the West. However, the decline of that narrative has not, Ferguson suggests, led to the implosion of the modern as a discourse of hierarchical differentiation. Rather, the modern remains as a powerful marker of status, success, high standards of living, and being "first class." Thus, dreams of collective progress have become replaced with a "new reliance on individual spatial mobility. How is one to escape the status of being 'a poor African'? Not through 'patience' and the progress of national or societal development, but by leaving . . . Not progress, then, but egress" (191–92).

Like Ferguson's informants, most Garifuna I knew put little stock in the idea of national development as they suffered from the high prices and low wages resulting from structural adjustments engineered since the early 1990s. Many also aspired to get away, viewing migration abroad as the most viable option to *superarse*, to better oneself (see England 2006, 149–186). For them, the idea of the modern implied questions of material and social status. Cinderblock houses were both "modern" and less affordable than "traditional" wattle and daub constructions. Access to education, electricity, and conveniences (e.g., refrigerators) marked a modern lifestyle, sometimes rendered as "regular" and "normal." Achieving that lifestyle hinged not on national development but on transmigration. However, such progress could be framed not simply as individual but familial and communal. Hometown associations abroad use resources derived from egress to produce progress in the place of origin. Likewise, parents use dollars earned abroad to invest in their children's education in Honduras. Educational certification remains a mark of personal betterment and social status even if everyone knows that a janitor in New York makes more money than a teacher in Honduras. Unlike what Ferguson claims for the parts of Africa where he works, in Sambo Creek dreams of development and modernization have neither decomposed nor become completely individualized. Rather, they have become reworked within transnational, ethnic circuits connecting a "backward," "rural" community to the margins of the centers of global power.

The idea of the modern also implies hierarchies of race and culture, as Garifuna are acutely aware. My friends noted that racism today was less virulent than in the past in part because Garifuna had raised their "level of life." This idea did not directly imply that a modern way of life had simply superseded the traditions of the past or that the latter were necessarily inferior to the former. In Sambo Creek, ideas of Garifuna culture, typically conceived in terms of "traditions" and "customs" specific to Garifuna and inherited from the past, are the subject of considerable metacultural commentary, debate, and ambivalence.

Garifuna I know expressed considerable pride in Garifuna culture, often with no more provocation than my gringo presence. Doña Luz delighted in demonstrating her practice of tradition and insisted I go with her on trips to other communities for funeral anniversaries, when older Garifuna women direct rites to honor the ancestors (see Kerns 1983). On one of these trips, she rode on the bus in crisp new jeans and a Tommy Hilfiger shirt, changing into traditional dress when she arrived. On another occasion, she traveled with her sisters, all dressed in identical, short-sleeved print dresses and head wraps that represent both familial affiliations and participation in the unique traditions of Garifuna spirituality. Doña Luz told me that when her grandsons were younger she spoke to them mostly in Spanish. Back then, the school prohibited children speaking Garifuna in the classroom. But after hearing a radio program from a Garifuna organization advocating that children learn the Garifuna language, she began to speak it more at home. Most of the youth I knew acquired Garifuna as a second language, but they did learn it.

Members of the older generations often identified the virtues of the past even as they depicted life "before" as more difficult and less modern than in the present. Before everyone planted the land, shared food with neighbors, and built manaca houses for each other for nothing more than drink and food. Many Garifuna, young and old, said that those houses were more comfortable than the cement houses of today; nonetheless, manaca houses also signify poverty, and very few people I knew in Sambo Creek wanted to live in them. Luz's grandson Marcos once commented on how things had changed compared to the time of his grandmother, laughing: "now the Garifuna is modernized up the ass." He also once saw the devil in a dream, dressed like a schoolboy.

Members of the same family sometimes disputed the importance of the cultural legacies passed down by the ancestors. Chino, the young man who I introduced at the beginning of the book, was resolute in his commitment to stay at home as much as possible, finding enough construction opportunities in town to make a living. He was proud that his daughters were learning to speak Garifuna and argued with his brother, a manager in a milk factory in San Pedro Sula, who enrolled his children in a bilingual English/Spanish school, caring little that they were not learning to speak Garifuna. For Chinos's brother, the Garifuna language offered no cultural capital in the labor market; the requirements of social mobility and economic security demanded leaving behind elements of Garifuna tradition that, to his mind, had little practical application. Although his disinterest in teaching his children Garifuna was not shared by most people I knew, many assumed that if a child did not spend significant time in a Garifuna community, the child would not learn the language.

The realms of "witchcraft" (*brujería*) and "magic" were particularly charged. This was not an arena I investigated systematically, in part because many people I knew tended to distance themselves from it. An informant in a study on Garifuna perceptions of tourism in another community noted that Garifuna would not discuss these issues with outsiders, claiming that locals "are irresponsible and lie about peculiar beliefs, such as magic and superstition . . . The Garifuna people do not want to be know for those matters" (Kirtsoglou and Theodossopoulos, 144). And with good reason. As discussed in chapter 2, spiritual practices have been vilified aspects of Garifuna culture, historically rendered by dominant discourses as evidence of the lack of civilization and even devil worship. Contemporary evangelical Garifuna celebrate the particularity of certain aspects of Garifuna culture such as music and dance but denounce belief in the power of the ancestors to affect the living. However, such processes have not produced the disenchantment of the Garifuna world. Successive generations of anthropologists have demonstrated the enduring importance of distinctive Garifuna religious traditions that mediate social relations across the geographical distance separating kin and community. For example, Jenkins (1983) showed how migration to the United States led to an increase rather than a decrease in *dügü* rituals, as transmigrants funded ceremonies for the ancestors. More recently, Johnson (2007) has compared religious practices in Honduras and the United States, analyzing how Garifuna religion has become increasingly reframed as a religion of the African diaspora.

Nonetheless, for some, "superstition," and "witchcraft" function as internal impediments to progress. One man lamented to me that a relative once sold land to pay for a ritual heal her daughter, representing the action as a waste of resources for the sake of superstition. Tyson offered the following commentary in discussing the difficulties of starting a business in a Garifuna community:

> Garifuna tend to have a dirty mentality because they are very negative. I'll be honest with you. The Garifuna always wants to hide in witchcraft. This is a factor. What is the country with the most witches in the world? Haiti. And it's the poorest. Why? Because the people do not have a thoughtful mentality. They are always involved in this stupidity, something that has been abandoned throughout the world. This is now part of history. Let's go to Africa. It is said that there are excellent witches in Africa. It is also a poor country, a poor continent, for the same reason. They don't have a fruitful mentality. They don't have the vision to go to high school, much less the university. This is what happens in the Garifuna littoral in Honduras. You make an investment and someone makes you sick with witchcraft. They are very negative. How are we going to go forward? Never. The indio [mestizos] will always be on top because he doesn't think that if he starts a *pulpería* (small store) someone will make him sick.

These were among the most scathing comments about Garifuna culture, Africa, or other parts of the African diaspora that I heard from a Garifuna. By and large, the image of Africa has been recuperated as a sign of pride, and the colors and iconography of Africa appeared frequently. Here, Tyson mines stereotypical images of Africa and Haiti to critique what he perceives as an unproductive, antientrepreneurial "mentality" among Garifuna. His comments hark back to an earlier era of modernization theory that rendered non-Western cultural difference as barriers to progress. In cultural arenas such as food, music, and dance, he could delight in the persistence of customs he viewed as inherited from Africa. But with respect to witchcraft, contemporary Africa and Haiti become sites of a negative diasporic identification, places with people who, like Garifuna, are mired in poverty, lack a "fruitful mentality," and are stuck in beliefs the rest of the world has left behind. Tyson dreamed of opening a small business after acquiring sufficient capital from working abroad, imagining the entrepreneur as an economic and ethnic hero in the struggle for individual and collective prosperity.

Negative evaluations of some elements of Garifuna cultural heritage, though by no means uniform and uncontested, reflect contemporary perspectives on socioeconomic mobility and the enduring ideological oppositions between modernity and tradition. The perspectives of Tyson on witchcraft and Chinos's brother on the Garifuna language posit that becoming a successful cosmopolitan subject requires leaving "unfruitful" customs behind. Affirmations of Garifuna tradition run up against forms of socioeconomic pragmatism that evaluate culture, in part, on the basis of its utility for progress. These doubts about the utility of customs in the contemporary world cannot be divorced from a long history of dominant associations of Garifuna culture with savagery and poverty. However, self-critical perspectives on Garifuna custom should not be simply reduced to internalized inferiority. Tyson's critique is not delivered in a register of shame or embarrassment but of dismay at modes of thought that, in his view, prevent forward-looking Garifuna from getting ahead. Still, Tyson could not completely separate himself from what he decried. He surprised me one day by saying that he thought someone was trying to harm him with witchcraft. I told him I didn't think he believed in all that and he said, "I don't." He then laughed and said: "Those who don't believe are affected the worst."

My friends often compared Sambo Creek to other Garifuna communities. They would tell me that if I wanted to find the "pure" and "authentic" Garifuna culture, the "Garifuna Garifuna," I should go to the Mosquitia (Mosquito Coast). There, they said, people speak little Spanish and live a traditional life of fishing and planting. The neighboring Indians flee at the sight of other people and the people live a "crude" and "primitive" life of mud houses, poor roads, no electricity, and limited opportunity; but they are more pure and traditional. Such discourses render "other" Garifuna as objects of nostalgia, pity, desire, and envy, suggesting the felt dilemmas of negotiating between progress and tradition and between becoming modern and remaining Garifuna. In Sambo Creek, a marginalized place hyperassociated with cultural difference, metacultural commentary marked shifting spaces of sameness and difference and pride and distance from the singularity of an authentic yet troubling subject rendered as not quite modern. Nostalgic ruminations for times past may reverberate with cultural revitalization projects, yet the stigmas historically associated with Garifuna traditions (of poverty, filth, and savagery) also resonate in local evaluations.

"For Sale": on the road to Sambo Creek, 2004. Land speculation has led to high real estate prices in the region. Photograph by the author.

Displacement

Not even the dead have enough land to rest in peace. Will told me this during my visit in 2004 as he showed me the grave of his grandmother Luz who had died the previous year. The cemetery in Sambo Creek lies on the north side of town along the coast, separated from the beach by a narrow footpath. There is no room for cemetery expansion and no land available for an alternative site. Graves have been dug so close to the ocean that once several coffins washed out to sea during a storm. Gravesites have also become more elaborate in recent years, as better-off families purchase concrete platforms and expensive headstones, but the land problem effects everyone: How can the ancestors rest in peace crowded precariously together in such a fashion? How can the living imagine a future without access to land?

The cemetery stands as a testimony to one of the most significant problems plaguing Sambo Creek: the lack of land to grow crops and even build homes. Powerful outsiders have long controlled significant portions of land surrounding the town's center along the beach. From what I could gather from oral accounts, Garifuna first settled in Sambo Creek sometime in the mid-nineteenth century, proceeding mostly from the communities of Santa Fe and Guadalupe.[4] Local legend says that the community was named after a Miskito Indian (called Sambos in English). By the 1880s, Sambo Creek was large enough to be included in government records, which listed the community as having a school and twenty-five *manzanas* under cultivation.[5] As in other Garifuna communities, residents historically combined wage labor, fishing, and agriculture, the latter characterized by shifting cultivation of plots typically cleared by men but planted and harvested by women. Sometime in the 1910s or early 1920s, the Suiza Planting Company (controlled by the owners of the Standard Fruit Company) acquired land for banana cultivation in Sambo Creek. They did so, according to older community members, through intimidation. The company abandoned cultivation by the mid-1920s due to banana disease (Ramos, 433). Some of the company lands became used once again by Garifuna for cultivation but were subsequently claimed by powerful outsiders.

In the early 1940s, a wealthy mestizo affiliated with the dictator Tiburcio Carías Andino appropriated a large portion of the land immediately surrounding the town center to create a cattle ranch. This act of land usurpation remains a particularly notorious example of mestizo racism and government abuse, as police from La Ceiba forced Garifuna to abandon their plots and borrow food from other communities. Most of this land remained in the hands of various outsiders until the early 1980s, after leading members of the community successfully petitioned the National Agrarian Institute (INA) to recuperate part of it. During that process, Felipe Suazo, owner of the general store and one of the wealthiest Garifuna residents, bought a large portion of the disputed land from the private owner, who was in danger of losing the whole plot. Suazo divided the plots and sold them to individuals on the condition that they construct a cement house with a zinc roof (McCommon, 63). In most cases, only Garifuna with relatives working at sea or in the United States could afford to buy land or build a home in this neighborhood, known as the Colonia Suazo. The Colonia Suazo thus developed into a class-differentiated enclave with well-built homes, ample yards, good electrical and water service, and a higher proportion of mestizos than the Colonia Libertad, built on the land recovered in the name of the community via the INA.

The local town council (*patronato*) divided the communal land into individual plots and distributed them to community members (Garifuna and mestizos) through a lottery. The first houses were constructed in 1983,

The center of Sambo Creek, 2004. The close proximity of houses reflects land scarcity in the town. Photograph by the author.

bringing only temporary relief to overcrowding within the town's center along the beach as plots were divided and subdivided over the following two decades. This neighborhood, where I lived with Luz and her family, has limited infrastructure, poor roads, and by the late 1990s had already become overcrowded, with little room for the building of new structures on family plots. The following map shows residential patterns in Sambo Creek in the year 2000. Note the extreme density in the town center and the Colonia Libertad compared to Colonia Suazo and the large tracts with low population density on the northern and western sections.

The crisis in land access is connected to a decline in agricultural production. Describing Sambo Creek in 1980, McCommon refers to a "shortage of unoccupied land in the main portion of the village" (734) yet also suggests that agricultural production was an important economic activity for many Garifuna families. By the time I arrived in the mid-1990s, few Garifuna worked the land as a primary means of subsistence or income generation. Local explanations for the decline in agricultural production typically pointed to mestizo encroachment and/or the younger generation's loss of interest in farming. Consuela, a woman in her late sixties who still

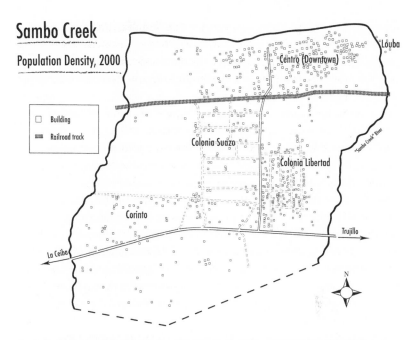

Sambo Creek, showing neighborhoods and population density. The center and Colonia Libertad are the most crowded parts of town. Map by Juan Mejia.

cultivated an agricultural plot, drew on both evaluations. I met Consuela through her daughter Selma, who came to my English class regularly. With the support provided to the household by transmigrant brothers, Selma had studied accounting in Tegucigalpa. Her mother reflected on the differences between the past and the present by noting: "Before the people worked the land. *Era más maltraba la vida* (Life was more difficult)." Before the school only went to the third grade but now youth study more. She mentioned Selma and laughed, perhaps at the thought of her daughter farming for subsistence. "The people of before sold in La Ceiba. They sold casabe, all that, because they worked the land a lot." I asked Consuela why people don't work the land as much today, noting that she still had her plot:

> Here in the colonia there are some that have their small parcels
> in order not to lose the tradition but this little bit of yucca only
> provides enough for one tub of casabe and that's it. And, well, the
> new neighbors that came were people that well, they robbed, they
> ruined your work. Look, they didn't let people live in peace. I still
> continue [farming] because I kept what I have and now I continue.

These new neighbors began to arrive in large numbers after the road from La Ceiba to Trujillo was paved in the early 1980s. "Behind the road came people from different communities or different sides of the country, people that didn't bring anything, that brought hunger and took for themselves what you had planted."

Consuela's comments sketch an ambiguous relationship to "working the land." On the one hand, she associates farming with a more difficult life in the past, characterized by hard labor and minimal education. She suggested that her daughter Selma, a graduate of secondary school and aspiring office worker, could leave behind that hard life of cultivating yucca and selling fruits, casabe, or other goods in the banana fields or streets of La Ceiba. On the other hand, when I asked Consuela why people no longer worked the land, she did not point to progress to provide an answer. Rather, she drew attention to the "new neighbors" (mestizos), outsiders who did not respect the property of Garifuna residents. Other Garifuna I know provided similar representations, asserting that the pigs and cows of new arrivals destroyed the crops of Garifuna, who did not have the custom of fencing off their land. In these accounts, a growing presence of outsiders, land loss, and the decline of farming went hand in hand.

Local accounts of land transfers highlight various forms of dispossession. Some narratives emphasize violent removal in the more distant past. Other stories highlight fraudulent land acquisition. One of the more notorious cases involves a former school director, who leveraged his position to acquire lands formally used for yucca cultivation (Brondo, 154). Some accounts depict poor and/or ignorant Garifuna selling land for a pittance out of necessity, while others highlight the inability of Garifuna to stop mestizos from squatting on land and acquiring title to it. As a result of such processes, much of the land once used for cultivation in the area known as Corinto became owned by mestizos.

For local Garifuna, land dispossession exemplifies mestizo racism. In an interview, Miriam drew direct connections between racism and land dispossession:

Here in Honduras, principally here in this village that is so small, there exists a lot of racism. A lot. A lot. Mainly among the indios [mestizos] here who simply like to see themselves as superior and before God we are all equal, right? This is what I think. The relations between the Garifuna are very distinct. An example. When a negra

(Black woman) lives with an indio (mestizo man), he doesn't marry her. When they live together there is always this racism. But to me it appears that a Garifuna man makes the india (mestiza woman) happy. In contrast, for the Garifuna woman there is always an obstacle. [MA: What would that be?]. To me it appears something among them, more among them. It shouldn't be that way. Before God we are all equal. From my point of view it exists a lot. They have even ruined the Black's land because you are calm and don't fight with them; they're left with everything because they see that all of this belonged to Garifunas. But what could you do when you had planted your yucca and they put in their cows, put in their pigs? You couldn't do anything because one is humble and they held all power because they didn't give any power to the Black, and it shouldn't be like that. Just like they have a right to live, so does the Garifuna. And Garifunas don't bother them. They always come to bother us.

It is worth comparing Miriam's two examples of racism—mestizo men refusing to marry Garifuna women and mestizo appropriation of Garifuna lands. Within Sambo Creek, Garifuna and mestizos alike often noted that interracial sexual relations, at least between Garifuna men and mestiza women, were more common in the present than in the past. Such a trend might be taken as evidence of racial harmony in the community. However, Miriam offers the opposite interpretation, pointing to a pattern in which Garifuna men marry mestiza women, yet mestizo men rarely marry Garifuna women. Other Garifuna women noted this pattern, explaining it primarily in terms of the attitude of mestizo men, who they depicted as desiring "negras" only for a good time.

Mestizo men I met sometimes made offhand remarks such as "Do you have a Black girl?," implying that Garifuna women were both attractive and available. Dominant representations of Garifuna have long rendered them hypersexual (Coelho 1955, 50). The growth of punta as the national dance-and images of Black sexuality in U.S. and Latin American media-reinforces these associations. Many mestizos I met asserted that they would not want a long-term relationship with a Black woman because they did not find them attractive, found them "too assertive," or would feel "ashamed" to marry them. These notions reflect a system of racialized patriarchy that renders Black women at the bottom of social hierarchies and beyond the pale of formal relations.

If Miriam's first example of discriminatory sexual relations foregrounds the gendered dynamics of racism, her comments on land dispossession do not overtly raise gender distinctions. Nonetheless, land displacement has gendered dimensions and, as Brondo (2006) argues, land loss and privatization disproportionately affect Garifuna women. Historically, land and home inheritance has passed primarily through matrilineal lines. As a result, more Garifuna women own homes than Garifuna men and familial usufruct rights for communal lands tend to pass from women to their daughters. Therefore, the transfer of land into private property involves a significant resource loss for Garifuna women to mestizo men and, to a lesser extent, Garifuna men. If accounts of land displacement often highlight the precarious status of women, they also lament community vulnerability. In this regard, it is worth noting that while the most visible leader of a movement to reclaim the lands possessed by the Castillo family was a Garifuna man, Garifuna women played a predominant role in the struggle. I will return to that struggle in chapter 6 but turn now to questions of racial categories, racism, and racial consciousness threaded through the previous discussion.

What's in a Name? Mestizo (Indio, Blanco, Ladino) and Garifuna (Negro, Moreno)

An analysis of identity terms provides a useful entry point into issues of ethnoracial distinction and discrimination. In interviews, as in daily conversation, informants often used a variety of different ethnoracial terms. For example, in her comments cited above Miriam consistently used the term "indio" or "india" to refer to mestizos. Indio, in this usage, does not refer to an indigenous group such as the Lenca or Miskito but to the majority population. In fact, although "mestizo" and "ladino" are the official terms of reference for the majority population, the terms "indio" and, notably, "blanco" (white) often take precedence in daily discourse among Garifuna and non-Garifuna alike.

During research on Garifuna in schools, I conducted a survey designed to identify students in a public high school based on their ethnicity. I got students to write their name, place of origin, grade, age, and "etnia" (ethnic group), and when I asked students what "etnia" meant, they, or the teacher, typically responded "race." I explained that the term meant their social or cultural group. In most classes, the teacher would ask students "Who are we?" Many students looked perplexed. Some laughed and said, "We're indios." Others said, "We're mestizos." In many classes, confused students would ask the teacher "Who are we?" and be told what school texts said they were—mestizos.

Students identifying as Garifuna (who did not fit the "we") had little trouble labeling their ethnicity, writing "negro," "negra," "Garifuna," or "negro Garifuna." A few even asserted that identity with phrases like "Black until death" (*Negro hasta la muerte*) or "Proudly Black." Likewise, the handful of Creole, Miskito, and foreign students responded with relative ease and consistency. The other students, even with their teacher's help, came up with various written responses other than "mestizo." Most of the alternative responses were "indio" and "blanco." A few students qualified mestizo with other terms such as "indios mestizos," "Spanish or mestizo," and "mestiza (blanca)." One student wrote "mulata" and another "*trigueña*" (a color term that can be used to describe dark-skinned mestizos or negros). Others listed their nationality (*Hondureño*), city, or religion. Several simply wrote, "I don't know."

When I told a mestizo friend who worked in the human rights movement about the survey, he asserted that terminological ambiguities reflected a crisis in national identity. I argue, instead, that the students' confusion over terms of self-reference stems primarily from their position as unmarked members of the dominant ethnoracial identity in the nation. As critical analysis of whiteness in the United States shows, the dominant ethnoracial category can become normalized almost to the point of invisibility as it becomes equated with national identity (Frankenberg 1993; Lipsitz 1998). Similarly, in Honduras the majority, dominant category can take on considerable ambiguity and collapses readily into the notion of "Honduran." We can return to the curious choice of the National Institute of Statistics to use the term "other" to denote 92 percent of the population, in contradistinction to "ethnic groups" or peoples such as the Garifuna or Miskito. Rather than view that gesture as a denial of self-identity to mestizos, I read it as a refusal to draw an equivalence between the dominant, "national" population and the Black and indigenous peoples who have been othered as racially and culturally distinct.

If mestizo is an ethnoracial category that does not have to speak its name because it stands for the nation, it is also a category permeated with the notion that Hondurans are primarily the product of European and Amerindian mestizaje. This point helps us understand how the terms "indio" and "blanco" can be used synonymously with "mestizo": "indio" and "blanco" refer to the purported racial bodies at the foundation of the representative Honduran. In use, they can stand not just for a part of that mix but also for the whole collective subject. Thus, students who said "we're indios" used a common label for the collective subject that their teacher called "mestizo." Likewise, those who used the term "blanco" could do so to highlight their own individual "whiteness" or to refer to mestizos as a whole.

While the terms "blanco" and "indio" can signify "mestizo," the terms simultaneously retain a hierarchical relationship inherited from colonialism. "Indio" often carries connotations of lower-class or peasant identity, poverty, backwardness, rurality, and violence, though it can also cull forth images of masculine rebellion, mobilized in moments of nationalist assertion.[6] In contrast, blanco signifies social status, political dominance, and physical beauty. Although Honduras has historically been characterized as one of the "least white" of Latin American countries, whiteness functions as a somatic norm (Hoetink 1967) in the social hierarchy. The national elite tend to exhibit lighter features than their less privileged compatriots. Fair skin and straight, blonde hair define the highest standards of beauty, reinforced by media images from the United States, Venezuela, and Mexico. Thus, the terms "blanco" and "indio" often refer to mestizos yet imply class and status distinctions.

Garifuna play on the distinctions, shifting from blanco, mestizo, and ladino in interethnic and formal settings to indio in more intraethnic and informal contexts, especially when critiquing mestizos. Garifuna invariably call those who steal, get drunk, start a fight, or make racist comments "indios." In an interview, Selma moved through a sequence of identity terms, from "blancos" to "those that say they are white" and finally "indios," in pace with a critique of how mestizos refer to Garifuna as negros. She thereby mocked their purported pretensions to whiteness and called them a racial name with no more distinction than her own.

As the terms "blanco" and "indio" represent the racial poles construed as embedded within the mestizo, the term "negro" marks a distinct racial type encompassing Garifuna and Creoles. The term "moreno," literally meaning "brown," typically refers to Garifuna. In the street, bus, and stores, I often heard mestizos calling out to strangers, "Hey negro," "Hey moreno," or "Trigueña." While they also hailed people with terms such as *chele* (light, white), *flaco* (skinny), or *gordo* (fat), rarely did I hear "Hey blanco" or "Hey mestizo." Blackness marked a difference worth noting, and the use of terms to refer to it (especially "negro") can take the force of an insult. Moreover, a tendency among some mestizos and Garifuna to use the terms "moreno" and "negro" interchangeably ignores distinctions between Garifuna and Creoles; the latter sometimes protest being called "morenos" to distinguish themselves from Garifuna.

In interviews and conversations, I often asked Garifuna what term they preferred—negro, moreno, or Garifuna—given that they are often used interchangeably in daily discourse. Several noted that Garifuna was the most correct and precise term. Others said they preferred negro because it referred to "all the Black races of the world." Tyson answered: "Negro. That's my color and that's how I'm represented on a world level. I'm of the negro race. You know. That's my representation. I'm of the Garifuna race but I'm negro. My color is negro. My language is what changes. Garifuna is my language. My color is negro." Another man answered with a shrug that it was all the same to him if you called him negro or Garifuna: "I'm Garifuna and in the second place, I'm negro." Such responses couch Garifuna as a type of Black, as part of the African diaspora. Yet in practice, the terms do not translate simply into an academic distinction between race (represented by the category Black/Afro-descendants) and ethnicity (represented by the more particular category Garifuna). Garifuna and Black are not merely nested identities but entangled properties.

In daily use, the terms "Garifuna" and "negro" are so interchangeable that they sometimes collapse into one another. That is, not only can "negro" refer to the category of people also called Garifuna but Garifuna can occasionally stand for the larger category negro. An interaction between Luz and her grandson Marcos exemplifies this point. Marcos came home one day saying that he heard that Nelson Mandela was coming to Honduras. (The Garifuna organization ODECO had invited Mandela to attend the bicentennial celebration of the Garifuna presence in Honduras, but he did not come.) Luz asked who Nelson Mandela was and Marcos replied "The president of Africa." After I interjected, "The president of South Africa," Luz asked, "Is he negro?" Marcos responded, "Yes, he's Garifuna." Luz simply nodded. On other occasions, I heard different Garifuna speak of *Isleños* Garifunas (Garifuna Bay Islanders) or *Jamaiqueños* Garifunas (Garifuna Jamaicans) in reference to people otherwise understood as Creoles or Jamaican Blacks. These are moments of linguistic slippage where the meanings of negro and Garifuna become interchangeable. Luz and Marcos are perfectly aware that Nelson Mandela is not, in one sense,

Garifuna; that the president of South Africa does not call himself Garifuna or speak the Garifuna language or otherwise share the cultural traditions specific to Garifuna, and that he is both Black and different from them. In the moment of their conversation, however, such differences mattered less than the question of shared racial identity as Black. When Luz asked "Is he negro?" and Marcos responded "Yes, he's Garifuna," the interchange made perfect sense because the relevant fact to be established about Nelson Mandela was his blackness. "Garifuna" can sometimes mean Black because today blackness is conceptualized as integral to being Garifuna.

The significance of these associations will become more evident in chapter 2 when we assess arguments that, in the past, Garifuna distanced themselves from other Blacks and from being Black. In the 1990s, Garifuna I know used the term "negro" with pride despite (perhaps to spite) the deprecatory meanings and insults that accompany it. Selma noted how Garifuna prefer the term "negro" over the term "moreno", calling attention to the shifting meaning of the term depending on the identity and intent of the speaker.

> I prefer "negro" because we say that we're of the negro race. For me, well, sometimes it depends on who is saying it. Between ourselves, I prefer to say negros. "Negros, we the negros, we the Garifunas" but at least here it's unusual to say "we the morenos" and things like that. Instead we say, "we are negros" because we're of the negro race. For example, when we see each other we say "Hello negra" but practically never "Hello morena" . . . But the race that says they are blancos from here, when they call us negros, now that's insulting. It's not the same as when Tyson or Marcos says "hola negra." They say "those negros" and when, for example, there's a soccer game, they say "those Black sons of whores."

For mestizos, "negro" provides the word of choice for a racial insult, while "moreno" functions as a more polite term. Garifuna, however, tend to embrace the term "negro" in favor of the term "moreno". When I asked Tyson about the term "moreno" he laughed and shouted to anyone within earshot: "Moreno! I'm not moreno. These indios, maybe they have moreno [brown] skin. Not me. I'm negro!" Garifuna, particularly of the older generations, will use the term "moreno" to describe themselves or the Garifuna language, but in moments of public self-affirmation negro has become the term of choice.

This analysis of ethnoracial terminology highlights the multifaceted and contested character of naming and labeling self and other. In Honduras, these practices render stark distinctions between mestizos and negros (Garifuna, Creoles) as distinct types. Blackness represents less one end of a color continuum than a form of otherness associated with distinct racial–cultural groups. Such distinctions are not absolute. People refer to the children of "mixed" mestizo-negro parents as "mulatos" and mestizos sometimes acknowledge Black ancestry. Nonetheless, dominant uses and meanings of identity terminology echo the ideological formations of Honduran nationalism, where the mestizo descends from the indio and the blanco while the negro represents a subject apart.

Harmonious Racism

Within dominant Honduran racial discourse, there exists a long tradition of denying the existence of racism. Take, for example, the following statement by a mestiza editorialist from a major newspaper during the 1997 bicentennial celebration of the Garifuna arrival to Honduras, where Garifuna activists had called attention to racism.

> In the first place, I have the well-founded impression that the majority of Hondurans that belong to the race called ladina are not racists and do not discriminate against negros, caribes, zambos, garifunas, etc. . . . here there has not existed major race problems. Nonetheless, because they remain a little separated and apart from the large cities, the populations called Garifuna are also marginalized in small hamlets and villages, living in a tribal manner. Something good has come from all this; the conservation of the culture of this ethnic group; the presence of a strong race, even stronger than ours, with vigorous bodies and perfect teeth, with men that are the pride of national sports and some men and women who have excelled in the professional field, in business, the arts and civil society in general.[7]

This passage minimizes racism through a series of different tactics: asserting that the majority of ladinos are not racists; suggesting that Garifuna marginalize themselves; and proffering positive images of Garifuna bodies, culture, and achievements. Yet even the positive evaluations of Garifuna have a double-edged character. Aside from the arrogance assumed by the very act of evaluating a people, the positive qualities attributed to Garifuna turn on a set of stereotypes. The zealous attention to the "vigorous" body belies the article's title suggesting that skin color should be irrelevant to God's children. The fame Garifuna acquire as soccer players situates them as high achievers in the arenas of bodily prowess and entertainment while success stories in the professional world and civil society appear as exceptions to the norm. Finally, the positive connotations of cultural conservation cannot escape the negative associations with "living in a tribal manner," fixing Garifuna in place and time. Fraught with contradictions, the text expresses racism even as it disavows it.

Tyson provided a contrasting account in an interview that same year:

> Here there is a system of racism that is, like, harmonious, no? OK. An indio pretends to be your friend, an indio pretends to get along well with you as a negro but behind your back your first name is negro and your last name is son of the big whore. . . . The negro that doesn't see this lives in nothing. He's empty. One has to have conviction against racism. Do you understand?

Tyson insists on the existence of anti-Black racism, which he characterized as "harmonious," hidden under the surface of friendly sociality. His account, in turn, relies on a stereotype of the mestizo as treacherous indio that he found reflected in the Bob Marley song "Who the Cap Fit," which treats the theme of a friend's betrayal. The music of Bob Marley and the Wailers and their message of racial consciousness, Black redemption, and human liberation were very popular in Sambo Creek. Tyson drew on a relatively obscure song to personify a "harmonious," hypocritical, hidden racism in the figure of the indio, who would eat your food and be your friend when times were good but turn his back once you ran out of money. Although we should refuse to let stand a stereotype of mestizos as untrustworthy and treacherous, Tyson's characterization of "harmonious racism" captures important aspects of contemporary racism in Honduras. It suggests that interracial relations may not be characterized by overt conflict or blatant oppression yet nonetheless entail subtle discriminations. It also calls attention to the hypocrisies of racial dominance and denials of racism. Harmonious racism is a provocative label for imagining Honduran racism in an era of official multiculturalism.

Garifuna I know often remarked that racism today was not as open as in the past. The "before" often remained unspecified, but the most virulent forms of racism were identified with the Carías dictatorship (1932–1948). In that era, I was told, Garifuna had little access to education beyond the third grade, were largely prohibited from attending secondary schools, were barred from many elite social clubs and certain public spaces such as the Central Park in La Ceiba, and in general suffered considerable humiliation and repression.[8] Don Cornelio Zapata, who lived in La Ceiba during this period, related:

> The police in that era were a bit drastic with the people of color. There was a police chief named Jiménez. Whenever he saw a negro he would push him from the sidewalk and if the negro said anything he took him off to jail. When there was a dead dog they grabbed a negro to get rid of it. This I saw in La Ceiba. Whatever dead man appeared they went to get negros to bury him.

Such memories, passed down to younger generations, recall the Carías regime as a time when Hondurans, particularly Blacks, had few rights and little peace. Some older Garifuna, such as Luz, portrayed it as a time of terror when Garifuna would retreat to their homes at the sight of mestizo strangers. During their own lifetime, younger Garifuna could point to certain improvements in their situation, such as expanded educational opportunities, increased social mobility, and the end of prohibitions on speaking the Garifuna language in schools. The musical genre and dance "punta" had become a national sensation in the 1990s, and, as noted previously, interracial sexual relations had become more common. Nonetheless, for most Garifuna I knew racism remained an intractable problem, less overt and noxious than "before," but a scourge that would probably always remain.

From my gringo perspective, everyday social relations between mestizos and Garifuna in Sambo Creek seemed both extensive and relatively free of friction. Garifuna and mestizos lived in houses interspersed among each other, conducted economic transactions on a daily basis, greeted each other warmly on the street, and chatted together waiting for the bus. However, members of both groups, particularly Garifuna, called my attention to the social distance between them.

Garifuna often critiqued local mestizos for isolating themselves, noting that they rarely attended their funerals and wakes or tried to learn the Garifuna language despite living in a Garifuna community. They also pointed out exceptions, the handful of "almost Garifuna" who embraced the Garifuna "environment," learned at least some of the language, and established close ties with Garifuna residents. Yet such exceptions proved the rule that mestizos typically sought to remain separate. As examples, they claimed that mestizos created parallel institutions, building their own Catholic church (two exist in the community) and creating their own Fair. Mestizos I knew in Sambo Creek admitted that "a little" racism existed among them but asserted that Garifuna also excluded them. One young man claimed that Garifuna dominated the community soccer team and refused to give up the field to let mestizos practice. Others argued that Garifuna had long dominated the town council. One teacher I knew worried that the possible implementation of a bilingual/intercultural education program in the community would threaten his job security, noting a (failed) movement to hire only Garifuna teachers in another community. Mutual recriminations of impeded sociality circulated between both groups in Sambo Creek.

Most Garifuna I knew ultimately asserted that race relations were better in their community than in the cities where they worked or studied. Given the lack of clear-cut class disparities between mestizos and Garifuna in Sambo Creek, everyday interracial sociality did not play out within obvious discrepancies of social hierarchy. Beyond the community, however, Garifuna encountered more overt expressions of social disdain as racial inferiors out of place. Almost all of the daily racial offenses suffered in random encounters with mestizos—where Garifuna would be hailed with the phrase, "Hey negro" or openly insulted with comments like "This one is too negro" or "very burnt"—occurred in the streets of major cities. Four different people reported instances where someone shouted "Turn out the lights, it's dark in here" to signal that a "negro" did not belong. These incidents occurred in a high school in La Ceiba (the offended party got in a fight with the mestizo offender), in factories in Tegucigalpa and San Pedro Sula, and in the municipal building of La Ceiba. In the latter case, a former teacher who had secured a prestigious post working for the city noted, "For some of those people it was strange to see a negro in such a position. They wanted me to leave."

Many Garifuna I know linked racism to class status, arguing that as their socioeconomic situation had improved overt expressions of social superiority had diminished. Selma, who attended secondary school in Tegucigalpa, noted that racism was no longer as visible as "before" but provided an example of the racial prejudices involved in gendered professional work.

What happens now is that [racism] is not out in the open because persons of the Black race study, go to the university, mingle with other people. Now they are free to be what they want because they are free to be equal to the rest. But in any case it will always exist. They are always going to have a preference. For example, if a negra with a degree in marketing goes to a bank for a job it is not going to matter who has more ability. They are going to employ the blanca. I also felt something of this once, from a teacher. A teacher of mine once said, "Ah, to work in Bahncasa [one of the principal Honduran banks] one must be tall, blonde, white, well dressed." I had chosen this career and so I said to her: "But teacher, if they aren't going to employ a negra in an important place then why should I keep studying?" She took it back. She was sorry about what she said but . . .

Selma shrugged her shoulders to suggest that the damage had been done, that the teacher could not take back a slip that voiced common sense notions of racial preference tied to the idea of "*buena presentación*" (good presentation) in secretarial and other professional work associated with women. Good presentation is often listed as a necessary quality for such jobs and implies notions of clean appearance, proper comportment, and physical attractiveness. It also privileges whiteness as a beauty standard to the detriment of "Indian" or "Black" features.[9] For Selma, and other Garifuna I know, experiences of racial prejudice were not simply anomalous expressions of individual prejudice but manifestations of deeper patterns of discrimination.

We lack the statistical data necessary to fully analyze structural patterns of racism in arenas such as employment, education, housing, policing, and so forth.[10] During fieldwork, I encountered a host of mestizo stereotypes concerning Garifuna. Many of the most common images of "negros"—as happy, fun, peaceful, humble, sexual, and as lovers of music and dance— do not overtly degrade. Indeed, many mestizos invoked such notions to offer ostensibly positive evaluations of Garifuna individuals and communities. Nonetheless, the significance of such stereotypes also lies in what they negate. The idea that Garifuna are happy, fun, sexual, and relaxed resonates with notions of tropical laziness and lasciviousness linked to the North Coast. As the popular saying goes, "Tegucigalpa thinks, San Pedro Sula works, and La Ceiba parties." In this racialized geography of the nation, the association of Blacks with tropical diversion tends to come at the expense of other qualities such as industriousness, seriousness, and intellectualism. Likewise, celebrations of the Black as athlete extol the virtues of the body while neglecting those of the mind. Attributions of sexual openness turn readily into accusations of hypersexuality.

Within Sambo Creek, mestizos sometimes rendered Garifuna as unproductive and backward. For example, during my first visit in 1994, I struck up a conversation with a group of young mestizo men at the bus stop. I asked them how people made a living in town, and they immediately launched into a discussion of "morenos." One said, "Well, we work the land but the morenos here don't do anything. They just fish and work abroad. Consume, yeah, but plant, no." Another joined in and said, "They look for coconuts." A third laughed and said "and ride bikes." The first concluded: "They don't do anything. Only the indios." These young men represented Garifuna as essentially unproductive through a series of negations. Upholding agricultural work as the standard form of production, they dismiss the primary activities of Garifuna men—fishing and wage labor abroad—and ignore the productive role of women in cultivation and vending. These images reflect historical evaluations of Garifuna that ranked them below mestizos via gendered understandings of economic production. An association between "morenos" and consumption runs alongside this ideology of production as the image of Garifuna (young men) becomes that of a people who "don't do anything" but ride bikes. A common joke linked a Garifuna love of music and consumer goods: "Behind a Black is a stereo."

Despite the official recognition of Garifuna as part of national identity, their cultural practices remained subject to derision. The Garifuna language was a common target of critique. One evening at the local pool hall, run by a man who had worked in Boston, I witnessed a mestizo in his mid-twenties chide a Garifuna man for singing in Garifuna, asking him why he sang in "moreno." The man retorted: "What!? You're telling me I can't sing in my own language, in what is mine? You're an indio, you sing in Spanish right? I'm Garifuna and I sing in Garifuna." The mestizo responded: "Hey everybody, I saw in the paper today an ad for a job in San Pedro Sula. Wanted: Someone who speaks Garifuna." I heard an almost identical version of this joke from a mestizo teacher as he explained his reservations concerning bilingual/intercultural education. The message of the joke is that Garifuna is a language with little practical utility, of a different order than Spanish or English. Garifuna told me that on occasion a mestizo would mock them for speaking their "garu garu garu" in public places. This derogatory mode of imitation exceeds a critique of its utility in the labor market by associating it with primitive forms of communication.

One day a mestizo bus driver, relaxing after work, struck a conversation with me. He said that he heard that I was a teacher and that was a good thing because the people in Sambo needed a lot of education. "Negros are very backward. They will never arrive at the same level as us or you but it's important to teach them." I rarely heard such blunt assertions of Black inferiority. Nevertheless, mestizo representations of Garifuna often hark back to previous images of a savage, backward tribe. Sambo Creek, with its concrete houses, latrines, a smattering of cars, and other "modern" goods, may have fewer visible signs of "premodern" life than in the past. Mestizos within the community sometimes attribute such "progress" to a change in mentality brought on by mestizos and mestizo–dominated institutions such as the school. Such discourses not only justify the mestizo presence in the community but, like much media commentary, imply that Garifuna cannot "develop" without the intervention of external forces. The image of Garifuna backwardness and primitiveness (the negative antithesis to the modern) still lies around the corner from the apparently benign stereotypes of Garifuna as relaxed, peaceful, and fun and from positive accounts of Garifuna traditions promoted by the state, international NGOs, and, of course, Garifuna themselves.

The anecdotes of stereotyping presented here, along with Garifuna stories of encounters with racism, belie an exceptionalist vision of Honduras as a country relatively free of racial discrimination. However, if racial prejudices, insults, and antagonisms become manifest in everyday life, they do not erupt every day. In the rhythms of daily life, most days, social relations between "negros" and "indios" proceed without overt friction and conflict. Tyson's identification of a "harmonious" mode of racism cited at the beginning of this section suggests that race relations are not what they appear and that racial antipathy undermines racial sociality. His representation of Honduran racism also serves as a call to consciousness: "One has to have conviction against racism." As I hope to have shown, many other Garifuna expressed such conviction, identifying racism as a problem informing and warping local social relations and hierarchies, the possibilities of socioeconomic advancement, and the realities of communal displacement.

That conviction, many implied, was relatively new. Tito, a young man in his early twenties who hoped to become a professional soccer player, responded to my question concerning how race relations had changed in his lifetime by invoking a more general shift in attitude among Garifuna in their collective self-evaluation as negros:

> There's a change now. There's a change because today the negro, that is the Garifuna race, now realizes that this race too is important because perhaps we have left the darkness where we negros lived. [Before] we felt humiliated among the indios but today no, because now we raise our heads and see straight ahead and now we know that we are not inferior to them.

Tito calls upon an image of collective enlightenment often associated with modernization discourse to suggest that Garifuna had recently "left the darkness" of racial humiliation. He does not denigrate Garifuna customs or traditions; in fact a few years after our interview, Tito would join a musical group that provided education on Garifuna culture and history. Nonetheless, his comments on racial consciousness converge with the widespread sentiment that Garifuna "progress" in material conditions and educational achievement, largely enabled by transmigration, were key to their improving position within Honduran society and their own self-image. The perception of a previously humiliated people, denigrated because of their blackness, jostles against the perception of an independent and proud people retaining their own unique traditions in the face of adversity. Garifuna struggles to confront racism and define themselves occur within the long shadow cast by the idea of the modern.

Tito's comments call attention to modes of historical narration that do not focus on Garifuna origins and cultural retention but on transformations in Garifuna self-perceptions and encounters with racism in recent generations. In chapter 2, we explore the historical trajectories of these transformations, analyzing racialization of Garifuna in the past and their responses to racial and cultural discrimination. If today Garifuna typically assert a Black racial identity and a particular cultural, "ethnic" identity as a people in confrontations with racism, how did they maneuver within structures of racial and cultural discrimination in the past? How has the production of Garifuna identity been entangled with blackness, perceptions of phenotype, and African origins? How and why did Garifuna come to embrace a public, assertive identification with blackness? How and why did cultural particularity and "ethnic identity" become constructed, affirmed, and politicized under the name Garifuna? Answering such questions requires attending to the dynamics of racial and cultural dominance and identity formation in the past. It also requires that we recognize that in the play of power relations, othering, and self-making, pat distinctions between "race," "culture," and "ethnicity" may not hold.

2

From Moreno to Negro: Garifuna and the Honduran Nation, 1920s to 1960s

During my fieldwork, I often turned to Don Alonso for help in clarifying historical puzzles. He typically answered my questions with stories from his fascinating life of extensive travel and numerous jobs—as deckhand, fruit company employee, municipal employee, fisherman, factory worker, and more. He spoke to me as one traveler to another even as I sought him out as an informant on things local. On one occasion, I came to ask him about the meanings of the words "negro" and "moreno" in the past. I had recently interviewed a former mestizo labor leader who had responded to my question concerning whether a particular person was negro by saying, "He wasn't negro, he was moreno." I knew what he meant; that the person in question was Garifuna rather than an English-speaking Black (West Indian or Honduran Creole) because the term "moreno" referred specifically to Garifuna. However, the stark opposition between negro and moreno violated present usage (Garifuna often call themselves negro), and so I asked Alfonso what the terms meant in the past. He responded with a vignette. Once, when he was young and working for the Standard Fruit Company (SFCO) (in the mid- to late 1950s), he was in the company hospital and the doctor asked him "Are you moreno or negro?" He replied: "I am negro, negro Garifuna." Alfonso told me, "I know that I'm negro. I don't want to distinguish myself from those others because we are all negros."

I asked him if he always felt he was negro, since his youth, and he said yes and mentioned that the teachers in school would always say a little about "our origins." He then talked about living in Belize in the 1960s, where he had discussions about racism and segregation in the United States, where whites would kick Blacks to the back of the bus. He followed how Martin Luther King, Malcolm X, and John. F. Kennedy tried to change things, but they were all killed. He stopped and asked me if the man I had spoken to earlier in the day was mestizo. When I said yes, he sighed and said: "Sometimes they believe that we're timid, that we're passive, but that's not the case." Historically, he said, Garifuna tried to remain apart from mestizos and to live "independent of the power of the state." I steered the conversation back to his sense of racial self, asking, "If, as you say, Garifuna come from negros and indios caribes, then do you feel more negro or indio?" He laughed and said, "Negro, clearly." I asked him if it had always been like that, and he said yes. I forged ahead, saying, "I read in a book that before Garifuna said they were more indio than negro, that they came from South America and didn't want to have anything to do with Africa." He said, "No, no. I think we always felt more negro," glancing at his arm. But then he added: "There are still people in Sangrelaya (a Garifuna community east of Trujillo) that look more like the pure Vincentino (person from St. Vincent); they have a whiter color than us."

If Alfonso initially explained the term "moreno" by pointing to how Garifuna were different from [other] negros, he refused any absolute distinction between them. He made clear that as a young man, in an interaction with a social superior during an era of clearly defined racial hierarchy, he was "negro, negro Garifuna," distinctively Garifuna but also like those others. On other occasions, Alfonso would draw out the difference as stereotypes, relating how Blacks in the United States were lazy or how Creoles felt superior to Garifuna. But he affirmed a Black identity for himself and insisted that he, and other Garifuna, had done so in the past. His comments rub up against one of the more intriguing yet least examined scholarly contentions concerning Garifuna history: in the past Garifuna identified with "Indian" rather than "African" origins, disassociating themselves from the category Black and other Blacks.

Anthropologist Nancie Gonzalez (1988, 1992a, 1997) articulates this argument most clearly, arguing "despite their evident debt from Africa and their proclivity to absorb foreign Blacks, for three hundred years they persisted in identifying themselves as purely Indian" (1992a, 403). "Only after the massive immigration to the United States following World War II--when they witnessed the awakening of groups of black power, did they begin to recognize their African heritage" (1992a, 427). Gonzalez draws on her own fieldwork in Livingston, Guatemala, during 1957–1958. At that time, Garifuna ". . . emphasized their South American origins, pointed out their ancestors had never been enslaved and carved out a distinctive heritage that denied any African heritage" (1988, 137). In a later publication, she asserts, "No one mentioned Africa. In fact they made a point of saying that they were in no way related to other colored peoples that I might know. Their ancestors had been light-skinned 'like you,' they would say, smoothing my arm" (1997, 200).

Similarities and discrepancies between the accounts of Alfonso and Gonzalez open a space to reconsider Garifuna forms of self-identification in the past and present. While their accounts converge on the idea that Garifuna ancestors had lighter skin than contemporary Garifuna and suggest the influence of Black politics elsewhere on Garifuna identity formations, their perspectives clash in the contention that Garifuna always felt negro (Alfonso) and the assertion that they rejected an African heritage (Gonzalez). They also conflict around the notion that Garifuna rejected any relation with "other peoples of color," as Gonzalez puts it. In what ways did Garifuna relate to ideas of African origins, groups understood as "Black," and the categories Black and Indian in the first half of the twentieth century? How, and why, did forms of self-identification and public self-representation change over time? This chapter traces different forms of self-representation among Honduran Garifuna in the period between the late 1920s and 1960s, arguing that we need to revise Gonzalez's thesis. First, I find little evidence that, at least in Honduras, Garifuna understood or represented themselves as "purely Indian" during the 1930s and 1940s. Rather, Garifuna, racialized as Black, appear to have understood themselves as part of that category yet emphasized their own historical and cultural particularity, distancing themselves from other Black groups and the stigmas of slavery and African origins. For them, acknowledging a Black identity did not necessarily imply an affirmation (or even recognition) of African origins or solidarity with other Blacks. Second, while I agree with Gonzalez that Garifuna developed new modes of self-representation after World War II, these developments cannot be understood simply as products of Garifuna encounters with Black diasporic politics elsewhere. We need to also situate them in relation to ethnoracial hierarchies, dominant discourses of blackness and cultural difference, and transformations in Honduran society that produced the conditions of possibility for antiracist mobilization in the 1950s. In the 1950s, Garifuna activists and intellectuals began to publicly affirm an identity as Black in projects directed against racial discrimination, emphasizing forms of oppression and struggle held in common by Blacks in their local struggles at home.

What follows, then, is a partial history of racial discourse, hierarchy, and exclusion on the North Coast and in the Honduran nation, with an eye toward interpreting the relationship between Garifuna and blackness. I draw on the scholarship of historian Darío Euraque (1996b, 1996c, 1998, 2003, 2004) and his important insights into Honduran nationalism, dominant racial discourses, shifting political conjunctures, and changing social relations among Garifuna, mestizos, and other Blacks. However, as Euraque suggests, the history of blackness in Honduras has yet to be written (2004, 172). This chapter analyzes various ways in which Garifuna produced discourses of race, origins, blackness, and belonging under conditions in which they were racialized as Black and rendered as primitive and backward, similar to Indians. In order to develop that account, we must first come to terms with a common understanding of Black identity as irrevocably tied to Africa and slavery.

Did Garifuna Identify as Black?

Reconstructing racial and cultural identity formations in the first half of the twentieth century is no easy task. Written accounts produced by Garifuna in the era are scarce, and accounts produced by outsiders (intellectuals, state officials, journalists) filter their voices through their own prejudices and projects. Reflections from contemporary Garifuna provide a crucial resource but may occlude the diversity of past perspectives through investments produced by more recent histories. Discourses of African ancestry, sentiments of belonging to the category Black, and affirmations of blackness tend to articulate with one another today in ways that they likely did not in earlier eras. An analysis of fieldnotes from anthropologist Ruy Coelho, who conducted fieldwork in Trujillo, Honduras, during 1947 and 1948, will help develop this point.[1]

Coelho, the reader might recall, was a student of Melville Herskovits and examined questions of acculturation and African cultural survivals among Garifuna (who he, following convention, called Black Caribs or Caribs). His dissertation offers little commentary on how Garifuna understood their own identity, but his fieldnotes report on the position(s) Garifuna, in particular men, take toward their ancestry. I quote him at length because his comments require close scrutiny and serve as a sounding board for later discussions. Coelho, like Gonzalez, stresses that Garifuna disassociate themselves from slavery and Africa:

> The worst insult for a Carib is to be called a slave. From the
> beginning I was aware of the importance of this fact. All the

old men . . . repeated the same thing: the Black Caribs were not
African, and have never been slaves (the two being tied up in their
minds). One of the phrases I heard many times when the subject
of the *gubida* cult was discussed is: "It is the cult of our race." It was
implied by [sic] that they, as a free and independent people had
their own language and their own religion, and don't submit to the
rulers of the moment, and adopt their customs.[2]

With regard to Garifuna accounts of their origins, Coelho says:

I don't think I have a complete and clear picture of the facts, but
the way the Caribs ignore their origins, and are always discussing that matter, is a very interesting point. They don't want to be
Africans, that is slaves, like the other Negros, French, English
and Creoles. I hear many people say: "My grandfather had long,
straight hair and was as white as you." But the other alternative is
being Indians and that they don't want either.[3]

Coelho goes on to compare Garifuna accounts of themselves to mestizo
constructions of national identity in relation to Indians.

In this respect their attitude is identical with that of the majority
of Hondurans, who are proud to say they have Indian blood, but
are emphatic in disclaiming any relationship with the Indians of
today. For the Indians seen in the streets of the big cities, or living
on their own territories, are a very poor sort indeed. Their stature
is short, their traits don't show the beauty celebrated by the old
writers of chronicles, their condition is miserable. The Negros are
much better off than they are, for the Indians form the lowest strata
of the population. Of course, those people had nothing to do with
the building of the monuments of Copán, or the organization of
the defense against the Spanish, a tradition dear to the heart of
every Honduran. Lempira, the greatest national hero, is represented as a tall man, reminiscent of the Plains Indians of American
films during the 20's. After that model, the Black Caribs built their
own ideal type of the Caribs of old, a proud, independent tribe of
warriors. . . . This is a modern creation, put together by scholars
of the group, with the help of bits of information contained in

hand-books, and bad articles and bad stamps of third rate ency-
clopedias.. . .Their imagination, unfettered by any facts, built up,
and goes on building up, many different theories. [Douglas] Taylor
has some articles published in a small local newspaper of British
Honduras, whose author maintains that the Caribs are an ancient
"civilized" African race, having once a written language, presumably in Arabic characters! And that is only one out of many.[4]

Finally, Coelho recalls a conversation between himself, fellow anthropologist Douglas Taylor (visiting from fieldwork in British Honduras), and
Sebastian Tifre, a young Garifuna man who Coelho hired as domestic
help and principal informant.

There is an interesting episode with Sebastian, that I could see in
its proper light only recently. Sebastian once asked Taylor and me
if all Negros came originally from Africa. We said no, and told
him about the Melanesian, who are also considered Negros. His
next question was, where do the Caribs come from. Taylor showed
him St. Vincent in the map and, pointing to the Northern region
of South America, and the Antilles, told him there were Caribs all
over there, and there were still many left. "Why do they say that
all Negros come from Africa, then?!", he exclaimed. In his mind,
Caribs and Negros are equivalent terms. Taylor showed him photos
taken in Dominica, and told him about the mixture of Indian and
Negro blood that is taking place today in the island. We could see
he was embarrassed and disappointed. But on the night of Christmas night he had forgotten all about the Caribs with Indian traits
he had seen, and only retained one fact: there are Negros who
originally came from places outside Africa.[5]

If Coelho's initial assertions correspond with Gonzalez's argument that
Garifuna did not identify with Africa and (other) Black populations in
the region, his comments ultimately suggest that Trujillo "Caribs" neither
possessed a singular, settled account of their origins nor viewed themselves primarily as Indians.

Coelho was perhaps too concerned with identifying the cultural origins of the Garifuna to take seriously their efforts to do so themselves. In
fact, he denies Garifuna authority to make their own history, highlighting

their "meager traditions" and reliance on dubious texts.[6] Nonetheless, his fieldnotes provide food for thought. Coelho describes a conversation with Sebastian Tifre and his friends: "There was a violent discussion over an eternal question: the origins of the Caribs. As usual, there were two parties: the Africanists and the Anti-Africanists. I was surprised to see Sebastian take position with the Anti-Africanists, I didn't know he felt like that."[7] Coelho records nothing of the debate between the "Africanists" and the "anti-Africanists." He does say that the anti-Africanists are "the great majority" and discusses an Africanist in the following terms:

> the case of Victor Lopez is not yet clear to me; his arguments are based on common sense: "Of course we are Negros. Look at our skin, look at our hair!" Why can he see those things, when the others are so blind about them? Victor Lopez, as steward on American ships, has been to New York and Chicago; perhaps he identifies himself with high class American Negros, and that led him to the acceptance of his racial affiliations.[8]

For Coelho, Victor Lopez, an "Africanist" who accepts the truth of his own blackness and its origins, differs from the majority who are in denial of their origins and, thus, their genuine "affiliations."

Setting aside Coelho's psychological evaluations, we can emphasize two points. First, Coelho's notes suggest that in Trujillo in 1947 not all Garifuna shared the same position on their origins. As an example of the variation, one informant identified Caribs as "descendants of the Jews, of the tribe of Mannaseh, to be more precise."[9] In general, it appears that the older generation of men asserted that Garifuna were never slaves and did not originate in Africa, whereas a younger generation of men, some of whom had worked and lived abroad, debated the question of African origins. Second, we cannot simply assume that the anti-Africanist position entailed a denial of being Black, a rejection of the idea that Garifuna were negros. Take the reported conversation with Sebastian Tifre, who clearly views Garifuna as negros but at the same time questions whether all negros originally came from Africa. While Coelho, like many scholars of Afro-America, may have understood blackness in terms of African descent and a healthy identity as the affirmation of African origins, the possible conjunctures and disjunctures between ideas of blackness and Africa, and between expressions of ethnic particularity and racial solidarity, require more nuanced modes of analysis. Although some observers claimed that "morenos" "do not want to be called negros" (Lunardi 12), later in this chapter we see several cases where Garifuna men acknowledged in public forums that they were negros and/or members of the race of color.[10] After all, calling someone else "negro" was not merely an act of interpellation, it was an insult and an accusation.

Ultimately, we need to situate the production of race, origins, and history within the atmosphere of racial discrimination and political oppression under the Carías dictatorship. Coelho reports that meetings of more than ten people were prohibited and any sign of political protest met with

Sebastian Tifre (on the right), principal informant of Ruy Coelho, Trujillo, late 1940s. Notice their style. Reprinted from The Black Carib of British Honduras by Douglas MacRae Taylor (Viking Fund Publications in Anthropology, #17, 1951) by permission of the Wenner-Gren Foundation for Anthropological Research, Inc., New York, New York.

swift reprisals. The local leadership of elders had become co-opted by the government, while clandestine political discussions were part of the rhythm of everyday life. Indeed, we learn from the fieldnotes that Sebastian Tifre was part of a group (perhaps the same that debated African origins) that denounced Carías's National Party, referring to the execution of Garifuna in the community of San Juan for allegedly smuggling arms in 1937: "During fifteen years, what has the dictatorship done to the Morenos? Nothing more than send them to be executed . . ." (Coelho, 57).[11] Not long after Coelho left Honduras, Sebastian Tifre spent two years in prison for daring to publicly voice his allegiance to the opposition Liberal Party (Centeno García, 98–99). We return later to the articulations between emergent movements in defense of Garifuna and broader political currents in Honduras at mid-century. First, we need to understand the processes of racialization and nationalism through which Garifuna, by necessity, maneuvered. Coelho provides a clue here, identifying a relation between nationalist productions of a heroic Indian past and Garifuna self-representations of their distinctiveness as an independent people.

The "Black Problem" and Indo-Hispanic Nationalism

In 1926, after much debate, the Honduran legislature named the national money after the tragic, rebellious sixteenth century Indian leader Lempira. Four years later, the national census identified the majority population in Honduras as "mestizo" without registering the category "mulato." For Darío Euraque (1996c), these events represent two moments in the state consolidation of Honduras as an indo-hispanic nation. Prior to the 1930 census, the majority population was officially rendered "ladino," a term inherited from the colonial era that then referred to people who were neither pureblood Spaniards nor Indians. "Ladino" originally encompassed a variety of descent categories, including negro, mestizo (the product of mixture between Indians and Europeans), and mulato (the product of mixture between Europeans and negros). The shift in terminology from ladino to mestizo identifies the majority population in Honduras as the progeny of the Spanish and Indians but not Blacks. The elevation of Lempira to the pantheon of national heroes thus articulated with efforts to minimize the history of African slavery and identify the presence of Blacks as a foreign contaminant to the national body.[12]

As Euraque insists, the consolidation of indo-hispanic nationalism in Honduras must be understood in relation to transformations of the North Coast from a region marginal to the nation into a burgeoning enclave economy dominated by U.S.-based fruit companies. The outlines of that history are well known.[13] In the last quarter of the nineteenth century, the banana trade rapidly expanded along the North Coast, attracting people from the interior of Honduras and as far away as Europe, Palestine, and China. Initially, numerous companies bought fruit from local growers, most of whom ran farms of modest size. By World War I, however, three major companies—The United Fruit Company (UFCO), the Vacarros Brothers (later named SFCO), and the Cuyamel Fruit Company (absorbed by UFCO in the late 1920s)—had gained control over the fruit trade. They established extensive landholdings; built wharves and railroads; and controlled transportation, prices, and markets, undermining competition in their spheres of influence. The ultimate result was the Honduran version of the "poverty of progress" (Burns 1982), abetted by generous government concessions. The map showing the banana companies reflects the respective spheres of influence of the fruit companies, with the SFCO railroads surrounding La Ceiba and subsidiaries of the UFCO controlling the areas near Tela and Trujillo. The lines marked "unfinished projects" were railroads that the companies promised to construct, which would have connected the coast to the interior; their failure to materialize reflects the enclave economy.

The first decades of the twentieth century also witnessed the growth of nationalist thought (Barahona 1991, 265). At moments of political conflict, the trope of the rebellious Indian within the Honduran was deployed toward defense of the fatherland. For example, Froylán Turcios—poet, novelist, diplomat, and director of several newspapers—organized a movement opposing the occupation of U.S. marines in 1924. The patriots protested North American treatment of Hondurans as an inferior race, referring to themselves as "unhappy Indians" and highlighting their "Indian blood" (Turcios, 52, 102, 119–23). Such affirmations of Indian ancestry echoed similar constructions of mestizaje elsewhere in Latin America.[14] The writings of the influential Mexican philosopher of mestizaje, José Vasconcelos, were well received in Honduras (Mejía, 336). However, if Vasconcelos acknowledged the contributions of all world races to the "cosmic race," Honduran models of mestizaje tended to focus almost exclusively on two branches: the European and the Indian (Euraque 1996c, 144).

The racialization of the authentic Honduran as "indo-hispanic" dovetailed with attacks on the immigration of so-called foreign races.

In the 1920s, arguments for immigration restriction focused on Blacks and other "problem races" rang from the voices of anti-imperialist patriots such as Turcios, prominent politicians from both major political parties, and, importantly, labor organizations (Euraque 1998, 158). For example, in La Ceiba a worker's organization called the Sociedad de Artesanos el Progresso staged a public rally against Black immigration, publishing a letter that took the familiar line: while companies grew rich off men of "African origin," "our co-nationals, our sad compatriots" suffered from hunger.[15] Labor organizations also complained that foreign Blacks were given positions of authority and that they mistreated national workers (Posas 1981). Immigration per se was not the question. The same worker's association quoted earlier encouraged the importation of Italians and Spaniards, "those that best adapt to our climates and customs and those that history has recognized as effective."[16] It also failed to mention Salvadorans, by far the largest group of immigrants (Escheverri-Gent, 301). In contrast, "the Black element" represented "little ethnic value," a "step backward in social advancement for their

Banana companies and their spheres of influence on the North Coast of Honduras, 1930s. Patterned after Kepner and Soothill (1967, 97). Map by Juan Mejia.

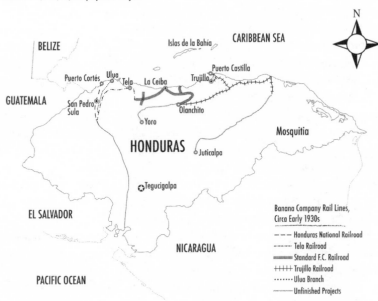

indisputable inferiority."[17] The Communist Party entertained this view, calling negros an "ignorant and deformed race whose mere presence invokes disgust and repugnance" (Argueta 1992, 62).[18] In 1929, despite objections by the fruit companies, the government of Liberal Party president Mejia Colindres passed a law restricting the immigration of negros as well as other races/nationalities identified as *arabe, chino, turca, siria, armenia, palestina*, and *coolie*.[19]

The English-speaking population of African descent in Honduras was diverse, the product of multiple migrations in the postemancipation Caribbean. As early as the 1840s, free people of color from the Cayman Islands settled in the Bay Islands (Davidson 1974, 74–79). These migrations initiated the group known today in Honduran as Creoles/negros Ingleses, who intermarried with other English-speaking Blacks from the Caribbean and Central America. By the 1870s, Blacks from elsewhere in the Caribbean—particularly Jamaica, British Honduras (Belize), and Barbados—began to arrive in significant numbers to work on the railroads and in the fruit industry, and some established small businesses (Chambers 2006). Soon, La Ceiba had a distinct neighborhood known as "Barrio Inglés" (Canelas Díaz 1999, 72–79). As North American fruit companies consolidated power in the early twentieth century, they imported Black workers who found economic opportunities severely limited in their home societies. The companies preferred West Indians because they spoke English, had prior experience in the fruit industry, and were perceived as subordinate subjects well suited to work in the tropics (Chambers, 65–66). Many of the West Indians were literate or skilled workers and held mid-level positions such as timekeepers, railroad engineers, and mechanics. Though diverse, the English-speaking population of African descent in Honduras came to share a sense of identity based on language, religious and social institutions (e.g., the Methodist and Anglican Church), and citizenship within the British Empire.[20] West Indian and Creole affinity with British and North American culture became juxtaposed with the perceived cultural inferiority of Honduran mestizos and Garifuna, who they sometimes conceptualized as "savage and uncultured" (168) in a pattern that echoed dominant representations.

Anti-Black agitation became associated with a variety of nationalist sentiments: resentment against U.S. imperialism; unfair company treatment of workers; competition over jobs; and racial hierarchy and purity. It also involved racial violence. Police routinely fined, jailed, and beat West Indians for petty offenses, and there were several unprovoked killings involving local officials (Escheverri Gent 1993). Although British officials rarely pursued cases involving their colonial subjects in Honduras, they admitted that Blacks suffered "systematic molestation."[21] In 1924, a delegation of labor leaders in Puerto Castilla demanded the immediate removal of Black workers, and when the UFCO failed to comply, several hundred armed mestizos attacked the West Indians, forcing them to take refuge aboard a Norwegian steamship.[22] Similar movements occurred in 1929. Non-Black workers threatened violence against Blacks at a moment in which companies were firing workers and reducing wages due to banana disease and global economic depression.[23]

The indo-hispanic nationalism officially enshrined in the national money, census categories, and immigration law entailed a vision of the Honduran population as a particular racial type whose most denigrated other, alongside "uncivilized" Indians, was the negro. Its most explicit object of attention and objection was the West Indian Black, but as a discourse of racial purity and degeneracy it encompassed all those understood as Blacks, raising the question: how were Garifuna implicated in the racial exclusions of indo-hispanic nationalisms?

Morenos between Race and Nation

Euraque offers a provocative answer to this question by locating elite discourses of indo-hispanic mestizaje and regional labor struggles within a longer trajectory of ethnoracial differentiation and politics on the North Coast. He contends:

> ... the 1920s effort to officially designate Lempira as the "representative" of the "other race" in "our mestizaje" involved a local racism that drew on a postindependence rejection of blackness, and especially a rejection of Garifuna blackness as a more local and immediate racial threat. This elite fear was magnified by the "threat" that non-Garifuna and non-Jamaican laborers perceived in the context of labor struggles on the banana plantations. This turned into an anti-imperialism channeled through the iconography of Lempira and via concrete efforts to deport black laborers that linked these mobilizations to a racialized nationalism from above and from below. It also included that Garifuna were deprived of resources— that is, land and commercial opportunities in towns like Tela and La Ceiba. (2003, 243)

These comments follow a lengthy discussion of population
where Euraque concludes: "the primary black population on the no
ran North Coast between the 1890s and 1930s and after continued to be
Garifuna. The primary 'Black threat' to the nation, in the 1920s then, was
internal and local" (2003, 242). Given the intensity of the hostility directed
toward immigrants in anti-Black discourse, we should be cautious in
accepting the claim that Garifuna represented the primary "Black threat."
Nevertheless, Euraque's argument points to intimate articulations between anti-Black racism and the subjection of Garifuna within regional
and national hierarchies.

The expansion of the fruit trade in the last decades of the nineteenth
century fomented intense competition over land ownership on the North
Coast. Garifuna who contributed to the settlement of what became the
major ports of Tela and La Ceiba lost land to newcomers from the interior of Honduras and abroad, often through coercion (López García 1994,
29–33). In Tela, Garifuna were forced to abandon their principal site of
residence and prime agricultural lands to make way for fruit companies.
Many resettled to another neighborhood in Tela or San Juan. In La Ceiba,
prosperous Garifuna families sold land, under the threat of forced removal,
to other cultivators.[24] In Nueva Armenia and Rio Esteban, social memories recall communal dislocation by the fruit companies during the late
nineteenth and early twentieth centuries. Likewise, individuals in Sambo
Creek abandoned or sold land below value under coercion from ladino
individuals or foreign companies.[25]

In some cases, powerful ladinos sought access to land and resources by
arguing that desirable areas occupied and used by "morenos" were national
lands. In 1896, Francisco Altschul sought government permission to exploit
a massive coconut grove in the Tela region, claiming that resident morenos
"having planted a very small number of coconut trees, take those of the
Nation for their own" (Soluri 1998, 82). A similar dismissal of Garifuna
production occurred in conflicts between moreno cultivators and ladino
ranchers in Iriona, Colón; the ranchers claimed, "what the moreno race
calls a crop is only miniscule plantings of yucca, made in the yards of their
houses that barely serve to maintain them" (1998, 81). In 1927, Francisco
Altschul (1928) sent a report on the Mosquitia to President Miguel Paz
Barahona. He described the inhabitants as:

> belonging to two races: the negra and the India. The first is repre-
> sented by caribes; and the second by three tribes, the zambos

[Miskito], sumos [Tahwaka] and payas [Pech]. The caribes or morenos, as they are called, probably arrived . . . several centuries ago,
proceeding from the island of St. Vincent, and are without a doubt
of African origin. They are [wage] workers and above all excellent
sailors and live in or on the coast. They are clean and to a certain
point civilized, as in times past there existed several schools . . . and
they were visited by from time to time by Christian missionaries,
some of them know how to read and write and the majority are or
consider themselves Christians, although they are frequently po-
lygamous and maintain some ancient rites, especially those of ritual
dances, very similar to the Voddoo of haitian negros. (299)

For Altschul, the caribes are "to a certain point civilized" *relative* to Indians, especially the "most backward" zambos and sumos, who he condemns for practicing polytheism and witchcraft, having no knowledge of
time and engaging in hunting and fishing rather than cultivation (300).
His report echoes other ethnological accounts of the Mosquitia, a region
long imagined as the dark, backward, savage, and untamed part of the
nation, sporadically produced since the Honduran state secured international recognition over the region in 1860. These reports drew implicit
comparisons between Garifuna and Indians in terms of their primitive
and heathen customs and civilized status while differentiating them along
racial lines (Barahona 1998, 19–28).

Evaluations of Garifuna productive practices merit particular attention. While the role of Garifuna men as wage labor and commercial actors
within the coastal economy might be recognized, the role played by Garifuna women in cultivation was denigrated. For example, one report draws
a distinction between the Caribs of the Mosquitia and those living to the
west, describing the latter as "more or less civilized, very intelligent, excellent sailors in the commerce of mahogany and tremendous and incorri-
gible runners of contraband" (Gomez Osorio, 285). In contrast, the Carib
men of the Mosquitia appear as lazy savages. "Like the zambos, they leave
the bulk of the agricultural work to the women, upon whom they live and
whom they consider veritable beasts of burden; the men are engaged only
in hunting, fishing and river or ocean navigation" (285). The predominance of women in agriculture was interpreted neither as evidence of their
own initiative or autonomy nor of a culturally sanctioned, gendered division of labor but as male indolence and dominance. This representation

confirms the savage status of the group and justifies their displacement from prime agricultural lands.

While accounts of the Mosquitia tend toward an ethnological mode of description that describes the customs, habits, and defects of clearly differentiated groups, representations of the burgeoning economy of cities such as La Ceiba tend to position Garifuna as out of place. Many accounts did not differentiate Garifuna from others understood as Blacks. Consider comments by three correspondents from Tegucigalpa describing La Ceiba at the turn of the century. The first describes the rapid progress of the North Coast:

> In the towns you will encounter cosmopolitanism: Germans,
> English, French, Spanish, industrious races that come from
> Europe, eager for riches, enduring the arduous, torrid climate and
> defying death. There are also other types of races, like Armenians,
> Arabs and adventurers of all types, gentlemen of industry or
> miracle. The fever of commerce is the issue of the day here. This
> port, though appearing small, has more commercial life than
> Tegucigalpa. (Miralda 1904)

The economic boom attributed to "industrious races" echoes fantasies of European immigration investing the nation with progress. It also effaces the history of those previously present; Garifuna had helped found La Ceiba and were a major part of the local workforce. In contrast, the author sets off the burgeoning city against (Garifuna) villages populated by "Africans": "On the coast you will see many small towns and villages . . . and the canoes vigorously pushed by the negro *Africano*, whose white teeth appear made to tear live flesh, and whose eyes appear like two embers that shine at the bottom of the eternal night" (Miralda 1904). Ignoring (or ignorant of) ethnic-cultural distinctions, the author depicts a feral, African blackness as a foil to the city's progress. Another correspondent acknowledges the presence of "morenos" but draws attention to nothing more than their suspect customs: "The morenos or caribes of this port are preparing a dance of the *mafia* (which signifies dance of the devil in their language) . . . These negros often celebrate this rite."[26] A third correspondent draws both a distinction and equivalence between caribes and negros in an account of working conditions on the docks, contending that the "humble workers . . . consist of caribes and negros, who–especially the later–don't give a whistle that they are swindled and sweat 4, 8 and more hours for a miserable pittance" (Labalenú 1903). The opposition to Black workers in labor competition could become explicit.

Hauling bananas in La Ceiba, 1927. Garifuna were a key labor source for the fruit companies, particularly on the docks. Photographer unknown. Photograph in possession of the author.

In 1905, the population of La Ceiba awoke to find dozens of handwritten notes strewn on the streets, all displaying a similar message to: "Burn La Ceiba like Belize. Burn Vacarro. There is no work for us, only for the negros. Let us burn them."[27] We can only guess if that chilling, anonymous message was intended to include "morenos" but, given the confusions, equivalences, and overlaps between the categories moreno/caribe and negro, we may wonder if the authors recognized a distinction. A decade later, Paulino Valladares, a founding intellectual of the National Party that would come to rule under Tiburcio Carías in the 1930s and 1940s, could attack Black immigration, citing "retarded ethnic elements, like the Caribs imported by the concessionary companies" (quoted in Euraque 1998, 162). "Caribs," of course, were native to Honduras.

The semantics of classification within the fruit industry highlight the ambiguous status of Garifuna as native nationals. A 1915 newspaper article breaks down the race and nationality of SFCO employees in the following manner:[28]

Hondurans	60%
Morenos	10%
Italians	5%
Americans	2%
American and Jamaican Blacks	8%
Other Nations	15%

. . .

Morenos are set apart from foreign Blacks yet distinguished from "Hondurans," lacking even a marked subnational category such as "Honduran Morenos." They appear as a race with no nation, awkwardly placed between foreigners and Hondurans. In fact, as John Soluri (1998) shows, with the rise of anti-Black agitation, the UFCO took pains to give a clear account of identity distinctions and national origins. In 1929, in the midst of intense anti-Black labor mobilization, the Truxillo Railroad Company (an UFCO subsidiary) sent a letter to the Honduran minister of development with employment statistics for eleven categories (1998, 240):

Hondurans	3,039
Other Central Americans	513
Bay Islanders	162
Honduran Caribs	463
South Americans	12
Mexicans	14
North Americans	201
Europeans	60
Asians	3
British Honduras	88
West Indian Islands	573

Avoiding the term "negro," the statistics were designed to demonstrate that objectionable races from foreign countries (the last three) comprised a relatively small portion of the company workforce. Honoring the racial and cultural assumptions of Honduran nationalism, the company lists "Other Central Americans" after "Hondurans" and then includes "Bay Islanders" and "Honduran Caribs," who comprise roughly the same number of employees as British Hondurans (Belizeans) and West Indians. The company letter also critiques a popular confusion of race and nation: "Naturally, *señor* Minister, the Honduran caribes and morenos who work for the company are generally taken to be negros, which perhaps creates in the mind of the people the erroneous idea of a large number of [negro] employees" (1998, 239–40). Around the same time, an anonymous government official made a similar point in a newspaper letter defending his inaction on Black immigration. "The hatred of Blacks has been so great and deep that in attacking them their adversaries have not taken into account the Honduran morenos who are our brothers and who form the majority of the men of color (*hombres de color*) that work in this port, many of them from the Bay Islands, where the English language predominates" (1998, 240). The need to clarify the national identities of populations reflects the conflation between "men of color" from Honduras and foreign Blacks, as blackness was rendered alien to the national body.

The fruit company statistics highlight the diversity of those labeled negro. By no means were all of the hated Blacks who spoke English and worked for the fruit companies recent company "imports"; some were born in Honduras to parents who had arrived in the nineteenth century. Rarely were distinctions between English-speaking Blacks born in Honduras and abroad registered within anti-immigrant discourse. An anonymous editorial in the *Diario del Norte*, titled "Negrura" (Blackening), condemns Black immigration and highlights the large number of negros in Tela, La Ceiba, and Puerto Castilla (ports with substantial Garifuna and Honduran-born English-speaking populations), "threatening tomorrow to cover the whole city."[29] The editorial notes, "this is not the first time that the indigenous Central American has crossed with the indigenous African, producing terrible physical and psychological combinations, and augmenting considerably the degree of ferocity of the population." The threat of "blackening" obscured distinctions between Blacks in terms of national origin, citizen status, and identities.

Even attempts at rendering clear who was who are confusing. Take the use of the terms "morenos" and "Caribs" in the letters from the Truxillo Railroad Company and the government official discussed above. We know that "moreno," like caribe, was a term typically used as a synonym for Garifuna (Gonzalez 1988, 136), but the Truxillo Railroad Company letter suggests that caribes and morenos are different groups, referring to "Honduran caribes and morenos who work for the company . . ." Perhaps moreno here refers to Bay Islanders, many of whom were considered negros or "people of color" and confused with foreign-born Blacks. The Honduran official states that many moreno workers come from the Bay Islands yet implies that other morenos come from the coast. Perhaps "moreno" was a term that could also signify "people of color" from Honduras, as distinct from foreign Blacks. It is hoped that future work will clarify the meanings of identity terms. The ambiguity of such terms is nevertheless revealing. A scholarly disposition to sort out the semantic confusion of identity terms should not blind us to the ways in which such confusion is integral to practices of interpellation and identification. In use, the label negro could wash out distinctions of language, culture, and nationality. Indeed, a key premise of indo-hispanic nationalism was that race, ethnicity, and nationality were bound to each other. Thus, particular efforts had to be made to assert that Caribs and Bay Islanders were also Hondurans. In the Honduran nation, the state of being Black and native was, at best, a paradox.

We can now turn to a consideration of some of the ways in which Garifuna navigated that paradox, focusing on fragments of evidence surrounding labor conflicts near Trujillo. In 1932, a correspondent for a regional newspaper reported on tensions in Puerto Castillo resulting from the scaling back of fruit company operations.[30] He investigated the "complaints of the morenos," "those pacific and prudent boys that we have known before, enduring the scorn of a 'superior race' and living three months on seven pounds of beans and a cluster of plantains a week."[31] Their political passions were directed primarily toward rival (mestizo) workers.

> For every shipment one of the "native" or "morena troops," as they are called by the blondes (North Americans), is employed and between them exists the sad rivalry of salary, which the company takes care not to dissolve. The natives accuse the morenos of being negros; and these, pure Trujillians, call the Hondurans of the interior *forasteros* [strangers] who come to dispute their means of subsistence.[32]

Mestizos asserted a status as national natives, denying that status to morenos on the basis of their blackness. The morenos, in turn, affirmed their own native presence in place and accused their rivals of being foreign to the coast, echoing in a regional idiom the nationalist argument that foreigners were stealing bread from native workers. Meanwhile, the UFCO benefited from the ethnoracial segmentation of the workforce (Bourgois 1989).

Several months before this report, a self-identified "moreno" named Sixto Cacho (1932) wrote an article for a North Coast newspaper titled "For the Morena Race and the Defense of All My Compatriots" that drew on indo-hispanic nationalism while appealing for the protection of morenos. I know little of Cacho save that in the late 1940s he lived in Tegucigalpa and housed Alfonso Lacayo, the first Honduran Garifuna medical doctor and an important activist of the second half of the twentieth century. Cacho speaks as a national citizen representing "morenos" as national subjects:

> The morenos that reside in Honduras are also its legitimate children; it behooves her to pay us attention so that we can give her the best

possible results. . . . in this century of lights Honduras should not be
content with a burden of illiterates; it should educate us so we will be
useful to the Nation.

The authorities should protect us, in one form or another; we
are negros, we know it, but unfortunately or fortunately we are
legitimate brothers of the *indo-latinos*; there are those that do not
know the history and probably balk at what is written; but it is very
certain, like the sun that shines on us daily.

I can demonstrate to whomever asks that the carib race that
populates the North Coast of Honduras descends from the
inhabitants encountered by Cristobal Colon, in the islands and
the mainland, during the discovery of America. (1932)

Cacho navigates the racial exclusions of indo-hispanic nationalism by
asserting a brotherhood with indo-latinos (mestizos) based on common
Indian ancestry. He does not, however, deny that morenos are Blacks,
admitting, "we are negros, we know it." In this sense (by identifying a group
of negros as legitimate Hondurans) he partially disrupts an indo-hispanic
nationalism that rendered negros outside the national body. Nevertheless,
for Cacho, being negro does not entail solidarity with foreign Blacks:

I request the protection of the moreno, as a legitimate Honduran. I request the good treatment of my race, which is peaceful, hard-working and honest; that our governments do not
permit foreigners to take away our bread and insult us on our
own soil; this happens in all the activities of the companies,
especially the Tela and Trujillo Railroad Co., where foreigners
distinct from North Americans are the preferred workers in
the workshops and the docks; while the latinos and morenos
do the roughest work, the Jamaicans and Belizeans direct us.
Are there no Hondurans who could direct the work on the
docks? Why this preference? Is there no one that can see this?
Yes, there is, but because the companies fix everything with
money, no one speaks, but I am ready to clarify things; with the
pardon of mister lawyers and mister authorities; as a Honduran I will always defend the rights of all my compatriots and
especially those of the morenos, who have no one to speak for
them. (1932)

Although Cacho does not identify a generalized "Black problem," he echoes arguments against foreign immigration from the perspective of native labor. Having established that morenos are legitimate Hondurans, he occupies that position to call for unity with mestizos in the face of company control and government corruption.

Cacho's arguments raise the question of whether some Garifuna joined the chorus of anti-immigrant sentiment and established common cause with mestizo workers. Given the imbrications of racial and immigrant discourse, and the racialization of Garifuna as negros, this seems unlikely, even though tensions between Garifuna and English-speaking Blacks (Honduran and/or foreign) were evident. The more prominent conflict at the time involved a "sad rivalry" between moreno and mestizo workers, each claiming the status of native against the other. What is evident is that the status of Garifuna as legitimate Hondurans was a problem, reflected in the care Cacho took to assert it.

On the Cultural Status of Garifuna

In 1930, Vicente Caceres (1930) published an article in a North Coast newspaper titled *"Chancunu: Dance of the Morenos."* Caceres was a leading educational administrator in Honduras who later directed a flagship normal school and served as a congressman during the Carías dictatorship. During a period of exile in the 1920s, he worked under José Vasconcelos in Mexico (Dodd, 246–47) and, upon his return, became a member of the Society of Geography and History of Honduras, a prestigious organization of intellectuals investigating Honduran history, geography, literature, and folklore. In his article, Caceres places the dance Chancunu (John Canoe) within the realm of Honduran folklore, paraphrasing a Garifuna named Martin Avila from the community of Tulian, who says:

> We the morenos of the colored race (*raza de color*) recognized as true Hondurans conserve our determined customs, [which are] perhaps little known in the rest of the Republic. For now I will speak about the dance because you asked me, sincerely desiring to inform the whole country so that they can see and appreciate how the Hondurans, true Hondurans, live without mixing ourselves now for various centuries, love with intensity that which our elders

taught us to enjoy ourselves and do not replace it for that which comes from the exterior perhaps with the purpose of extinguishing the little that remains of our ancestors. (Caceres, 7)

Avila goes on to briefly describe the dance and concludes by inviting the president to witness a performance.

In this instance of reported speech, Avila suggests that morenos (of the colored race) are true Hondurans not despite but because they maintain racial purity and traditional customs. His comment that morenos remain unmixed assuages, at least indirectly, fears of Black miscegenation degenerating the nation. If Sixto Cacho makes an appeal to national belonging through invoking ancestral similarities with mestizos, Martin Avila stresses the perpetuation of distinct customs despite alien pressures. For his part, Professor Caceres highlights the importance of folklore to the modern nation:

> ... nations of modern culture and civilization try to conserve their respective folklore. ... Like the Chancunu there are traditional dances among the indígenas of Intibuca, La Paz, Comayagua, Yoro, Colon, etc, accompanied by songs that record the primitive spirit of the autochthonous race. There must be a rebirth of the old times, the vigor and greatness of those that have preceded us, utilizing what of theirs remains to us in form of tradition, poem, song or dance, today, when there still remains something of the ultimate examples representative of the national race (7).

In Honduras, the promotion of folklore coincided with the consolidation of indo-hispanic nationalism[33] and served as an intellectual instrument for creating a modern nation that attempted to resuscitate the Indian past in the service of the present. Caceres's effort to include morenos within Honduran folklore was the exception rather than the rule, as other investigations of folklore tended to either ignore Garifuna or render them beyond the pale of modern civilization.[34]

An important early example is *Traditions and Legends of Honduras*, by Jesús Aguilar Paz (1989), originally written in 1931. Aguilar Paz was one of the most distinguished Honduran men of letters: professor of chemistry, congressman, cartographer, member of the Honduran Society for Geography and History, and an intellectual architect of official indo-hispanic nationalism. His book, based on extensive travel, documents myths, legends, and customs of Honduras, many associated with Indians. It echoes the call of Caceres to record the curiosities particular to the nation, and one section titled "La Fiesta de Cupita" provides a firsthand account of a Garifuna ritual.

Aguilar Paz notes the ethnological variety and mixing that has occurred in an "under-populated and indefensible country," listing the "old Spanish families, the Saxon descendant . . . the yankee, the negros Africanos, the native mestizos [mestizos criollos], the zambos and indios with their regional names; nonetheless, all in a nominal crucible of nationality" (1989, 165). Aguilar Paz represents Garifuna as African Blacks deported to Honduras from St. Vincent, living in hamlets that appear "like the paintings of African villages, primitive and of simple organization in their government" (1989, 165). He elaborates this image of the primitive, depicting mud and thatch houses stuck together in disorder. He mocks the "garruler la" of guttural speech and recoils at the "Fiesta de Cupita," introduced as "question of the diabolical Mafia, of the black star that twinkles in the shadows, in the web of night, the wave of the bat of evil . . ." (1989, 165). Aguilar Paz most likely witnessed a dügü or chügü, Garifuna healing and spiritual rituals dedicated to the appeasement of the ancestors.[35]

Although the practices of "negros Africanos" are nominally included within this account of legends and traditions of Honduras, they represent less the nostalgic fantasy of a national past than the dark nightmare of its primitive present. Aguilar Paz revisits earlier ethnological descriptions of Garifuna yet exceeds them in a poetics of disgust and fear. The heathen ceremonies and rude life of the morenos, "living remnants of African life," serve as counterpoints to civilization and demonstrate the weakness of the nation (1989, 168). In the subsequent two decades, the search for folklore tended to omit Garifuna from consideration, typically focusing on the interior and Western regions of the country rather than the North Coast and Mosquitia.

Here, as with the newspaper correspondent who evoked cannibal fears of the "negros Africanos" of La Ceiba, the use of "Africano" to modify "negro" accentuates not only foreign origins but the purported savage, uncivilized characteristics of the group. The trope of civilized/uncivilized was inherited from the nineteenth century and common throughout Latin America. Blacks and Indians could appear on both sides of the dichotomy, evaluated on their perceived assimilation to cultural norms such as sedentarism, wage labor, and Catholicism (Ng'weno 2007b, 104). In countries such as Brazil, Cuba, and Colombia, African-based cultural particularities became identified with the antithesis of civilization and modernity (Andrews 2004). Religious practices perceived as derived from Africa, rendered in terms of superstition and witchcraft, inspired particular repressive

Postcard mailed in 1926, location unknown. Notice the "manaca" house. This posed image of ethnic difference resembles postcards of later years. Postcard in possession of the author.

Costa Norte de Honduras - Una familia Caribe

attention as signs of otherness, rendering Blacks beyond the pale of civilization and its successor trope modernity (Andrews, 22–23; Palmié 2002). In
Honduras, Coelho reported that the "wildest stories circulated" about Garifuna religion and that such stories justified police repression against it (49).

Representations of Garifuna as a problem reflected not only the perceived
racial difference of Garifuna from the national type but also the problem
that living difference, whether Black or Indian, represented for ideologues
of a modern, indo-hispanic nation.[36] The glorification of Lempira and
celebrations of the ancient Maya were accompanied, as Coelho noted, by
disdain for contemporary Indians. Likewise, neither folkloric nor ethnological discourses produced respect for living indigenous culture as alternative modes of being in the world. They were accompanied by projections of
the already accomplished assimilation of indigenous peoples in the Western
part of the country[37] and the need to civilize the "savage tribes" of the untamed Mosquitia. Such contradictions between the affirmations of Indian
heritage and efforts to assimilate indigenous peoples also characterized the
modest efforts toward promoting *"indigenismo"* in Honduras.[38]

In the mid-1950s, Jesús Aguilar Paz led a government mission to the
Mosquitia and produced an overview of the "problems of the aboriginal
population in Honduras" (1955) that makes explicit the similarities and differences between Garifuna and indigenous peoples (indígenas). He lists and
describes five distinct indigenous groups-Misquitos/Zambos [Miskitos],
Payas [Pech], Jicaques [Tolupanes], Sumos[Tahwakas]-before turning to the
morenos, who "although not indígenas de America, form a racial group (of
African origin) that speak their own dialect and because of their human
and cultural condition have problems similar to the other aboriginal tribes"
(1955, 360). Aguilar Paz notes that the morenos are "improving" due to their
"social and commercial association with the Atlantic littoral" but stresses
that their sanitary conditions, economic situation, religious beliefs, and
mental evolution remain, like the indígenas, in a deplorable and primitive
state because of their separation from ladino civilization.[39]

In this taxonomy of difference, a racial distinction between negros and
indígenas intersects with an evaluative grid based on perceived assimilation to civilization. Its geography of racial-cultural difference is linked to
ideas of the relative success or failure of colonialism, the state, and capitalism to integrate the potentially unruly margins of the nation. Garifuna,
straddling the boundaries between the backward, neglected Mosquitia
and the North Coast enclave economy, are understood as both Blacks and
an "aboriginal population" with cultural conditions similar to indígenas.

They appear slightly superior to indígenas on account of their role in the regional capitalist economy and contact with ladino civilization but nonetheless remain a problem. Garifuna, when rendered distinct from other Blacks in terms of language, customs, and culture, were placed within a savage slot similar to that occupied by Indians. Moreover, within discourses of mestizaje there was no space for Garifuna to simply assimilate into the national body, for their blackness always marked their difference and ready conflation with the foreign.

Left Mobilization and Antidiscrimination

In the same decade that Jesús Aguilar Paz published his piece on aboriginal populations, Garifuna activists began to publicly confront racism within the context of movements against political oppression and U.S. imperialism. In conversations with Garifuna on differences between the past and the present, I often asked them when social conditions and racism began to improve. Almost everyone pointed either to the famous 1954 strike of fruit company workers or to the regime of President Ramon Villeda Morales (1958–1963), whom they credit with promoting social and educational reforms that extended to Garifuna communities.

Villeda Morales was the first Liberal Party president to hold office since 1932, and his rise to power owed much to the 1954 strike, the most significant event in the labor history of Honduras.[40] Sparked by UFCO dockworkers in Puerto Cortes, the strike spread throughout the company and then to the SFCO. The strike garnered widespread support from workers, teachers, students, artisans, peasants, and even wealthy merchants, who engaged in sympathy strikes or provided financial assistance. Standard Fruit employees settled within a few weeks but UFCO employees remained on strike for sixty-nine days.

The events of 1954 left a complex legacy of democratic reform, authoritarian retrenchment, the suppression of radical politics, and heightened popular consciousness (Argueta 1995, 205–52). After the strike, unions secured recognition and, eventually, increased benefits, while the companies reduced the workforce and marginalized radical labor leaders. Pressures for political reform contributed to a military coup in 1956 and a year later, the congressional election of Villeda Morales to the presidency. Villeda Morales, a "self-styled urban petty bourgeois reformer" (Euraque 1996a, 70), brokered a deal with the military that reflected its increasing power; in exchange for the military's support, Villeda Morales granted it constitutional autonomy from civilian control. He paid the price for that pact, falling in a 1963 coup amidst (false) charges of communist sympathies that obscured political contests within the Honduran elite, the rising profile of North Coast businessmen, and the perceived threat that the government's tentative agrarian reform represented to the UFCO. Although by no means a radical, his presidency marked a period of relative political openness, state modernization, and economic reform. As president, Villeda Morales courted Garifuna as political allies: he visited several communities; denounced the 1937 murders at San Juan; and recruited Garifuna for the Presidential Guard through regional Liberal Party networks (Euraque 2004, 216–18). His presidency also helped open space for public campaigns against racism.

In the year Villeda Morales took office, a group of young Garifuna men in La Ceiba created the Sociedad Cultural Lincoln (Lincoln Cultural Society), which combated racial discrimination and affirmed the blackness of Garifuna. According to reflections of one of the founding members, Santos Centeno García (1997), the Society "struggled for the social and political recognition of the Honduran negro via the quest for social justice" (85). The Society protested practices of racial discrimination and segregation in La Ceiba, defending the rights of Black students, teachers who were denied positions, and citizens when they were denied admittance to casinos, hotels, and restaurants (86). For example, the Society petitioned the president concerning an incident in which a young Garifuna couple was prohibited from dining at an elite restaurant. Villeda Morales ordered the governor to advise the owners that if the practice continued the restaurant would be closed (95).

Many of the leaders of the Society were active in the labor movement, affiliated with the clandestine Communist Party, and received support and advice from its leaders. In order to understand those connections, it is important to reflect on the resurgence of the radical left, in particular the Honduran Revolutionary Democratic Party (PDRH), established in 1946. Leading intellectuals of the PDRH were influenced by the "October Revolution" in Guatemala, advocated political transformation in Honduras, and challenged the exploitation of the fruit companies. The PDRH dissolved in 1954 due to divisions between liberals and communists, who (re)established the Communist Party in Honduras in that same year, less than a month before the famous strike (Argueta 1995, 145–65). The PDRH newspaper *Vanguardia Revolucionaria* circulated widely on the North Coast, championing worker's rights and denouncing the fruit companies. The paper also deployed a discourse of race that recognized, and in some cases actively promoted, negros as Honduran workers. Some articles identified individual victims of company authorities as morenos, and the paper published a series of letters from Triunfo de la Cruz denouncing the usurpation of community lands. [41] One article describes the suffering of the "people of color" in Tela, noting that indio workers shared the same fate.[42] To be sure, the indio, here referring to mestizos, remained the representative type. A group of nurses wrote a letter complaining that they were victims of "cruel racial discrimination" because the UFCO paid employees from the United States four times what they paid Hondurans. The nurses stressed that "we the complainants are not negros but mestizos like all other Hondurans, or the majority."[43] Nonetheless, the balance of racial discourse within *Vanguardia Revolucionaria* departs from depictions of negros as foreign threats to the nation.

One lead article published in 1950, titled "Racial Discrimination" (Urbina 1950), explicitly takes up the question of racism in Honduran society. The author was Nicolas Urbina, a teacher and important figure within the PDRH and, subsequently, the Communist Party (Argueta 1995, 157, 165). Urbina plainly states that in Honduras "negros are discriminated against. That is, treated poorly, considered as inferior beings" (1). He draws a comparison between fascism and the hatred of the Honduran government toward Blacks, invoking the assassinations of Garifuna in San Juan. Urbina affirms the physical and intellectual equality of negros, citing examples of outstanding teachers and students (who, from their surnames, were likely Garifuna) and "a moreno named Laboriel, a "torchbearer of the arts" who "sings to the negro slave and invites him to fight to liberate himself" (3). He also identifies and condemns racist practices and ideas: that negros cannot dance with indios or sit in first-class sections on the train; that they were born only to haul bananas and do not have the same rights as blancos. Not surprisingly, the article urges Blacks to support the PDRH and unite with other workers on the basis of class consciousness, so that all can leave the "degrading position of slave laborers" (3).

Tellingly, Urbina concludes by noting that his article was inspired by the complaint of a negro that *Vanguardia Revolucionaria* had also forgotten them. "This article recognizes and expresses that complaint, a party of the people can never forget a sector as ill-treated, vilified and humiliated. The democracy, friends, is for all" (3). A few months later, a self-identified moreno named Luciano Flores, writing from Guatemala, wrote an article for the paper telling young morenos to affiliate with the PDRH in opposition to the "despotic regime" that benefits the bourgeoisie while morenos lack opportunities to study and live a life "that has not passed that of being that of the primitive man, that is, of hunting, fishing and working as the worst paid peon" (1).

The racial discourse in *Vanguardia Revolucionaria*, though sparse, provides some tantalizing insights into the ways in which the Honduran left began to reevaluate the "Black problem." While a concern with racism remained subordinate to the imperatives of class struggle, the condemnation of racial discrimination within Honduras by a leading leftist represents an important moment of articulation between class politics and antiracism and suggests an acknowledgement of Black subjects as part of the nation. Nonetheless, we are ultimately confronted with more questions than answers on the relationship between antiracism and the Honduran left. To what extent did those labeled negros participate in the labor movement and left politics? To what extent did left and labor organizations question anti-Black racism? In what ways did popular mobilization, especially the strike of 1954, alter the contours of everyday racial encounters and racism? Did the silence around "foreign blackness" indicate the enduring vilification and resentment of English-speaking Blacks, their inclusion within class politics, or their declining relevance to the politics of labor and nation?

Current research throws only flashes of light on these questions. Many older Garifuna say that most Garifuna supported the strike of 1954. Some Garifuna men held low-level leadership positions within union sections, but there were few if any Garifuna in high-level positions on strike committees, unions, and left organizations. According to Euraque (2004), the two major negro labor leaders at the time of the strike were English-speaking Blacks. Euraque also notes that during the strike in La Ceiba, a group of dockworkers, mostly mestizos, threatened English-speaking Black dock bosses in their own neighborhood. After the strike of 1954, many English-speaking Blacks in La Ceiba, particularly those from the West Indies, reportedly left Honduras. Prohibited from entering the country since the late 1920s, West Indians from other parts of the country, particularly Trujillo, had left in large numbers in previous decades (Chambers 2006). As the immigrant dimension of the "Black problem" receded, as new possibilities for political representation emerged, and as civil rights and anticolonial

movements gained momentum elsewhere, Garifuna developed an antiracist politics that affirmed a Black identity.

The struggle against anti-Black racism was ultimately taken up not by
the Communist Party or other mestizo-led organizations but by Garifuna
affiliated with the radical left as well as individuals with ties to the Liberal
Party, such as Alfonso Lacayo. Lacayo served as a member of the solidarity committee for the national university during the strike of 1954, and, in
1959, he gave a talk to the Lincoln Cultural Society condemning ongoing
practices of segregation in La Ceiba. By then, activists had publicly recognized commonalities of struggle with Blacks elsewhere. According to
Santos Centeno García, "the struggle of Black Hondurans clearly identified with the struggle of the revolutionary movements of negros in the
United States" (86). The very name of his organization, honoring the U.S.
president who signed the Emancipation Proclamation, implicitly marked
an affiliation with Black slaves and their descendants.[44] If, as Coelho
asserted in the late 1940s, the older generations of men wanted to have
nothing to do with slavery, a decade later transformations in the public
representation of what it meant to be Garifuna, and black, were well underway. As elsewhere in the Caribbean world, young Garifuna men (and
likely women) were taking up, in their own fashion, what Richard Wright
called "the frenzied gospel of racial self-assertion-that strange soul-food
of the rootless outsiders of the twentieth century" (vii). The Lincoln Cultural Society dissolved when a military coup overthrew Villeda Morales
and communist as well as Liberal Party activists suffered repression, but
racial activism would reemerge and take on new forms, as morenos came
to publicly assert an identity as Black and Garifuna.

Conclusion

This chapter has identified changing Garifuna self-representations in relation to social and political transformations in Honduras in which they
played a part. That trajectory of identity formation can perhaps best be described as a matter of shifting emphasis from Black diasporic differentiation
toward Black diasporic affiliation. The available evidence suggests that from
the late 1920s through the 1940s public representations tended to highlight
the ethnic particularity and national standing of morenos/Caribs vis-à-vis
others labeled negros in relation to the state consolidation of indo-hispanic
nationalism, virulent anti-Black racism, and, by the mid-1930s, the political

repression of the Carías dictatorship. As we saw in the comments by Cacho, Avila, and Tifre, such efforts at differentiation did not necessarily entail a rejection of being "negro" and/or members of "the race of color." Instead, they involved negotiating the terms of racial ascription within nationalist discourse and contested relationships to two of the stigmas intimately associated with blackness, Africa and slavery. Attributions of those stigmas to West Indians and Honduran Creoles served as a means of distinguishing morenos from other peoples of color within a context of competition between racialized groups and of racial discourses that rendered blackness a foreign intrusion that threatened to degenerate the nation. In this period, negative images of Africa predominated in Latin America and, more generally, the West (Herskovits 1941; Drake 1958). Moreover, in Honduras associations of blackness with the foreign raised the stakes of asserting African origins. Given the intensity of anti-Black racism, is it little wonder that Garifuna sought to distinguish their particularity and native status, even as their racialization as negros made any simple erasure of blackness impossible?

For at least some Honduran Garifuna, a political identification with blackness, tied to a reconsideration of African origins, became available in the 1950s. The development of a politics voiced as antidiscrimination altered the terms of engagement with racial exclusion and hierarchy. Led by educated young men tied to reformist and/or radical political projects, it contested the terms of the "Black problem" by naming and attacking racism. Though focusing on the defense of morenos, it drew inspiration from the struggles of Blacks elsewhere and, it appears, evinced comparatively little concern with asserting distinctions from other Blacks. In the process, questions of African origins and blackness took on new meanings. In 1958, Alfonso Lacayo wrote an article in a newspaper sympathetic to Villeda Morales that attempted to come to terms with discourses of mestizaje that rendered negros a problem, identifying "new elements of African descent that occupy settlements disseminated on the North Coast speaking a French patois and others that occupy our cities with saxon customs and have English as their language, coming respectively from the French and English colonies."[45] Lacayo thus positions Garifuna and Creoles as similar subjects, Blacks distinguished primarily by their colonial histories. He also insisted on the importance of African ancestry in Honduran history and within the majority population. Ironically, Lacayo had worked under Jesús Aguilar Paz for two years in the early 1950s and also briefly stayed in the house of Sixto Cacho during the late 1940s. If Aguilar Paz was an important figure in imagining Honduras as an indo-hispanic nation and Cacho asserted an affinity between Garifuna and mestizos based on shared descent from Indians, Dr. Lacayo reportedly once said, when a mestizo called him a negro, "Shake your genealogical tree and you will see a negro fall" (Molina 2006).

Another example of Garifuna intellectual production suggests similar affirmations of being negro in connection with antiracist discourses. In 1957, a young Livio Martínez Lalin completed his thesis for training to be a teacher, "The Moreno Inhabitants of Honduras."[46] Reflecting forty years later, Martínez Lalin said that he wanted little to do with the new, "communist" Garifuna organizations, but he did write against racism. His thesis drew inspiration from the example of Booker T. Washington, "a negro slave from the United States who educated himself and later founded a University to educate the negro slaves of North America" (2). The text provides an interpretation of moreno customs and traditions, favorably compared to those of the "rural mestizo community." Martínez Lalin initially treads carefully around the subject of racial discrimination in Honduras, asserting that "racial discrimination does not exist in the country in comparison with that which prevails in the United States" and suggesting that only uneducated mestizos viewed morenos with disdain (6). By the end of the thesis, the evaluation of Honduran racism takes a stronger tone, as Martínez Lalin impresses the need for his society to overcome a "superiority complex" and the "antiquated hatred" of the moreno.

Curiously, Martínez Lalin offers a brief account of the morenos as a group originating from a shipwreck of African slaves who united with "tribes of the Mosquitia" in Central America, saying nothing of St. Vincent. This account suggests the absence of a universal, standardized account of Garifuna history and origins in this period, at least relative to the present. As we saw earlier, Coelho suggests that multiple origin narratives circulated, even if, especially among older Garifuna men, there was a clear sense that they were always a free people with their own language and religion. In 1963, Dr. Alfonso Lacayo would sponsor young Canadian scholars and encourage them to investigate the history of his people. According to posterior reflections, Dr. Lacayo was uncertain about Garifuna origins and wanted to know: "Why do we speak a distinct language? Why are our customs different from the rest of the population?" (Lacayo Sambulá, 47–48). The result of this collaboration was an account of Garifuna history based on written sources and eighty interviews with elder Garifuna men and women (Beaucage and Samson 1964). In a preface to the work, Lacayo presents it as a contribution to the "new history of our country," "a chapter concerning the migration to this country of a human group that, like it or not, constitutes a powerful ingredient in our nationality" (2). To the best of my knowledge, the work is the first academic publication to use the term "Garifuna." In 1964, Martínez Lalin also wrote two short articles that, instead of using the term "moreno," speaks of "The Authentic Garifuna Christmas" and "The Garifuna Culture."[47]

The word Garifuna did not come out of thin air but had long been used by "morenos" or "caribes" to refer to their language and themselves. In the 1920s, Eduard Conzemius noted that "In their own language the Central American Carib call themselves 'Garífuna' or for short 'Garif' . . ." (184). What appears new was the use of the word as a form of self-reference by Garifuna within Spanish language discourse to others, involving an implicit assertion of the right to self-representation. "Garifuna" is a term that, like "Carib," differentiates a specific cultural and ethnic identity and, unlike moreno, carries no necessary semantic connotations of blackness. Yet we have seen that the route from the terms "moreno" to "Garifuna" involved a certain affirmation of being negro, an engagement with Africa and slavery, and, most crucially, a confrontation with anti-Black racisms. The story told by Don Alonso at the beginning of this chapter captures the imbrications of racial affiliation and ethnic distinction when he contested a question concerning whether he was moreno or negro with the assertion, "I'm negro, negro Garifuna." The play, tension, and overlap between the particularity of being Garifuna and being members of the category Black would continue to inform future political projects and everyday existence into the era of official multiculturalism.

3

Black Indigenism: The Making of Ethnic Politics and State Multiculturalism

On April 12, 1997, Garifuna commemorated the 200th anniversary of their arrival to Central America in an official ceremony funded by the Honduran government. The Garifuna organization ODECO coordinated a week of activities that included panel discussions on topics like economic development and "the Garifuna woman," cultural events such as a secular performance of the healing ceremony dügü, and the unveiling of a bust honoring Dr. Alfonso Lacayo. The events grew better-off Garifuna residing in Honduras and other countries, a smattering of other people from the African Diaspora, the national media, and the presidents of St. Vincent and Honduras. Although some activists grumbled that money could have been better spent on more pressing needs, the state-sponsored celebration put Garifuna in the public eye, at least for a moment. It also captured something of the spirit of the day, when ethnicity became a key mode of social protagonism and the nation was being reinterpreted as "multiethnic."

Celio Álvarez Casildo, the president of ODECO who had become the most visible Garifuna leader in Central America, delivered a "National Plan for the Development of Garifuna and Afro-Honduran communities" that demanded twenty-five million dollars for infrastructure, health, and educational services needed to "compete in a new century with high scientific and technological development, where the possibility to receive, direct and disseminate information becomes fundamental to move forward" (Fernandez 1997). Álvarez Casildo also reminded the Reina government of an agreement it had signed the previous October to provide Garifuna communities with land titles. Earlier in the week, he told the press, "This is the moment in which the Black people of Honduras struggle to leave the invisibility in which we have existed for two centuries, fighting for lands that have been taken from us by the state, foreigners and the military"

(Pavón 1997). He thus took the occasion to demand visibility and inclusion, albeit within the recognizable framework of "development."

President Reina responded by saying that his administration was paying more attention to ethnic groups than any regime in history. He was surely right. A partial list of initiatives promoted during his presidency includes completion of the process ratifying Convention 169 on Indigenous and Tribal Peoples of the International Labor Organization (ILO); an agreement to title, amplify, and regulate (*sanear*) Garifuna lands; a new legal office, the "Special Prosecutor for Ethnic Groups and Cultural Patrimony"; a program called "Our Roots" designed to improve infrastructure in ethnic communities; the declaration of Garifuna as a "national monument" with their own day; and the creation of a bilingual/intercultural education program. The decree establishing that program announced: "Honduras is a multiethnic and multicultural country. . . ." (República de Honduras 1994)

President Reina presented the audience a vision of progress in which ethnic groups would play a key role:

> The new century will be marked by the current technological
> revolution in which we are living. And if we are not direct protago-
> nists in it, we can take advantage of it all the same because being
> a people of multiethnic origin we are prepared to develop, for the
> natural and geographic advantages of our country, an ecotour-
> ist industry in which you, above all, can be effective protagonists,
> taking advantage of the force of your dances, the originality of your
> foods, the happiness of your character and the natural beauty of
> these islands and all of the Atlantic littoral of Honduras. (1997)

This vision of national prosperity (implicitly tied to foreign dependence) was yoked to a denial of racism and a reworked frame of nationalist mestizaje.

> In Honduras there does not exist sectarianism, xenophobia or
> apartheid and for this we are a marvelous country of tolerance. The
> happiness and extroverted character of the Garifuna has favored
> the taciturn air and timidity of the Toltecas [sic—there are no
> "Toltecas" in Honduras] and Lencas and the character of both have
> benefited all of us who should feel happy to be mestizos. (1997)

President Reina's discourse reflects contradictions within state-sponsored multiculturalism. He valorizes ethnic groups, includes them as integral to the nation, yet falls back on stereotypes of introverted Indians and extroverted Blacks. He implicitly maintains distinctions between Blacks and Indians even as he draws equivalence between them as ethnic groups with their own names, cultures, and personalities. Honduras becomes conceptualized as a multiethnic nation, yet the "we" of the nation implicitly remains "all of us who should feel happy to be mestizos." If these paradoxes flow from the speech of one man, what might we expect of conflicts characterizing ethnic politics as a whole?

This chapter analyzes the development of organized Garifuna politics, from the mid-1980s to the mid-1990s, when at least parts of the Honduran state and law came to embrace multiculturalism and ethnic rights. How and why did the multicultural paradigm come into being in Honduras? How did Garifuna activists and state representatives struggle over the meanings of multiculturalism and ethnic rights? What forms of ethnorepresentation, racial discourses, and diasporic identifications did activists and others construct as they rendered Garifuna "visible"? I argue that Garifuna activists played an early and key role in the formation of the Honduran ethnic movement, working from a model of indigenous rights and helping define Honduran multiculturalism as incorporating peoples rendered distinct in racial terms. In the process, they called into question commonsense assumptions concerning the concept of indigenous that equate it as a cultural condition or status with the category of Indian. Their strategies echoed developments elsewhere in Latin America and allow us to explore the complex relations between multiculturalism, blackness, and indigeneity.

Blackness, Indigeneity, and the Multicultural Turn in Latin America

Honduras is one of many countries that has taken up the mantle of multiculturalism and redrawn laws to recognize "ethnic rights." During the 1990s, most Latin American states instituted constitutional or other legal reforms, establishing collective rights for ethnic groups, most prominently indigenous peoples. A wave of literature has documented reforms delimiting a regime of rights specific to certain collective subjects concerning land and/or territory, bilingual/intercultural education, customary law, political representation, and others.[1] Laws vary from country to country, but a clear pattern has emerged in which groups of people understood to bear identities and cultures distinct from majority and/or dominant populations become subjects of special juridical regimes and bearers of distinctive rights.

Scholars have offered a variety of explanations for these reforms. Some depict them primarily as the result of a pan-American indigenous movement and its international allies, particularly environmental organizations (Brysk 2000). Others highlight structural transformations in governance and the economy. Deborah Yashar (1999), for example, argues that the indigenous movement emerged largely in response to neoliberal reforms that compromised the viability of indigenous communities and undermined their relationship with the state. She, like Donna Lee Van Cott (2000), views state accommodations of ethnic rights as an effort to restore the legitimacy of states that have "democratized" under the adverse terms for social welfare imposed by neoliberalism. Another line of analysis emphasizes the curious role of multilateral institutions such as the World Bank and Inter-American Development Bank—architects of neoliberal "reforms" that push privatization and free markets—in promoting ethnic rights (Offen 2003). These explanations are not necessarily incompatible, and taken together, they point to the array of social institutions, ideologies, and movements that shapes ethnic politics. Nonetheless, we can identify a certain fault line in evaluations of ethnic politics and state multiculturalism, between accounts that tend to celebrate the forward march of ethnic movements and state reforms (e.g., Brysk 2000) and those that express caution, highlighting how multicultural reforms can be encompassed within neoliberal governance (Gros 1997; Hale 2002, 2005). I return to these issues in chapter 4, focusing here on the relationship of blackness and indigeneity in the recent turn toward multiculturalism.

If official multiculturalism recognizes certain collective subjects, how does that process occur, and what kinds of subjects are recognized? Literature on these issues in the 1990s was dominated by discussions of populations understood as indigenous peoples to the neglect of those understood to be "Black." Volumes dedicated to Latin American multiculturalisms focused almost exclusively on indigenous peoples; the rare justifications for excluding Blacks in analysis of ethnic movements suggested that Blacks were engaged in urban-based struggles that shared little with indigenous mobilization (e.g., Yashar, 77). Yet, as some scholars noted, mobilization of rural Black communities occurred in a number of Latin American countries—for example, Colombia, Ecuador, Nicaragua, Honduras, and Brazil—and blackness increasingly came to appear "like indianness" (Wade 1997). As early as 1992, Whitten and Torres noted:

> Black political movements are gathering strength in a number of countries, including Brazil, Colombia, Venezuela and Ecuador. Some of these challenge discriminatory practices through the courts and seek greater black participation in the electoral arena. Others champion "blackness" and black heritage, reclaiming black history and insisting on respect for the black contribution to national culture. Still others seek territorial autonomy for the indomitable maroon communities which survive to this day. (1992, 15)

The latter politics gained traction during the 1990s in a number of Latin American countries as rural Black communities pressed demands for recognition of cultural difference and similar rights as indigenous peoples, above all to collective land and territory. In some countries, most prominently Colombia, Black communities acquired titles to lands and were afforded collective rights resembling those of indigenous people (Wade 1995; Grueso, Rosero, and Escobar 1998; Restrepo 2002). By the turn of the millennium, multilateral institutions such as the World Bank and Inter-American Development Bank had directed increasing attention to "Afro-Latinos" or "Afro-descendants" and developed a series of initiatives concerning them. Thus, at least some Blacks became rendered in terms of ethnorepresentation, previously reserved primarily for indigenous peoples, as collective subjects with distinct cultures, identities, and histories.

Nonetheless, the status of Blacks within contemporary multiculturalism remains, in most countries, ambiguous. For example, the 1998 Ecuadorian Constitution enumerates a series of rights concerning indigenous peoples and then adds a final provision stating, "the state recognizes and guarantees the rights of Black peoples in all respects that apply (en todo aquello que les sea aplicable)" (República de Ecuador 1998, Artículo 85). Presumably, those rights apply only to those Blacks who can demonstrate similarities with indigenous peoples. Juliet Hooker (2005a) argues that throughout Latin America states have granted indigenous peoples collective rights to a far greater extent than to Blacks. She attributes "indigenous inclusion" and "black exclusion" to the criteria used to recognize collective rights, namely notions of cultural difference rather than racial discrimination or social marginalization. In most of Latin America, Blacks and

Indians have been differently positioned within what Peter Wade (1997) calls "structures of alterity." Indians tend to be viewed as distinct, bound "ethnic" groups with separate cultures and a key component of the national past, whereas Blacks are often portrayed as racially "other" without bearing corporate identities and distinctive customs and traditions. Thus, Blacks have been at a relative disadvantage compared to Indians in securing rights and recognition within multicultural regimes, and only those (mostly rural) Blacks who can position themselves as sharing the same conditions of a typified view of indigenous peoples can take advantage of multicultural citizenship reforms. Contemporary multiculturalism in Latin America is deeply informed by racial–cultural discourses and assumptions that often reproduce a dichotomy between indigenous and Black subjects.

The politics of Garifuna identity in Honduras disrupts straightforward distinctions between blackness and indigeneity. The Honduran version of multiculturalism represents perhaps the clearest case in Latin America where indigenous and Black populations have become "recognized" ethnic subjects with an equivalent institutional status (Anderson 2007; Restrepo 2007). Since the early 1990s, all state laws and initiatives directed toward indigenous peoples include "Afro-Hondurans" as well. The sections that follow explore how that particular form of multiculturalism developed out of a series of interrelated processes, including previous ethnorepresentations of Garifuna as Blacks with similar cultural characteristics/"problems" as Indians; transformations in dominant discourses of racial–cultural difference during the 1970s that positioned Garifuna as an "ethnic group," a representative of national folklore, and a tourist attraction; and the formation of an ethnic movement in the 1980s, modeled on a discourse of indigenous rights, in which Garifuna played a key role. I explore the possibilities and attractions offered by the indigenous rights paradigm in a sociopolitical context where the state asserted the absence of racism in the nation.

The chapter also analyzes how the lines between indigeneity and blackness were both reproduced and blurred in the ethnic movement and state multiculturalism. A racial distinction between indígenas and negros was maintained even though Garifuna, as Blacks, also came to occupy a cultural–historical position equivalent to indigenous and, in some cases, asserted a status as indigenous. I title the chapter "Black Indigenism" to highlight the ways in which Garifuna politics opens spaces to conceptualize blackness and indigeneity not simply as distinct identities but as subject positions that can overlap one another in social struggle. Nonetheless, the analysis in this chapter and the next refuses to simply celebrate the "inclusion" of Garifuna within the purview of ethnic rights but keeps a critical eye on state multiculturalism as informed by projects to shape and contain ethnic politics while remaking the image of the Honduran state and nation.

This perspective requires that we revisit the question of visibility, a trope commonly used to refer to the marginalization of Blacks and the lack of cultural recognition afforded them in Latin America. If Garifuna activist Álvarez Casildo marked the 1997 Bicentennial as a watershed in drawing attention to his people, that Garifuna had already been rendered visible was a condition for the event to have taken place at all. In fact, the bright light of ethnorepresentation—shone by anthropologists, state officials, activists, cultural performers, and other experts—had rendered Garifuna visible for quite some time. Moreover, since Garifuna have been interpellated as Black, being "invisible" as an unmarked national citizen was impossible. The focus of this inquiry, then, is not on whether Garifuna are, or have been, "visible" or "invisible" but on what becomes visible and invisible about them within processes of ethnorepresentation, where notions and representations of culture, peoplehood, indigeneity, and blackness combine in shifting and unstable configurations.

Ethnorepresentations, Folklore, and Tourism before Official Multiculturalism

Media coverage of the Bicentennial reflected the particular ways in which Garifuna have become "visible" to the nation. Newspaper articles and editorials not only paid some attention to governmental and social "neglect" of Garifuna but also provided celebratory, stereotypical images of them. A passage from an article titled "Rites and Traditions Encompass the Legendary Past and Present of the Garifuna People" exemplifies the contradictions:

Their cinnamon skin, the firmness of their bodies, the happiness reflected in the corner of their lips and their white teeth, plus the rhythm of an incomparable cadence, joined together in the Garifuna dancers who show the world their punta, a purely religious dance, the expressive force of a people who fight to exist in between governmental indifference and the almost total incomprehension of the population who believe they are part of something exotic, without being aware that they too are Hondurans.[2]

The striking attention to bodies, along with the photographs that accompany the text—of women dancing in flowing skirts and traditional head wraps, of men playing wooden drums, of a shirtless boy fishing, and of an old woman as an icon of the ancestors—does little to dispel the notion that Garifuna are "part of something exotic." Those white teeth appear again, not as fangs that would tear live flesh but as signs of health and happiness. Garifuna are now Hondurans not despite being seen as exotic but precisely because they are rendered exotic.

Representations of Garifuna as a culturally distinct Black group that was "part of the nation" did not simply arise with the ethnic politics of the late 1980s and 1990s but had precedents in previous decades. As we have seen, during the first half of the twentieth century Garifuna tended to be portrayed as racial and cultural others, within the nation but not of it. However, by the early 1970s, constructions of folklore—previously concerned almost exclusively with Indian and peasant contributions to the nation—began to incorporate Garifuna as part of national identity and as tourist attractions.

The transformation of the annual fair in La Ceiba exemplifies this change. In 1972, the municipal government and national Office of Tourism sponsored a "Caribbean Festival of Garifuna Dances" as part of the fair. According to posterior reflections, the festival drew 2,000 Garifuna performers and helped transform a regional event into an international Caribbean-style "carnival" with pageants, parades, and a week of merriment and licentiousness (Pineda 1996). From a historical perspective, the prominence of Garifuna dance groups in the transformation from fair to carnival is remarkable. In the 1950s, Garifuna were excluded from participating in the city fair and publicly ridiculed for crowning their own queens (Centeno García, 87–88). In the 1970s, Garifuna dancers became a cultural attraction key to remaking the image of La Ceiba as a tourist destination.

The first festival was coordinated by Armando Crisanto Meléndez, a Garifuna artist and intellectual best known as the head of the *Ballet Folklórico Garifuna*. The dance group began in Tegucigalpa in the early 1960s as an effort to bring together Garifuna living in the capital (Flores Lopéz 2000). In 1976, the newly created Secretary of Culture, Tourism and Information sponsored the Ballet Folklórico Garifuna.[3] The Secretary consolidated state institutions dealing with national cultural patrimony, living ethnic difference, and tourist promotion (Herranz, 232), sponsoring an investigation of Garifuna culture in which Crisanto Meléndez played a key role. In the early 1980s, it published several folklore texts that focused primarily on the various "ethnic groups" of Honduras, including Garifuna (Muñoz Tabora 1984a, 1984b). By then, the renamed *Ballet Folklórico Nacional Garifuna* had acquired an international status, having toured Latin America, North America, and Europe.

We can locate shifts in state representations of peoples increasingly labeled as "ethnic groups" within broader political transformations in Honduras in the early 1970s. This period is best known for a military reformism under General Oswaldo López Arellano, the same man who came to power in the 1963 coup (Sieder 1995). López Arellano had ruled Honduras until 1971, when Ramón Cruz of the National Party was elected president. Cruz lasted barely over a year, when López Arellano returned to power. According to Euraque, this coup was a product of three levels of conflict: (1) the old clashes between the Liberal and National parties; (2) disputes over representation in business organizations (in part a conflict between traditional, rural elites and "modernizing" industrialists, mostly located on the North Coast); and (3) "continuing strife pitting traditional landlords and the new rural bourgeoisie against peasants and workers in rural Honduras" (1996a, 149–50). By the late 1960s, worker and peasant organizations had regained some of the militancy of earlier years and the coup received widespread support from them (1996, 153). The new regime began an agrarian reform program that is often credited with diffusing conditions that might have led to revolutions similar to those in Guatemala, El Salvador, and Nicaragua.

A new, state-sponsored cultural politics emerged during this period that shaped the policies and programs of state agencies such as the Secretary of Culture, Tourism and Information even after the fall of the government in 1975 (Euraque 2004, 134–40). The government sought to foster economic development and lessen dependence on the United States through agrarian reform, forest development, industrialization, and tourism. It also sought to break with cultural dependence through promoting national popular culture and "integrating marginal sectors into development" ("Minorías Étnicas," 31). The "marginal sectors" now included not just the poor and peasants but also the "cultural minorities." To be sure, this recognition of ethnic diversity refused to identify ethnic marginalization with racial oppression. An article titled "Ethnic Minorities" in the Secretary of Culture's journal asserts:

There are few existing cultural minorities and the high degree of *mestizaje* has produced a nation where racial synthesis is not a governmental aspiration but a social fact ... This excludes, without a doubt, the existence of oppressive or exclusive politics, there having been no preference for any race in particular. Nonetheless, the necessity of social–economic development has produced a government obligation to define the attitude towards these sectors of the population. ("Minorías Étnicas," 30)

Ethnic subjects thus became the object of a new kind of attention, even as state representatives minimized their numerical presence, denied state racism toward them, and maintained a vision of nationalist mestizaje. Similar contradictions also characterized the "ethnic" discourse of President Reina in the 1990s.

Media discourses also linked Garifuna to folklore and tourism. In the 1970s, Honduran newspapers began to publish articles on picturesque Garifuna communities. For example, an article titled "Garifuna Folklore in the Enchanting Landscape of the Caribbean" describes the communities near La Ceiba (Corozal, Sambo Creek, and Nueva Armenia) as places comfortably straddled between tradition and modernity and primitiveness and civilization.[4] This journalism departs significantly from ethnorepresentations found earlier in the century. The travel account of Jesús Aguilar Paz, which rendered such communities scenes of savagery, was replaced by mostly positive, if patronizing, images of accessible difference. As if informing readers of the amenities available at a hotel, the article notes: "The *morenales* are blessed with the services offered by civilization, like electrical energy, drinkable water, churches, police and adequate communications ..." Despite these influences, "these populations jealously guard their ancestral customs, like their typical foods, rites, music and primitive dances ..." The text suggests that Garifuna have managed to maintain their traditions while becoming integrated into modernity, taking pains to show images of church and cross that "confirm the Christian faith" of the inhabitants. It avoids any depiction of threatening difference in spiritual practices and beliefs, focusing instead on the now familiar trinity of food, music and dance (consumable culture). Living difference appears not as a threat but as a curiosity and a promise.

As proponents of Honduran folklore had argued in the first half of the twentieth century, truly "modern" nations incorporate premodern difference as part of what makes them unique; by the early 1980s, Garifuna had become a central element of that discourse, increasingly directed toward tourism. The use of the term "Garifuna" itself is significant, particularly considering that Garifuna promoted it over terms such as "caribes" and "morenos." The term highlights an "ethnic" identity that marks a culturally specific people meriting respect and acceptance. The new forms of ethnic recognition were far from radical and typically failed to challenge, or even acknowledge, racism. Garifuna continued to confront a variety of forms of racial and cultural discriminations, from stereotypes of their spiritual practices as witchcraft, to prohibitions on children speaking the Garifuna language in school, to discrimination in employment practices. We thus cannot mark a simple transformation from discrimination to equality but need to identify a shift from outright exclusion to ambivalent inclusion. Ultimately, state discourses of ethnicity would be confronted by collective rights mobilization, as Garifuna and other peoples created national organizations to represent themselves to the nation-state, reshaping the folkloric mold in which they were cast.

Before proceeding to that part of our story, we should pause to consider the interventions of Garifuna intellectual Armando Crisanto Meléndez, who played a key role in many of the government initiatives involving Garifuna culture. In the 1970s, Crisanto Meléndez wrote several newspaper

Postcard from the 1990s depicting women dressed for a ritual occasion. A poster of the same image adorned many state offices. (Courtesy of Juan Antonio Bendeck, Imapro, El Progresso, Honduras.)

articles whose titles—"Brief History of the Negro in Honduras" (1972a), "Garifuna Dances and their Significance Should be Known by Hondurans" (1972b), and "The Garifuna Culture and the Principle of Nationality" (1976)—reflect a concern with identifying Garifuna (and Blacks) as part of the Honduran nation. Meléndez suggests that the failure to recognize the Afro-Honduran presence represents an affront to national dignity: "In lacking these elements many of us Hondurans are castrated mentally, because we have assimilated foreign cultures" (1976, 20). This critique of cultural dependence serves as a prologue to a brief discussion of Garifuna history and culture. Here, as elsewhere in his writings, Crisanto Meléndez emphasizes the African dimensions of Garifuna ancestry. He does acknowledge a history of interracial mixture on St. Vincent, describing Garifuna as "descendants of Africans of West Africa mixed with Amerindians" and noting that the Garifuna language is "basically Arawak," with influences from the Carib language and West African languages (1976, 20); but on the whole he frames Garifuna as a people of African descent.

We see this emphasis reflected in his use of the prefix "Afro," an increasingly popular form of reference for blackness in the Americas during this period. We also see it in an article (1972a) he published for the Festival of Garifuna Dances, where he highlights the agency of Africans, particularly men, in the historical formation of Garifuna on St. Vincent. In a presentation for the First Congress of Black Culture of the Americas (held in Colombia in 1977), Crisanto Meléndez identifies Garifuna as the product of successive waves of shipwrecked Africans who came into contact with Carib Indians and peoples of mixed Carib-African ancestry (1988). In the initial encounter, Caribs provided refuge to the Africans, only to enslave them. Worried by the "disobedient spirit" of the Africans, the Caribs decided to kill all Black male children, but the Blacks rose up, killed many Caribs, and "escaped with their wives and children" to the mountains (1988, 89). This group became augmented by later shipwrecks (in 1635 and 1675) of African slaves, many originating from Nigeria. These slaves "adopted the cultural and linguistic traits of the Caribs as a protection against their capture" and, by the eighteenth century, gained control of St. Vincent (1988, 90). This version of Garifuna history emphasizes the heroic agency of African men (over that of Indians and African women) in the making of the Garifuna people. In many ways, it echoes accounts by British planters in the eighteenth century who argued that Black men usurped Indian women and a Carib identity to claim native status on the island (Anderson 1997).

Crisanto Meléndez reverses the moral–political evaluation, highlighting the resistance of African-descended Garifuna to slavery, colonial oppression, and, later, to marginalization and acculturation.

Crisanto Meléndez also marks out a complex relationship between Garifuna and slavery. In a poetic passage, he highlights the creative spirit resulting from both African cultural legacies and American encounters, simultaneously claiming an exceptional status of Garifuna with regard to slavery and forms of solidarity with the descendants of African slaves.

> The Garifuna people came into being in the land of the Caribbean Sea, after the discovery of the American continent, and therefore there lives in this people the world encounter between three continents: America, Africa and Europe. The creative force that lives in this culture expresses the response of a people with deep roots in a strange land that is not of their origin (*arraigado en tierra extraña de su origin*), the YORUBA people of Africa, as well as the unification of Amerindian elements and the integration of European elements. Although the Garifuna were never slaves, we heard the sorrows sung by slaves imprisoned in the plantations. . . . (1983, 7)

As we saw in chapter 2, during the 1940s young Garifuna men with political inclinations debated whether Garifuna were African, while their elders differentiated themselves from other Black populations and a history of slavery. In the 1950s, activists affirmed a Black identity as part of the Honduran nation and positioned Garifuna as part of the Black diaspora; so too did Crisanto Meléndez.[5] What distinguished him, and his era, was an emphasis on the endurance of cultural traditions and the African origins of the Garifuna people, who had become "deeply rooted" in lands *outside* of Africa.

Further historical investigation is necessary to trace how Garifuna encountered and imagined "Africa" in the 1960s and 1970s, but the focus on Africa in the work of Crisanto Meléndez cannot be understood apart from transatlantic currents of Black mobilization and identity formation. Garifuna had long been attuned to Black activism and political ideologies elsewhere in the world (Centeno García, 105), particularly in the United States. One activist related that during his political formation in the late 1960s and early 1970s, the most important Black political figures were Martin Luther King, Malcolm X, and Angela Davis, representatives, respectively, of civil rights, Black nationalist, and Black Marxist politics. The political messages and style of Black popular cultural figures such as Muhammad Ali and Bob Marley also influenced younger generations.

In the late 1990s, Tyson remembered the TV miniseries *Roots* when it was aired in Honduras during his youth in the early 1980s. Back then, only a few people in the community had televisions, and they would charge ten cents to watch. The whole town stopped when *Roots* came on. Tyson cringed when he remembered how the slave catchers punished Kunta Kinte for running away by cutting off part of his foot. Tyson could make negative evaluations of contemporary African cultures (see chapter 1), but he identified with a history of slavery, responding to a question I asked him about what it meant to be Black in the following terms:

> As you can know, the Black was always enslaved by whites. So in those hard times there were white hunters that hunted Africans like they were dogs. . . . So the difference is here in economic power, until today, because Blacks, since the beginning of the history of slavery, were prohibited from going to school. They sold them in chains. They were at the bottom. Because imagine a man the same as you comes to sell you. You're an object. Now you're not a human being. So this influenced racism, you know. And when Blacks asked for a few rights during . . . John F. Kennedy. When was that? [MA: In the '60s]. In the '60s. Imagine. It wasn't long ago. That was practically yesterday. How could we be seen? Before any race we were inferior because we were the ones enslaved, even though before they [slaves] were indios. They were slaves of the Spanish but they were kept weak. That was how they went to Africa to bring people here.

As we see later, Tyson's construction of blackness departs significantly from that of activists, but his concern with slavery and racism reflects the recovery of African origins represented in the work of Crisanto Meléndez and a long history of antiracist struggle within and beyond Honduras. In the era in which Crisanto Meléndez was exploring African ancestry, Garifuna activists had revitalized a project to combat racism under the auspices of a new organization called the *Black* Fraternal Organization of Honduras (OFRANEH), which, in another twist in identity formation, would turn toward *indigeneity* as a route of struggle.

OFRANEH and the Formation of "Autochthonous Ethnic" Politics

During the 1980s, a national movement that came together under the label of "autochthonous ethnic groups" began to form. The history of that movement has not been written, but its origins can be traced to political–cultural organizations representing indigenous peoples and Garifuna established in the 1970s.[6] These include Moskitia Asla Takanka (MASTA), an organization originally designed to represent the peoples of the Mosquitia (and now specifically oriented toward the Miskito), a Tolupán organization fighting land displacement (Stocks 1992), and OFRANEH, created by Garifuna in 1977. Contemporary activists trace the development of OFRANEH to previous efforts to organize against racial discrimination, such as the Lincoln Cultural Society. One story attributes OFRANEH's origins to the antiracist initiatives of Erasmo Zúñiga Sambulá, who, in 1973, protested the absence of Black workers in the construction of the wharf at Puerto Cortes, denouncing the racism facing the Black population and demanding respect for human rights (Chala Santiago, 43–44). The persistence of racism played a key role in galvanizing the formation of OFRANEH. Many of its activists had cut their political teeth within the Honduran labor movement and/or the Liberal Party, and some had been members of previous organizations that fought racial discrimination. OFRANEH did not receive official recognition for several years because of concerns that it had "separatist" tendencies and would incite division within the nation (Euraque 2004, 235). The state document granting the organization juridical personality identifies its fundamental objective: "to group together and represent all Garifunas of Honduras as a means to assure their integral improvement and full integration into Honduran society."[7] Rather than read the phrase "full integration into Honduran society" as promoting cultural assimilation, we should interpret it as promoting equal acceptance and opportunity along the model of civil rights. Another objective reads: "Promote the diffusion of the Garifuna culture, in our communities, as well as in the rest of the country."[8] During the early years, the organization promoted cultural events and small-scale development projects but faced internal rivalries over leadership and direction.

However, by the mid-1980s, activists began to raise the political profile of the organization and embark on a new strategy that involved creating alliances with other ethnic groups. Roy Guevarra Arzú, a key figure in OFRANEH during the 1980s and early 1990s,[9] noted: "We want to collaborate and progress together with the other ethnic groups, who do not have organizations" (Chala Santiago, 45). Similarly, Nancie Gonzalez identified the organization's "dual strategy of linking themselves with other blacks . . . [and engaging in] joint efforts with other ethnic minorities" (1988, 209). If OFRANEH had been born, at least in part, out of desire for racial equality, it came to emphasize a politics of ethnic rights in alliance with indigenous struggles for collective recognition and rights. How did that happen and work?

In an interview with me in 2004, Roy Guevarra Arzú said that the strategy of aligning with other ethnic groups emerged after a case of land conflict in the early 1980s in which local Garifuna, the Honduran state, and a U.S. citizen held competing claims over land in the area of Puerto Castilla (near Trujillo) that was used for a U.S.-sponsored military training center.[10] The U.S. citizen, Temístocles Ramírez, had rented 12,000 acres from the National Agrarian Institute in the early 1960s, which he subsequently purchased. In the early 1980s, the Honduran government designated the property for use as a U.S. military training base, primarily for El Salvadoran troops. Ramírez demanded compensation for the lands while the government argued that he was in violation of the Honduran constitution (which prohibits foreigners to own land within forty kilometers of the coast) and the 1974 Agrarian Reform Law (which limited the amount of land that can be owned by individuals). Several Garifuna families who cultivated plots in the area were removed to make way for the base. In addition, Garifuna from Trujillo argued that they were the rightful owners to some of the land, based on a land grant provided in the early twentieth century. Though supported by the local Catholic Church and trade unions opposed to the military base, Garifuna claims were ignored and the state eventually compensated Ramírez. (The base was shut down in 1984 over the land disputes.) This conflict acted as a catalyst for Garifuna to link land issues to the plight of other ethnic groups. Guevarra Arzú noted:

So, after we had a meeting during the struggle we realized that there were other sectors like us that were being affected by landowners, timber merchants, land-holding politicians and landowning military officials and at this time there was the Honduran Indigenous Institute, right? So we wanted to embrace each other, create a single [front] . . . well, first insert ourselves but we realized that, well, as a Black population it was difficult because the idea

from the indigenous side was different and so we said "alright" and
we took away from that a process of unification.[11]

These comments require some unpacking. It is significant that OFRANEH
began to pursue alliances with "the indigenous side" in relation to land
struggles. The Puerto Castilla dispute was symptomatic of an intensifying
problem of land dispossession in the 1970s and 1980s created by, according
to a later report by OFRANEH, "an avalanche of usurpations motivated
by the supposed arrival of tourist investments to Honduras. Politicians,
military officials and landlords appropriated lands that they distinguished
as favorable for investments" (2002a, 6). Moreover, land reform policies in
the 1970s did not redistribute land from the rich to the poor, but rather
"encouraged displaced peasants to migrate to the more sparsely populated
coast where land tenure was unclear" (England 2006, 111), where ethnic
groups did not have legal title to communal lands and resources. Collective land and territorial rights were a well-established component of indigenous movements in Latin America, which had grown in size and strength
in the 1970s and early 1980s (Van Cott 1994; Díaz Polanco 1997). Also, the
1982 Honduran constitution acknowledged indigenous land rights (albeit
vaguely). Article 346 reads: "It is the obligation of the state to dictate measures in protection of the rights and interests of the indigenous communities that exist in the country, especially those concerning the lands and forest
where they are located" (República de Honduras 1996). Garifuna, simply as
Blacks, had no institutional means to claim collective land rights; but as an
ethnic group similar to indígenas, they could pursue a land agenda.

Guevarra Arzú suggests that Garifuna leaders hoped to tap into existing institutional spaces oriented toward indigenous peoples, citing the
Honduran Indigenous Institute (IIH). This organization was created in 1974
by mestizo intellectuals with the purpose of working for the benefit of "our
indígenas" (Flores Andino, 27). Its founding members included Horacio
Moya Posas, a former director of the National Agrarian Institute, and intellectuals who had worked in the field of folklore, including the venerable
Jesús Aguilar Paz. The IIH was not a government institution. Unlike many
Latin American states, the Honduran government never created an indigenous institute, a fact that reflects the absence of a systematic, centralized
state politics directed toward indigenous subjects. In the late 1970s, the IIH
attempted to increase awareness of indigenous issues in Honduras, though
with minimal indigenous participation and limited impact. Nonetheless, in

the early 1980s the institute did promote the idea of a national indigenous law and helped create a space for dialogue between social scientists, state actors, and indigenous professionals. By the mid-1980s, other organizations directed by Honduran professionals had emerged in the name of the indigenous. A Garifuna professional named Tulio Mariano Gonzaléz was a leading figure in one of them, the Honduran Council of Indigenous Promotion (COHPI). This organization was a predecessor to The Honduran Advisory Council for the Development of Autochthonous Ethnic Groups (CADEAH), established in 1988. The shift in terminology from "indigenous peoples" to "autochthonous ethnic groups" reflected an effort by Mariano Gonzaléz, Guevarra Arzú, and others to expand the indigenous framework to include groups understood in racial terms as Black—Garifuna and Creoles.

Guevarra Arzú would play a key role in this effort from his position within the state planning agency, the Secretaría de Planificación, Coordinación y Presupuesto (SECPLAN). In 1987, SECPLAN sponsored a meeting known as the "First Seminar with the Autochthonous Ethnic Groups of Honduras." Coordinated by Guevarra Arzú, the event drew together state agencies, ethnic representatives, and private organizations with an "indigenist" orientation, including the aforementioned IIH and COHPI. The seminar was attended by representatives of Garifuna, Miskito, Tolupán, Pech, Tahwaka, and Lenca. As noted previously, organizations representing the first three groups had been established in the mid-1970s. Organizations representing the Pech and Tahwaka were created in 1985 and 1987, respectively. These organizations are called "federations" and based on a model of political representation established by peasant and worker organizations (Barahona 2004, 229–30). The leadership is elected in a general assembly and acts as the political representative of the people to the state. Federations representing the other ethnic autochthonous groups were created within a few years: Lenca in 1989, Creoles in 1990, and Chortí in 1994.

The 1987 SECPLAN workshop discussed a diagnostic of the situation of the "ethnic autochthonous groups" to promote their "ethnodevelopment" in conformity with the national development plan (SECPLAN, 3). The seminar also sought to conceptualize "a legal framework adjusted to the requirements, preservation and incorporation of these groups into development and their definition as cultural patrimony of the nation" (3). At the meeting's conclusion, ethnic representatives issued a series of demands. These include, among others, that the government study the health situation of the ethnic autochthonous groups; that the National Agrarian Institute fulfill agreements to provide Tolupán communities with land titles; that the state return the lands near Puerto Castilla that "historically and legally belong" to Garifuna communities and to pursue "other similar cases in the rest of the country" (Anexo 3). Representatives also promoted a "Law for the Protection of Autochthonous Ethnic Groups." Key features of this law included provisions on recuperation, regularization (*saneamiento*), and titling of lands; recognition, protection, and promotion of autochthonous ethnic languages and cultures; recognition and conservation of traditional forms of organization; recognition of rights to exploit and commercialize natural resources; and direct political participation, especially in the National Congress (Anexo 3). Although the law was never passed, these provisions—with modifications—continued to figure prominently in Honduran ethnic politics and reflected the agenda that had emerged from the pan-national indigenous movement and indigenous rights regimes in international law (see Brysk 2000).

The 1987 workshop provides insight into how Garifuna became positioned within the state as an ethnic group like indígenas. The diagnostic produced for the meeting was written by a team of four government officials and two academics from the national university. Garifuna professional Roy Guevarra Arzú, representing SECPLAN, was the coordinator. The text provides a taxonomy of different groups that categorizes them according to geographic–cultural–historical criteria in the following manner:

> Mesoamerican Groups ("of high agricultural and sedentary cultures"): The Chortí of Western Honduras.
> Circum-Caribbean Groups ("hunting and fishing cultures, nomadic, and semi-nomadic"): Sumos (Tahwaka) and Payas (Pech) of the Mosquitia.
> Groups of the Cultural Frontier ("who share both Mesoamerican and Circum-Caribbean Features"): These include the Xicaques (Tolupán), Lenca, and "Afro-Caribbean Black groups" (*grupos negros afro-caribeños*), identified as the Garifuna and "English-speaking Blacks" (Creoles).

Finally, the diagnostic glosses Misquito as "an ethnic group of recent formation, a product of the mix of Black populations with circum-Caribbean indígenas" (SECPLAN, 7).[12]

The taxonomy merits close scrutiny. The distinction between the first two categories echoes a common social science distinction between "highland" and "lowland" indigenous cultures in Latin America. It also echoes a colonial distinction between the "forest tribes" of the Mosquitia and the relatively "civilized" groups of the interior of Honduras, characterized by their greater assimilation to mestizo norms and integration within colonial and national governance (Cruz Sandoval 1984). The third category of frontier groups is the most interesting one. It marks the racial distinctiveness of "Afro-Caribbean Black groups" yet also includes the Lenca and Tolupán. The groups placed within this category constitute four of the five largest ethnic populations in Honduras. In effect, the taxonomy highlights the *commonalities* between the most numerically significant groups. Garifuna and Creoles are positioned together as racially distinct from the other groups, but they are also represented in cultural terms as similar to those groups. Accordingly, the diagnostic proceeds to emphasize the common history of all the ethnic autochthonous groups as "products of the situation of colonial domination," as sharing "a more or less common socioeconomic situation" of intense land and resource loss, of poverty and lack of access to social services, and as "possessing very rich cultural structures, of old and enormous traditions that have still not been valorized by the Honduran nation state" (SECPLAN, 8–9). Within this characterization, Blacks appear like indigenous peoples or, more accurately, Blacks and indigenous peoples share common historical, sociological, economic, and cultural conditions.

The terminology of "autochthonous ethnic groups" (*grupos étnicos autóctonos*) also reflects, and helps to produce, a form of equivalence between racially differentiated subjects. In use, the term could clearly encompass both Black and indigenous groups. The word "ethnic" alone would serve this purpose, so it is instructive to analyze the adjective "autochthonous." In a general sense, the term refers to the condition of being the native inhabitants of a particular place. As such, it is often used synonymously with indigenous/indígena. However, in the Americas the term "indigenous" also typically functions as a synonym for "Indian" and has racial connotations, in the sense that Indian is not just a cultural category but carries connotations of descent from the pre-Colombian inhabitants of the Americas. The term "autochthonous" did not have that same direct association with Indian; it could thus serve as a racially ambiguous label to denote a "native" or "indigenous" status. As etnias autóctonas, Garifuna, though considered "Black," became represented in the same terms as indigenous peoples, as long-standing occupants of territory who bear non-European linguistic and cultural "traditions" and the same collective rights as indigenous peoples. Creoles seem to share that status, even though they appear to have had little involvement in state ethnic politics at this time.[13] This equivalence between ethnic groups soon became incorporated into state law and programs. In fact, in the early to mid-1990s, legislation and presidential accords employed the phrase "etnias autóctonas."[14] The legal language later shifted to the phrase *"pueblos indígenas y afrohondureños"* (República de Honduras 2004), but state initiatives concerning indígenas also include afrohondureños.

The question of the relationship between indígenas and negros and blackness and indigeneity—and where Garifuna fit within them—was by no means settled in the 1980s. The term "etnias autóctonas" facilitated forms of solidarity that left open the question of whether Garifuna were indigenous. Tulio Mariano Gonzaléz, director of CADEAH in the late 1980s, described the reasoning behind the use of the term: "It was to consolidate two interests, the ethnic groups that were here in Honduras before the arrival of the Spanish colonizers and the ethnic groups that arrived after the colonizers . . . We wanted to put etnias autóctonas because for us at that time the word covered all of the ethnic diversity in Honduras." He also noted that the term was used to end a fruitless discussion concerning whether Garifuna should be considered "indígenas." The label "ethnic autochthonous" allowed for those racialized as distinct to pursue a common agenda as equivalent subjects. Today, some Garifuna activists—most notably in OFRANEH—readily assert that Garifuna are indígenas without denying that they are also Black.

The story I have told of the early days of ethnic mobilization is a partial account, one that does not pretend to account for the full range of actors and perspectives in ethnic politics during the 1980s. A complete account would bring us into the dynamics of each federation and the peoples they represent, their relations to other civil society organizations such as the Catholic Church, and the transnational dimensions of the emergent indigenous rights paradigm. I have sought here only to demonstrate the key role played by Garifuna in the formation of Honduran ethnic politics, which established a certain Black–indigenous equivalence reflected in the category "ethnic autochthonous groups." I have also suggested that the movement emerged in complex dialogue with elements of the Honduran state at a moment when these groups were increasingly acknowledged as culturally distinct subjects.

With the formation of federations representing most of the ethnic autochthonous peoples by the late 1980s, ethnic activists sought to increase their own autonomy. In 1989, representatives of the federations announced that "the interference of persons from outside of our peoples" had "systematically restricted and limited the peoples' direct participation" in their own organizational process.[15] Over the next couple of years, they would create a "Confederation of Autochthonous Peoples of Honduras" that united the federations and supplanted or absorbed previous organizations that acted in the name of ethnic groups. In the 1990s, the movement would acquire a more confrontational politics and place increasing pressure on the state to recognize the collective rights of ethnic autochthonous peoples. In the case of OFRANEH, a new generation of activists, eventually led by women, would radicalize a politics of indigeneity into the new millennium.

From Convention 169 to Article 107: An Overview of Garifuna Activism and State Multiculturalism in the 1990s

On October 12, 1992 (Columbus Day in the United States and the "Day of the Race" in Honduras), a new Garifuna organization called ODECO organized a demonstration in La Ceiba, dubbed the "Peaceful March of Resistance: Indigenous, Black, Popular." The march not only drew Garifuna but also representatives of indigenous, labor, and environmental organizations, as well as the Catholic Church. The slogan "Indigenous, Black, Popular" had come out of earlier transnational meetings among activists discussing how to protest the quincentennial "celebration" of the conquest of the Americas.[16] In 1995, ODECO held a similar protest and issued a series of demands that reflected the close association between Garifuna and indigeneity established in the 1980s:

1) Order the protection and return of the lands of Garifunas and Indígenas.
2) Promote reforms to Article 6 of the Constitution of the Republic such that indigenous languages and Garifuna are official languages.
3) Develop bilingual, bicultural education, incorporating into the National System of Education the human, linguistic, historic, and cultural values of the Black and indigenous community.

4) Regulation and implementation of ILO Convention 169.
5) Indigenous and Black participation in the different powers of
   the state. (ODECO 1995)

As seen in chapter 4, over time ODECO placed less emphasis on articulations with indigeneity, but in the early 1990s it was crucial to define Black
struggles in close proximity to indigenous rights.

OFRANEH retained that emphasis and played an important role in the
Confederation of Autochthonous Peoples of Honduras (CONPAH), the
organization composed of ethnic/autochthonous federations established
in September 1992. In the early 1990s, federation leaders protested land
usurpation, organized campaigns against environmental destruction,
promoted land titling, denounced the assassination of leaders involved in
land rights activism,[17] and worked toward securing participation in state
programs and policies. They also lobbied the government to pass Convention 169 of the ILO on Indigenous and Tribal Rights. Convention 169, created in 1989, replaced an earlier convention that indigenous and human
rights activists critiqued as assimilationist. The new convention contained
provisions on indigenous land, resource, and territorial rights; linguistic
and cultural rights; and consultation procedures that exceeded anything
in Honduran law (Anaya, 58–61). The Honduran government ratified
Convention 169 in 1995, during the regime of Liberal Party president Carlos Roberto Reina.

Many of the programs created during the Reina administration had been
negotiated during the previous regime of Rafael Callejas (1990–1994). The
Callejas government, best known for instituting neoliberal reforms, passed
environmental legislation that recognized the rights of ethnic autochthonous groups and laid the groundwork for a United Nations funded program
called "Cultural Rescue," the first state-sponsored program in cultural preservation. During his tenure, the National Agrarian Institute, working with
an NGO led by Garifuna intellectual Salvador Suazo, provided land titles
for twenty-two Garifuna communities. A "multicultural" agenda had thus
begun to take hold in the midst of neoliberal reforms, but the recognition
of ethnic rights was limited to a few scattered and incomplete initiatives.
Moreover, the state passed laws that threatened the interests and well-being
of ethnic groups. For example, the government's Agricultural Modernization Law—heavily influenced by the U.S. Agency for International Development (Jeffrey Jackson, 23–55)—encouraged capital-intensive agriculture and

land privatization to the detriment of small-scale agriculture. The congress passed Decree 90/90 to circumvent prohibitions on foreign ownership of property in Article 107 of the Honduran Constitution. The law permits foreigners to buy land for residential purposes or approved tourist projects. For Garifuna activists, the decree reflected a state priority in promoting foreign investment over protecting communal land rights. These tensions would come to prominence in conflicts over government efforts to reform Article 107 later in the decade.

Ethnic politics acquired heightened visibility early in the presidency of Carlos Roberto Reina (1994–1998), who came to power on the back of popular discontent with the policies of Callejas but who continued neoliberal reforms. In July of his first year in office, more than 4,000 people marched to the capital of Tegucigalpa to present a series of demands to the national government, completing a "Pilgrimage for Life, Liberty and Justice" that began in the department of Intibucá in Western Honduras. The Pilgrimage was organized by the Consejo Cívico de Organizaciones Populares de Intibucá (COPINH), an organization that had begun in 1993 as a coordinating agent of various "popular" organizations in Intibucá.[18] According to COPINH's own narrative, its original goals included unifying regional popular organizations (peasant, ecological, labor, and human rights organizations), rescuing Lenca culture, defending the environment, and struggling against discrimination. The organization initiated direct-action political tactics such as occupying government offices to demand the closing of sawmills that colluded in forest destruction without providing benefits to local communities (Barahona 2004, 242). COPINH soon took on the character of a federation primarily representing the Lenca people. It thus placed the indigenous subjectivity of its "base" in greater relief, as "the unknown face of Honduras began to discover its indigenous face, a face of resistance and national identity" (COPINH 2004). The movements in Intibucá echoed similar developments elsewhere, most notably in Chiapas, Mexico, where an uprising born out of prior leftist, peasant movements presented a masked yet publicly indigenous face in early 1994, the same year in which COPINH organized the historic march to the capital (Harvey 1998; Collier 1999).

As protestors arrived in Tegucigalpa and occupied the National Congress, the national press reacted mostly with sympathy, noting that for the first time indígenas had marched en masse to the capital. The press was particularly captivated by the large banner of Lempira, the Indian leader who resisted the conquest and whose name adorns the national money. COPINH transformed Lempira from a symbol of the Indian ancestry of the mestizo nation into a symbol of living indigenous and popular resistance. Although the majority of those marching identified as Lenca, representatives of the Pech, Garifuna, Tolupán, Miskito, and Tahwaka also joined the protest. Leaders presented a series of demands, the most publicized of which included a moratorium on logging in disputed areas, the removal of the governor of Intibucá, and the creation of indigenous municipalities in the region. The government created an emergency commission to negotiate with representatives, including a member of OFRANEH who served within CONPAH. The forty-eight promises covered a range of demands, such as the building of infrastructure, the investigation of assassinations and illegal logging, the inclusion of ethnic representatives in the planning of nature reserves, and the delivery of land titles. Although many of the initiatives were directed toward Lenca communities, the emergency commission also made promises to other ethnic groups. For example, the government promised not to install a refinery in Puerto Castilla, for long a preoccupation of Garifuna activists in the Trujillo area. The government also promised a few concessions to OFRANEH in a conflict concerning the Cayos Cochinos, a series of small cays that had been made into an ecological reserve, prohibiting the extraction of resources by local fisherman. In that struggle, Garifuna who relied on the cays for subsistence asserted rights as an indigenous people under ILO Convention 169 (see Anderson 2000, 220–30; Brondo and Woods 2007).

Diverse social subjects—people cast as Blacks in the case of Garifuna, "peasants" in the case of Lenca—articulated a politics of indigeneity as a paradigm of struggle with the potential to challenge dominant visions of national development. COPINH joined the confederation CONPAH in 1994 and over the next several years would coordinate other marches to demand compliance with previous promises. COPINH demonstrated a globalized political vision involving a popular, antineoliberal orientation also prevalent in OFRANEH (see chapter 4). One demonstration expressed solidarity with indigenous peoples in Chiapas. Another protested nuclear tests conducted by the French (Barahona 2004, 246–47). The warm media reception that the indigenous protests received in 1994 reversed course in 1997, when COPINH demonstrators tore the head off a statue of Columbus on the Day of the Race. Whether or not they destroyed the statue intentionally remains a subject of debate. One activist told me that it was an accident—the statue collapsed as they climbed it to dump red paint on it—but the protestors decided to make the most of the situation and celebrated the fall of Columbus. They were vilified in the press as "savages." Rather than defending the leaders of COPINH, the Special Prosecutor for Ethnic Groups and Cultural Patrimony Eduardo Villanueva prosecuted them for destroying a material manifestation of national culture. The incident exposed the contradictions between the dual mandates of his office, between defending peoples acting in the name of anticolonialism and preserving an artifact of national patrimony that commemorated colonialism.

While OFRANEH often played a role in multiethnic demonstrations in the capital, Garifuna organizations came together to hold their own demonstration in 1996 called the "March of Drums." The land titling process initiated in the Callejas years had stalled, and a coalition of Garifuna organizations tenuously united under the "National Coordinator of Black Organizations of Honduras" (CNOH) to secure an agreement from the government. The Coordinator incorporated representatives from the most important Garifuna organizations, including ODECO, OFRANEH, a Garifuna woman's organization, representatives from Garifuna town councils, and NGOs headed by veterans Tulio Mariano González and Armando Crisanto Meléndez. The head of the Coordinator was Celio Álvarez Casildo of ODECO, whose well-financed organization acquired the buses to transport several thousand Garifuna from coastal communities and cities to the capital. The demonstration was held, once again, on the anniversary of the "discovery" of the Americas.

I attended the march, joining protestors as they arrived at the Presidential Palace. We waited while a government commission negotiated with Garifuna representatives. The protest had a festive air. Men and women danced punta to drum beats that had earlier lent the march noise and rhythm. They were dressed in a wide range of Afro-diasporic styles, from the hip-hop fashions associated with the United States to the dreadlocks and cowry shell jewelry that evoke a "roots" aesthetic. The colors of Africa were prominent. Demonstrators came with signs demanding land rights and an end to racism and chanted slogans that were standards from left protests ("A people united can never be defeated") and indigenous actions ("The earth is our mother"). None of my friends from Sambo Creek could come, so I joined a group from the nearby community of Corozal, who were excited about the opportunity to push forward their land claims.

One of the young men in the group became ill, and I went with him to see a doctor. When I returned a few hours later, the government and Garifuna representatives had signed an agreement stating that the National Agrarian Institute (INA) would initiate a comprehensive land titling program for Garifuna communities. Garifuna had won an important victory but even at the time it seemed too easy.

Despite the hope generated by the accord, land titling and resource rights remained a subject of intense conflict between competing visions of development, tourism, ecological preservation, property ownership, and ethnic rights. The 1996 agreement committed the INA to provide titles to community lands and included provisions for the regulation of illegally acquired lands (*saneamiento*) as well as the expansion (*dotación* or *ampliación*) of lands to meet community needs within a period of six to eight months, in accordance with ILO Convention 169 and agrarian law. The INA was slow to produce titles, delivering seven at the end of 1997 and eight in 1998. Titles for the rest of the Garifuna communities were produced between 1999 and 2004. More crucially, OFRANEH and many local community leaders considered the titles seriously flawed. For example, Sambo Creek and two nearby communities received land titles in 1997. Occupying more densely populated areas than Garifuna communities in the Eastern departments of Gracias a Dios and Colón, the titles covered a limited area, barely exceeding the neighborhoods where people had built homes.[19] The town councils (*patronatos*) of these communities signed a complaint detailing their objections to the titles.[20] They argued that the land titled was a fraction of what they deserved, based on previous measurements. They also critiqued the titles' failure to recognize the "right to administer and utilize the natural resources that exist in our territories," including those related to rivers, lakes, lagoons, forests, beaches, and the ocean. The language here draws on the concept of territory, understood in Convention 169 as the total environment in which a people secures subsistence and reproduces its culture. Community leaders also argued that the titles upheld existing private property titles, making the process of land regulation impossible.

The question of recovering lands illegally appropriated from a community constitutes one of the more problematic issues in the process of land titling. Garifuna activists argue that foreign fruit companies, national businessman, military officials, tourist developers, and peasant "invaders" have illegally obtained lands traditionally occupied and/or used by communities. State officials admit that non-Garifuna have sometimes acquired land through illegal means but uphold the sanctity of private property. In practice, the National Agrarian Institute rarely questions the validity of existing private property titles, especially those of the elite. Although the presidential accord promised investigations of "irregular" land acquisition, the government failed to deliver. During the subsequent presidency of Carlos Flores Facussé (of the Liberal Party), some Garifuna communities were able to extend their community titles, but the land problem remained a contentious arena of conflict, both at the level of individual communities in dispute with third parties and at the level of negotiations between Garifuna organizations and the state concerning territorial rights. In short, the titling process did not resolve land problems but, as seen in chapter 4, set the conditions for future conflicts. Here, I conclude my account of major developments in the 1990s with a brief discussion of struggles over a proposed constitutional reform.

During the summer of 1998, the National Congress initiated a proposal to reform Article 107 of the Constitution, which prohibits foreigners from owning land forty kilometers from any ocean or national border. Foreign investment in coastal lands had occurred throughout the twentieth century: in the form of concessions, partnerships with Hondurans, or through violations of the law. Nonetheless, proponents of tourist development within and beyond Honduras (the U.S. State Department supported the reform) understood Article 107 as a threat to "land security" and an impediment to foreign investment. The proposed reform would allow for the sale of state, *ejidal* (communal), and private lands to foreigners on the condition that they be used for tourist development.

OFRANEH and ODECO immediately protested on the grounds that the reforms would facilitate the usurpation and sale of lands within or near Garifuna communities, violating their collective rights and threatening their collective existence. They were careful to emphasize that they did not oppose tourism but a model of capital-intensive tourism in which the only role for Garifuna would be as cultural entertainers and unskilled workers. OFRANEH staged a series of protests outside of the National Congress, joined by ODECO and an environmental organization. They secured an agreement from the president of the Congress to hold further discussions. But in November of 1998, on the heels of the devastation wrought by Hurricane Mitch, the Congress pushed through the first stages of reforming

Article 107 on the grounds that tourist investment was crucial to national reconstruction. Garifuna activists protested once again, helping to form a coalition of environmental, peasant, and labor organizations; the ethnic confederation CONPAH; and the left leaning political party Partido Unificación Democrática (PUD). The coalition was called the "Front for the Defense of National Sovereignty."[21]

Opponents of the reform cast it as another elite effort to sell the nation for their own benefit. They argued that the reform would sacrifice sustainable tourism in favor of corporate tourism, which would displace communities and destroy the environment, as had occurred in Cancún, Mexico. The reform contained no regulations for land transfers and would thus benefit rich landowners who had illegally acquired lands and could sell them at a high profit. Such unregulated sales would come at the expense of sustainable environmental practices and the productive activities of indigenous and Black peoples, independent producers, cooperatives, and even agribusiness. The movement against the reform of Article 107 thus articulated the defense of ethnic territorial rights with the defense of other marginal sectors and the environment, within a nationalist language that framed neoliberal reform as neoimperialism. CONPAH produced a T-shirt during the campaign that visualized this position. An arm clothed in yankee colors (red, white, and blue) extends a stack of money to another arm offering a piece of the Honduran flag. Between them hovers a Black face wearing a traditional Garifuna head wrap, presiding as the spiritual guardian of nature and nation.

In the media, supporters of the reform cast the opposition as a selfish, recalcitrant ethnic minority. For example, Otto Martin Wolf (1998), a regular columnist for the national daily *La Prensa*, ridiculed Garifuna aspirations to engage tourism beyond the role of waiters:

> Someone should tell the presidents of the Sheraton, Melia and Marriott Corporations that come to build here that they should not worry about sending hotel managers, to leave the chefs in France, that they do not need to send trained and professional staff because they can choose the personnel they need from Garifuna. . . . Because I am sure that those that complain about possible "humiliating jobs" that tourism will generate have confidential information concerning the training of the Garifuna population in hotel management.

Wolf went on to critique Garifuna for denying others the opportunity to share the benefits of tourism, continuing the sarcasm: "And the rest of us, who are barely 99.99% of the population should remain calm here in sweet Honduras, contemplating neighboring countries full of tourists with wallets replete with travelers checks" (1998). Sedimented stereotypes of a backward people impeding national progress thus resurfaced in the afterglow of the Bicentennial celebrating the Garifuna presence and multiethnic Honduras.

Efforts to marginalize opponents of the reform as a tiny, backward segment of the population impeding development failed to derail the movement articulated around the "Front for the Defense of National Sovereignty." The opposition culminated in a demonstration of at least five thousand people affiliated with dozens of organizations, held yet again on October 12, Day of the Race. The National Congress signed an agreement not to pursue the reform. During the protest, police opened fire into the crowd, killing two members of a peasant union and wounding at least sixteen others. The government shelved, at least momentarily, reforms to Article 107 but, as seen in chapter 4, the subsequent administration would introduce a different variant of neoliberal land laws effecting Garifuna territories that would prove more difficult to challenge.

Black Indigeneity and State Multiculturalism

This chapter has provided a partial account of how the ethnic paradigm came into being and how Garifuna activists positioned themselves at the heart of it. If Garifuna political organizations of the 1950s and the 1970s were born out of struggles against racial discrimination, during the 1980s they developed a new strategy of aligning themselves with indigenous peoples under the sign of ethnic autochthony. The two modes of struggle are not mutually exclusive and Garifuna activisms brought them together. In 1987, just two months before the important SECPLAN workshop, Garifuna marched in the May Day workers parade to demand equal treatment in employment, holding signs declaring: "Racism is not a Myth in Honduras" and "Garifuna are Hondurans too."[22] Four years later, Horacio Martínez—a leading figure in OFRANEH in the early 1990s—would define Garifuna as an "Afroamerican nationality that has its own culture, its own traditions, its own language and its own religion," emphasizing both that the organization had opened many battles against anti-Black discrimination and shared similar conditions to other etnias autóctonas.[23] The latter orientation involved a novel politics in which Garifuna activists represented themselves as a traditional people with the same status and rights as indígenas, raising the question of the relationship between blackness and indigeneity. The focus became the collective cultural rights of rural communities rather than quotidian discrimination in urban areas. Ultimately, the concern with racial discrimination did not disappear but was partially subsumed within the indigenous rights paradigm, remerging in more overt forms after Garifuna received recognition as a people.

Locating Garifuna within the indigenous rights paradigm had many attractions and possibilities. It facilitated alliances with other minorities facing similar problems and struggles. It allowed activists to tap into the small number of indígenista institutions in Honduras and the pan-American indigenous movement. It presented a framework to address cultural and linguistic oppression and claim rights to cultural and linguistic difference. It helped turn stereotypes of Garifuna primitiveness into valorized traditions. The paradigm brought to the fore the problem of access to land and resources, rendering rural communities the center of political concern. Like (other) indigenous peoples, Garifuna would mobilize an image of themselves as stewards of the environment, protecting that which Western modernity destroyed. Indigeneity thus provided a language through which collective claims could be made and heard; it made Garifuna a collective subject that the state and other actors could recognize as legitimately distinctive. Garifuna, though identifying and identified as Black, became "visible" as a collective subject to the state, indigenous and environmental organizations, international NGOs, multilateral institutions, and the public media by appearing in the same metacultural frame as indigenous peoples.

In the 1980s and early 1990s, a discourse of racial discrimination had little hope of gaining traction with the state compared to the indigenous rights paradigm. The Honduran state could admit the existence of ethnic groups and include Garifuna, but like most Latin American states, refused to admit the existence of racism (Banton 1996; Dulitzky 2005). President Reina's comments at the Garifuna Bicentennial that Honduras has "always been a country of tolerance" echoed a common denial of racism by state officials and mestizo intellectuals (Anderson 2001). This discourse of "racial exceptionalism" (Hanchard 1994) depicts harmonious race relations and the relative absence of discrimination, with a particular emphasis on contrast with the United States or South Africa. In Honduras, as in most Latin American states, antiracist discourse has historically proven insufficient as the primary means of achieving recognition and rights from the state. OFRANEH could not name racism when applying for legal personality in the late 1970s; only in the last few years has the state officially recognized racism as a problem within Honduran society. Sustained debate on racism and a politics directed toward establishing state initiatives to combat racial discrimination emerged only after the recognition of Garifuna as an ethnic autochthonous group.

Honduras is not the only Latin American country where subjects identifying as Black have articulated their struggles with indigeneity. In Colombia, Ecuador (Walsh and Garcia 2002; de la Torre 2005), Nicaragua (Gordon 1998; Hooker 2005b; Goett 2006), and Peru (Greene 2007b)— to name a few—activists have represented Blacks as distinctive "ethnic groups" or "peoples" with collective cultural rights, with varying degrees of success. Given the close associations between such rights and indigeneity in the region (Ng'weno 2007a), efforts by Blacks to assert a distinct ethnicity or peoplehood necessarily become entangled with questions of indigeneity. These encounters play out differently across the region, and, in general, Blacks have achieved fewer rights than indigenous peoples as their status as cultural others remains in question (Hooker 2005a).

The case of Colombia, with the most extensive legislation directed toward Black communities (Wade 2002), is particularly instructive. Constitutional reforms enacted in 1991 recognized a comprehensive set of cultural and territorial rights for indigenous peoples and produced a related but distinctive set of legal initiatives for Pacific Black communities. During the reform process, activists had to work hard to convince state authorities that Blacks could be considered ethnic groups with unique cultural and social characteristics (Grueso, Rosero, and Escobar, 199). Although the 1993 Law 70 concerning Black territories recognized Black communities as ethnic groups, it also depicted "blacks as invaders [of 'vacant lands'], in contrast to indigenous peoples who always had original land rights" (Wade 1995, 35). Moreover, the legislation limited the recognition of Black territories to the Pacific Basin, compromising the ability of Blacks in the other regions to secure land rights (Ng'weno 2007a, 423). According to Ng'weno, legal recognition of Black ethnicity remains conceptually distinct from that of indigeneity on the basis of distinct relationships to territory: "In sum, the state does not visualize Afro-Colombians arising from their territories, as they do for indigenous communities. Instead, it sees them as having come to occupy them in a relatively recent past" (2007a, 427).

Honduran state multiculturalism is distinctive in that it incorporates indigenous and Black subjects (Garifuna and Creoles) within a single paradigm of collective rights and legislative framework. Black subjects, like indigenous groups, are legally understood as ethnic groups and peoples. Moreover, some forms of Garifuna activism push beyond an equivalence between Black and indigenous identities, to assert Garifuna indigeneity. These developments do not simply reflect past Indian–African amalgamation or the fact of Garifuna cultural differences, as if representations of cultural difference do not involve institutional mediation. Rather we need to see the production of a legal equivalence between indigenous and Black subjects in Honduras as a product of layered histories of difference production. As we saw in chapter 2, mestizo intellectuals and officials in the nineteenth and twentieth centuries drew comparisons between Garifuna and Indians as problematic others with distinctive customs. In the 1970s, Garifuna became rendered representatives of folkloric difference and tourist attractions. Early in the formation of ethnic activism and multiculturalism, Garifuna activists from OFRANEH adopted a discourse of indigenous rights and aligned with (other) indigenous peoples, helping to shape the contours of a state multiculturalism that incorporated peoples differentiated along the lines of race within the same paradigm. Indigeneity remained the normative center of ethnic recognition, but unlike elsewhere in Latin America, in Honduras those identified and identifying as Black could claim a cultural position legally equivalent to those identified and identifying as indigenous.

To be sure, the equivalence and entanglement between blackness and indigeneity remain the subject of continued debate and contestation. In the late 1990s, leaders of federations representing the Misquito, Tahwaka, and Pech told me that they were never entirely comfortable with the unification of the "negros" with their struggles (see chapter 4), but they did not question the status of Garifuna as a people. The Honduran state and multilateral institutions find multiple ways to deflect Garifuna political claims, but they still consider Garifuna a pueblo. In fact, discourses questioning Garifuna rights to difference sometimes insist on their similarities to mestizos. We can end where we began, at the Garifuna Bicentennial, where the Minister of Culture, Rodolfo Pastor Fasquelle, made an extraordinary speech. Pastor Fasquelle, a distinguished historian, was a key government protagonist in negotiating ethnic demands who spoke often and with authority on culture and identity. At the Bicentennial, he told the audience:

> (I must) remind the Garifuna where they come from. One cannot invent oneself according to one's whim or preference. To try to pass as African is just as questionable for a Garifuna as it would be for Carlos Roberto Reina to dress like a Lenca or for me to presume to be British or a Pech Indian just because I have these ancestors. Like all other Hondurans, the Garifuna are mestizos, from the Arawak Indian and the African Black. To pass as the product of just one of these ancestors is to falsify one's identity, to forget the other complementary component, to betray the ancestors who they are trying to erase from their collective historical birth certificate. (1997)

The Minister of Culture does not question the ethnic status of Garifuna on the basis of their blackness. Rather, he highlights their Indian ancestry to show that they, too, are of mixed descent and thus mestizos, implicitly the same as other citizens. Pastor Fasquelle once questioned the indigenous status of the Chortí by suggesting that they were simply peasants with few cultural attributes of the Indian. He could not make that kind of claim about Garifuna, whose cultural difference had been a subject of folkloric fanfare for over two decades. He could only suggest that they were falsifying identity by denying Indian ancestry. The irony, of course, was that Garifuna had mobilized and acquired cultural recognition within a framework based on indigenous rights, even as many among them emphasized a Black racial identity. For better or worse, their status as an autochthonous ethnic group legally equivalent to indígenas could not be denied, even by the most dissimulating of cultural experts.

4

Paradoxes of Participation: Garifuna Activism in the Multicultural Era

In retrospect, the Reina years represented something of a high point for ethnic activism in Honduras in terms of mass mobilization, favorable media attention, and recognition of ethnic rights by the state. A leading activist in OFRANEH told me in 2004 that Hurricane Mitch (which devastated Honduras and Nicaragua in 1998) marked a shift for the worst in state politics and that the space for negotiation, dialogue, and concession had contracted as the neoliberal project of market expansion and capital-intensive tourism advanced. Her comments contrasted with the discourse of state officials I had recently interviewed. This expanding body of experts on ethnic issues emphasized the increased participation of indígenas and negros in state laws and programs. Even the "Special Prosecutor for the Ethnic Groups" Yani del Cid, a critic of much government practice and policy, told me that new spaces of participation and consultation had emerged.

That a Garifuna activist and government officials offered different evaluations of state politics hardly came as a surprise. However, as I began to look closely into developments over the past several years, I wondered if they might both be right. Was there increased participation with less dialogue? Had state and multilateral institutions expanded attention to ethnic issues without altering the paradigm of progress characterized by its opponents as "neoliberalism?" How were Garifuna organizations positioned, and positioning themselves, within spaces of participation in the name of "ethnic," "indigenous," and "Afro-descendant" inclusion? In this chapter, I continue to examine Garifuna activisms and state initiatives concerning ethnic rights after the emergence of official multiculturalism, focusing on developments during the regime of President Ricardo Maduro of the National Party (2002–2006).

The inquiries in this chapter speak to two recent theoretical discussions: critical analysis of the relationship between neoliberal governmentality and multicultural politics and assessments of the relationships among Black politics, cultural rights, and antiracism in Latin America. If the early literature on indigenous movements in Latin America emphasizes resistance to national assimilation (e.g., Stavenhagen 1992; Díaz Polanco 1997), later work sounds a more cautious note, interrogating the effects of official multicultural recognition and politics. For example, in her study of the Guatemalan Maya movement, Kay Warren (1998) warns against the depoliticizing potential of state initiatives that, "in the name of reform and decentralization," may ultimately "foster tactical political alliances to constrain alternatives, remove important issues from the realm of political debate and generate images of rural life that further naturalize inequalities" (205). Charles Hale (2002, 2004, 2005, 2006) takes this perspective further, arguing that official multiculturalisms may represent a "menace" to their presumed beneficiaries, diffusing the transformative potential of ethnic activism and reinscribing racial hierarchies.

Hale coins the term "neoliberal multiculturalism" to label an "emergent regime of governance that shapes, delimits, and produces cultural difference rather than suppressing it" (2005, 13). He argues that

> Encouraged and supported by multilateral institutions, Latin American elites have moved from being vehement opponents to reluctant arbiters of rights grounded in cultural difference. In so doing, they find that cultural rights, when carefully delimited, not only pose little challenge to the forward march of the neoliberal project but also induce the bearers of those rights to join in the march. (2005, 13)

We should not understand "neoliberal multiculturalism" in functionalist terms as the systemic production of ethnic politics in accordance with the "logics" or needs of capitalism (e.g., Žižek 1997). State versions of multiculturalism are sometimes confronted by visions of ethnic rights that contest neoliberalism (Speed and Sierra 2005). For example, the Zapatistas' cultural–political experiment creatively articulates indigenous rights, cultural autonomy, Mexican nationalism, and Marxian critiques of neoliberalism and capitalism (Collier 1999; Nash 2001). In Bolivia, the frustrations and expectations of neoliberal multiculturalism helped lead to regime change and what Postero (2007) calls postmulticultural politics. Nonetheless, in Honduras as in many other parts of the region, the contemporary politics of official multiculturalism creates difficult choices for activists: participate in state projects at the risk of compromising demands, or critique state initiatives at the risk of marginalization and loss of influence.

The phrase "neoliberal multiculturalism" best glosses a dominant project that aims to wed multicultural reforms with neoliberal initiatives, a project that produces contestation as well as adherence, often by the same actors. As Hale argues, the state and multilateral institutions that advance various forms of neoliberal, multicultural projects "cannot readily fix the cultural–political meanings that people produce and affirm as they mobilize" (2005, 13). As seen later, state and multilateral institutions attempt to mitigate the oppositional potential of multiculturalism, in part, by marginalizing organizations that explicitly contest neoliberalism (see Hale 2004). They do so, I argue, not via simple exclusion but through a politics of participation. In an era of ethnic recognition, "participation" provides a particularly compelling arena to examine contesting visions of rights and governance, to analyze the ways in which ethnic activists both engage with state and multilateral institutions and combat the politics of those institutions.

"Participation" is a ubiquitous term within discourses of political democratization, sustainable development, and ethnic rights. Ideologues from the political right and left can agree that democratic reform requires the active participation of civil society. Promoters and critics of development both know that without local participation, projects designed to improve communities or preserve the environment will fail. Ethnic rights advocates insist that they have the right to participate in programs and decisions that affect them; only a retrograde institution would deny that principle out of hand. Yet if everyone agrees on the importance of participation, they diverge sharply over what it means, the proper procedures for enacting it, when it is really present, and when it is empty rhetoric. In practice, participation is often rendered less a question of social justice than a matter of incentive structures, recruiting, and even creating stakeholders in projects of governance and resource extraction (Hayden, 61).[1] Rather than simply take participation as a good, we need to inquire into its political life as an *instrument* and *object* of struggle.

This argument adds to recent work that critically analyzes "participation" as a discourse and practice of governance that may produce unintended political effects. For example, in an analysis of relations between a conservation organization and local inhabitants of a national park in Indonesia, Li (2007) shows how participatory procedures operate as tactics of government designed to produce particular kinds of subjects, structuring the terms of discussion and debate while rendering conflict as a problem of misunderstanding rather than of divergent interests between authorities and "participants." At the same time, she demonstrates how the frustrated expectations generated by participatory models can ultimately provoke political challenges (218). Similarly, Postero (2007) analyzes how a "popular participation" law ostensibly designed to empower indigenous people actually sought to curb confrontation and promote integration of indigenous leadership with the government. In practice, participatory procedures produced new forms of exclusion by reinforcing traditional political parties and expert forms of knowledge at the expense of traditional forms of leadership. However, participation within conditions of disempowerment helped produce a "new form of citizen activism" involving confrontational politics and novel protagonism in the electoral arena (163). In both cases, efforts to render "participation" a technical procedure to mitigate confrontation did not simply produce subjection but also led to subversion (see also Ng'weno 2007b).

My contribution to this analysis lies in showing how "participation" itself serves as a tool of political struggle as the subjects of participatory discourse employ it back on institutional representatives to challenge their structures of engagement. Indeed, the participatory regulations of the World Bank became deployed by OFRANEH to challenge a bank-funded state project and national legal regime of property behind it. Multilateral institutions have been particularly influential in promoting "participation" as a mode of governance, responding to complaints of exclusion by people negatively affected by development projects and increasingly skeptical of "the credibility and representativeness of third world states" (Ng'weno 2007b, 232–33). OFRANEH leveraged both of these concerns in debunking a state program's effort to assert legitimacy via its participatory procedures.

The chapter begins by tracking debates over the meaning and practice of participation at a moment of its purported realization, a "consulting" meeting between state officials and representatives of ethnic federations. I highlight the constraints on political discourse implicit in this forum, challenges to those constraints, and differences among activists in their tactics of working with (and against) the state. I expand this discussion by analyzing competing perspectives on land and territorial rights. After the failed effort to reform Article 107 of the Honduran Constitution, the state developed initiatives that ostensibly recognize communal land rights yet, according to critics, also threaten their dissolution. OFRANEH once again led the effort to defend Garifuna territorial rights, drawing on indigenous rights and positioning Garifuna as indigenous. This does not simply involve an instrumental appropriation of the language of indigenous rights to achieve preestablished goals but also an ongoing encounter with indigenism as a political project in motion.[2] I show how OFRANEH links a politics of indigenous territoriality to a critique of neoliberalism, contesting recent state laws and programs that attempt to locate collective rights within a free-market framework. The ironies of participation take center stage in a conflict between OFRANEH and a government program of land regulation funded by the World Bank. I argue that the government program used a mode of participation that marginalized OFRANEH and exacerbated divisions among Garifuna activists, while OFRANEH used World Bank regulations on consultation to contest the "neoliberal" program.

The final part of this chapter turns to a discussion of the two principal national Garifuna organizations—OFRANEH and ODECO—and analyzes differences in their modes of ethnoracial representation, politics, and alliances with other sectors. Whereas OFRANEH continued to pursue (and radicalize) a politics of "Black indigenism," which ties Garifuna to indigenous activism and rights, ODECO increasingly came to emphasize the particularity of "Afro-descendants" and forged its closest relations with organizations representing Afro-descendants in other Latin American countries. By the end of the millennium, ODECO's politics of what I call "Afro-visibility" focused attention on the problem of racial discrimination and promoted antidiscrimination measures within the state. At the same time, ODECO tends to take a less oppositional stance on the neoliberal politics of the state and multilateral institutions than does OFRANEH. The divergent modes of ethnorepresentation and politics pursued by the two principal organizations once again reveal the dynamic and multiple configurations of identity politics. They also provide an opportunity to reflect on the relationship among cultural rights, civil rights, and antiracism. The chapter thus concludes with an effort to reassess critiques of cultural rights activism in ways that do not simply oppose cultural rights and antiracism. I suggest that the radical edge of Garifuna political formation lies less in a predetermined logic of identity categories (Black and indigenous) or identity politics (civil rights vs. cultural rights) than in the articulations between identity-based claims and refusals to accept dominant, neoliberal modes of institutional power.

Notes on a Consultation

In late July, 2004, I attended a meeting of the "Consulting Group" of the government Program to Support Indigenous and Black Communities (PAPIN). I was invited to the meeting by Carlos Palacios, a mestizo who worked for PAPIN as an expert on indigenous affairs. I had met Palacios four years earlier, when he worked in the office of the Special Prosecutor for Ethnic Groups. Like many state officials I met, Palacios welcomed my inquiries into the dynamics of state politics and ethnicity and encouraged me to see how participation worked.

PAPIN involved an eclectic assortment of projects and, what interested me most, a process of institutional dialogue between ethnic federations and the state via a Consulting Group. PAPIN received most of its funding from the Inter-American Development Bank (IDB) (in loans) and the Austrian Trust Fund (in a grant). From the IDB's point of view, the Consulting Group would produce "a better understanding of the issues affecting indigenous and black populations" and "bring those populations nearer to the pertinent government institutions and vice-versa" (Inter-American Development Bank n.d., 2–3). The meeting I attended involved considerable debate over the meaning and practice of participation and anxieties over relations with state institutions.

The consultation was a two-day affair held at a hotel in Tegucigalpa. The Secretary of Government and Justice, the state agency overseeing PAPIN, ran the meeting. The officials were mestizo men, with the exception of Omar Cacho Gil, a Garifuna who coordinated PAPIN, and Marquez Martínez, a Miskito working for the parent office. A representative from the Inter-American Development Bank (IDB) was also present. She mostly observed the meeting but occasionally interjected to highlight a priority of the IDB or explain problems in the delivery of money. A conduit to funding, she was probably the most powerful person in the room. There were two representatives from each of the ten ethnic federations, representing the nine recognized ethnic groups (the Lenca have two federations,

ONILH and COPINH). The majority of those representatives were men, although six of the federations were represented by at least one woman. There were also representatives from two Lenca and Miskito communities where program projects in culturally sensitive infrastructure construction (dubbed "ethnoengineering") were underway.

This was the fourteenth meeting of the Consulting Group. We sat around a large conference table, government officials seated at the head. The main themes of discussion included the state of the infrastructure projects (which were not going well); a program for training Black and indigenous women leaders (also characterized by problems and delays); a proposed office that would centralize state ethnic politics; and a recent property law. I focus on the latter two themes but it should be noted that throughout the meeting federation leaders voiced critiques of consultation processes and the lack of respect afforded to indigenous peoples. These complaints ranged from requests for better food to objections that state officials often portrayed informal discussions as formal consultations. My own presence became a source of dissent.

In the introduction to the meeting, PAPIN coordinator Omar Cacho Gil told the group that I was there to observe the process. After the first break, I asked the government official in charge of the next section—the highest ranking member of the Secretary, who was important enough to wear two cell phones—if he could ask for permission on my behalf to record the meeting (already being taped for the minutes). When he did so, one of the representatives of OFRANEH laughed and everyone else remained silent. I did not tape the meeting and my account here is based on my notes. On two occasions later in the meeting, representatives cited the lack of prior consultation concerning my presence as another example of the lack of respect shown them. I had told the representatives of OFRANEH of my invitation, and they expressed no objection to my presence; but in the meeting they made it clear that I was not affiliated with them and that the government needed to consult with the federations on who could be present.

Everyone agreed that consultation was important, but its organization and execution were subject to contestation. This became particularly evident in the response to a PowerPoint presentation by Marquez Martínez on the proposed creation of the "Indigenous and Black Peoples Support Unit" (UAPIN). Martínez was a young Miskito professional who had recently come to work for the Secretary of Government and Justice after consulting for the World Bank. He promoted the unit as a centralized space within the state to coordinate issues relevant to indigenous and Black peoples. Some of the more notable of its functions included formulating "public politics of attention to indigenous and Black Peoples"; elaborating development plans and programs ("in a participative manner"); assisting in legal reforms; serving as an interlocutor between the government and peoples; and acting as the government representative before multilateral institutions and transnational NGOs. According to Martínez, the Support Unit would provide indigenous and Black peoples a single office to hold dialogues with the government and greater access to state institutions, resulting in a more coherent state politics.

His proposal was met with hostility. The most vocal critics were the two representatives from OFRANEH (Gregoria Flores and Amilcar Colón) and Aurelio Ramos, president of the Miskito federation MASTA. Gregoria Flores was a former president of OFRANEH who remained a leading figure in the organization. Throughout the event, she was one of the most insightful critics of state politics, drawing on previous histories and comparative examples to highlight government failures. A state official I interviewed referred to her, with a mixture of sexism and respect, as a warrior. Less than a year after the meeting, she was wounded in a shooting while collecting testimony to present to the Inter-American Court of Human Rights. The police said that it was a simple case of attempted robbery, but human rights groups gathered evidence that she was warned to desist from land rights activism. Amilcar Colón had been elected coordinator of OFRANEH in 2003; in 2005, he would lose that post as a result of internal disputes in the organization. At the meeting in 2004, the two OFRANEH representatives presented a united front.

Critics of the proposed office identified two problems. The first revolved around the lack of prior consultation in the proposal's formulation. Amilcar Colón began the discussion with a dramatic flair, making sure that the government's tape recorder was on before stating: "we were never consulted about the election of the figure." All the activists who spoke agreed that the proposed document was invalid, even as a starting point for discussion, because it had been produced without any input from the federations; to begin consulting now was a farce. The second critique focused on structures of participation between activists and the state. Federation representatives worried that the office would act as *the* voice for indigenous and Black peoples, compromising both their independence and access to the state. Aurelio Ramos and Gregoria Flores raised the situation of Kuna organizations in Panama, where the creation of a centralized government office had produced a channel of selective access to state institutions and international funding.[3] The proposed office was potentially dangerous because the intermediary would prefer certain organizations over others and compromise the federations' independence. Representatives of OFRANEH and the Lenca federation COPINH—the most confrontational organizations—were particularly vocal on this point. Amilcar Colón argued that OFRANEH had spent years creating spaces of dialogue and could gain the ear of the state by bringing "six trucks" (of protestors). A representative of COPINH echoed the sentiment. A small, pregnant woman who spoke infrequently but with authority, she noted that the intention behind the proposal was not necessarily bad but that "We have the last word. We have to consult the bases. The buses are well prepared if we want a meeting with [the Secretary of] Education." Referring to the argument that Martínez should be accepted because he was Miskito, she noted: "The young man is indígena. The government likes us to kill ourselves but the more problems we have, the more we are united." Her comments spoke indirectly to a previous moment of tension between representatives of MASTA and OFRANEH.

Although Aurelio Ramos and Gregoria Flores voiced similar critiques of the proposed office, they came into conflict after the official from the Inter-American Development Bank asserted that the bank wanted a permanent office dealing with indigenous issues. In response, Ramos said that the proposal, though defective, represented a good opportunity. He also chided Gregoria Flores for implying that she did not want such an office. Flores countered that although the government was obliged to create a valid interlocutor with the peoples, the interlocutor should not be an individual or a small office. The proposal would bureaucratize indigenous peoples yet again. She insisted that the peoples must define their own politics. If the representative of MASTA made a point to demonstrate a willingness to work with state and international institutions on this issue, the representative of OFRANEH reiterated her skepticism.

This moment of discord reflected a recent history of tensions between federations. As discussed in chapter 3, in the early 1990s, most of the key organizations representing indigenous and Black peoples in Honduras participated in the CONPAH. By the end of the millennium, serious fissures had developed among the members of CONPAH. In fact, key leaders within MASTA, the Lenca federation ONILH, and the federations representing the Pech and Tahwaka had attempted to create a new coordinating organization that would exclude OFRANEH and COPINH. As I discuss elsewhere (Anderson 2007), these divisions had multiple sources, including competition between activists over access to funding and projects; sensibilities of racial distinctiveness; and disagreements over political tactics. Miskito leaders who I interviewed in 2000 (including Aurelio Ramos) represented their relationship with OFRANEH in complex terms. On the one hand, they asserted that the coordination between "negros" and indígenas in a single space of struggle distinguished the Honduran ethnic movement from others in Latin America. On the other, they argued that OFRANEH and COPINH had dominated CONPAH, suggesting that those organizations' political belligerence could not be embraced by all and threatened to compromise the movement. Although MASTA sometimes coordinated mass protests in the geographically isolated Mosquitia, they did not have the capacity to produce the mobilizations that had placed COPINH in the center of indigenous politics and that OFRANEH, to a lesser extent, could also effect. The alternative confederation MASTA promoted failed to take hold and was denounced by COPINH and OFRANEH as a divisionary tactic of government institutions and the World Bank.

The effort to create an alternative confederation to CONPAH contributed to deep suspicions of state intervention in ethnic organizations. These histories remained implicit at the 2004 meeting and were evoked by Flores' assertion that the various peoples needed to develop their own politics apart from state initiatives. During the second day, federation representatives met on their own to discuss their priorities. Within a year, most of them would sign a call for renewed "unity of indigenous and Black peoples" (OFRANEH 2005a). That unity, however, was tenuous, and the former institutional coordination between OFRANEH and other indigenous organizations remained elusive.

The PAPIN consultations were circumscribed by the structure of the meetings, oriented around the presentation of information, state initiatives, and project reports. To be sure, the framework was flexible enough to allow ethnic representatives to voice their concerns and request meetings with other state officials. What remained absent was space for substantive dialogue on the broader political, economic, and cultural frameworks employed by the state and multilateral institutions, even though one of the program's mandates included strengthening the legal framework of Black and indigenous rights. An analysis of a discussion in the meeting over a recently passed property law underscores the limits imposed on the subjects of consultation, limits not necessarily accepted by those same subjects.

Critiquing a Property Law

The new property law—*Ley de Propiedad Decreto Número 82-2004*—went into effect at the end of June 2004 and included a chapter "On the Process of Regulation of Real Estate (*Propiedad Inmueble*) for Indigenous and Afro-Honduran Peoples" (República de Honduras 2004, 41–43). At the PAPIN meeting in July, project administrators brought in a legal expert, Romeo Ucles, to explain the law, though it became clear that some of the activists knew it better than he did. He spent most of his presentation promoting the virtues of the law, designed to "strengthen and bestow juridical security to title holders of property, to develop and execute a national politics that permits national and foreign investment and the access to property on the part of all sectors of society" (República de Honduras 2004, 6). Ucles cited a study from the Harvard Institute of International Development on the costs of inefficient property regimes; in Honduras, property registration was twenty times more expensive and seventy times slower than that in developed countries. The result was an irregular, closed property market characterized by conflict, corruption, stagnation, and lack of access to property rights among the majority. According to Ucles, the law would reduce transaction costs, create mechanisms to settle conflicts, and facilitate property registration for excluded sectors. In essence, he reiterated neoliberal wisdom on the importance of property rights for development and poverty reduction adopted by the World Bank, Inter-American Development Bank, and United States Agency for International Development (USAID) (Stocks 2005, 89). He also related additional benefits concerning the recognition and titling of communal lands in accordance with ILO Convention 169, which, he said, "I imagine you take as your bible." He closed by noting that although resolving land issues would not be simple, the law would solve most problems.

In the ensuing discussion, members of various federations contested the compatibility between indigeneity and market logics. The first volley came from MASTA activist Edy McNabb, who had a close working relationship with the government. He argued that the chapter evoking Convention 169 had been "mechanically inserted" and that indigenous peoples viewed

the land not as a market asset but as "mother earth." McNabb annunci-
ated a stock position in indigenous movements that pueblos indígenas
have a special relationship with the land that cannot be captured by Western logics of ownership and resource extraction. The representatives of
OFRANEH reiterated this position and focused on specific problems with
the property law, arguing that it conflicted with Convention 169. The heart
of the contradiction lay in articles recognizing the rights of "third parties."
Article 97, for example, states: "The third party who has a property title in
lands of these peoples and who has had and possessed the land covered by
that title has the right to continue possessing and exploiting it" (República
de Honduras 2004, 42). OFRANEH activists argued that these provisions
attenuated collective rights by upholding the legality of private property
titles held by outsiders and compromised the peoples' ability to resolve
conflicts. Moreover, they suggested that the law would actually incite land
invasions by powerful outsiders confident in their ability to secure private
titles that would be upheld under the law. OFRANEH also condemned a
provision in the law allowing communities to dissolve collective property
regimes in favor of individual titling.

Ucles responded that his purpose was neither to attack nor to defend
the law—it was approved—but to inform meeting participants of their
rights. Asserting, "It is important that you know your rights," he argued
that problems would have to be resolved not with arms or illegal occupations but with "paper," within the boundaries of the law. Of course, activists were pushing the point that the law did not adequately recognize
indigenous rights. A Miskito representative noted the contradiction, arguing that indigenous rights were historic rights and not rights granted
by the state. He provided examples of how "ancestral rights" were violated
in the Mosquitia. By the end of the discussion, Ucles was simply repeating
that, though there were always abuses of the law, problems and conflicts
would have to be resolved legally, a point reiterated after he left by the se-
nior official of the Secretary of Government and Justice. Even that position
was contested, as Gregoria Flores suggested that when the state upholds
illegality, peoples still have the right to justice. The previous summer, her
organization had convoked an assembly of Garifuna community members who repudiated a previous version of the law and urged Congress to
consider the "Garifuna territorial law" submitted by OFRANEH. Despite
a meeting of government officials with activists to discuss the property
law—where Ucles served as a consultant—the version passed by Congress

took little account of the principal objections. State officials, who rendered the discussion a pedagogical exercise to "know your rights," ignored that history.

From OFRANEH's perspective, the property law represented a step backward in the recognition of indigenous rights and a continuation of policies favoring land acquisition by the rich. A number of Garifuna communities, located on the valuable coastline, are embroiled in conflicts with some of the most wealthy, well-connected men in Honduras, such as Miguel Facussé and Jaime Rosenthal. Miguel Facussé is the uncle of former president Carlos Flores Facussé (1998–2002) and author of the National Development Plan during the administration of Carlos Roberto Reina. He has vast landholdings and financial interests in Honduras and may be the richest man in the country. Since the early 1990s, he and Garifuna from the municipality of Limón have disputed ownership of lands that Facussé intends to use for tourist development and African palm plantations (England 2006, 165). Rosenthal is a former vice president (from the Liberal Party) and a wealthy businessman. He owns the newspaper *El Tiempo* and has investments in a wide array of companies. Rosenthal and members of the Garifuna community of San Juan are engaged in disputes over the legal ownership of land where Rosenthal has installed a hotel (CCARC 2003, 4: 36). OFRANEH argues that the property law works in the interests of such powerful landholders and potential investors, by recognizing the rights of third parties in indigenous territories.

The existing property law rests on an ideological framework that promotes the market as the benevolent motor of development under the theory that an efficient property regime will facilitate capital investment. The granting of land to the poor or indigenous peoples becomes justified not so much in terms of social justice or wealth redistribution as in terms of economic dynamism. As Marquez Martínez (2003) noted when he worked for the World Bank, "For the government it is important to define land tenancy in the northern region as an important condition to promote the development of private sector investment in tourist activities" (15). The World Bank and Inter-American Development Bank also identify land security as a precondition of capital investment. We return to other state initiatives concerning land conflicts, but first we need to look closer at the alternative visions of land tenancy held by OFRANEH, who articulate a discourse of indigeneity and territoriality with a critique of neoliberalism as neoimperialism.

OFRANEH and Territoriality

The principle of territoriality is a central component of many indigenous movements in the Americas and has become (partially) codified in international agreements on indigenous rights such as ILO Convention 169. In some countries (e.g., Colombia, Brazil) state legislation concerning indigenous and (some) Black peoples recognizes the principle of territoriality (Roldán Ortiga 2004; Stocks 2005). Within these spheres, the concept of territory typically refers to a geographic area in which culturally differentiated peoples reproduce their distinct way of life. Convention 169, the most important juridical resource for territorial claims in Honduras, identifies territory as "the total environment of the areas which the peoples concerned occupy or otherwise use" (Anaya, 307), including natural resources, oceans, rivers, and so on. In some interpretations of international law, indigenous territorial rights have been understood not simply in terms of ancestral possession of specific areas antedating colonialism but also in terms of the principle that formal rights to occupation, ownership, and use of territory are necessary for the survival of peoples and cultures. As one analyst puts it, the concept of territory "relates to the collective right to survival as an organized people, with control of their habitat as a necessary condition for the reproduction of their culture, and for their own development, or as Indigenous experts prefer, for carrying ahead their 'plans of life' and their political and social institutions" (Kreimer, 2). In this sense, indigeneity marks a cultural condition requiring a territorial basis for its sustainability.

In contemporary rights discourse, assertions that indigenous people have a special relationship to the land and practice environmental stewardship become mobilized in critiques of the destructive practices of capitalism and neocolonial states. OFRANEH attributes the misery of indigenous and Black peoples to "an economic structure based in the pillage and destruction of mother earth" (2005a), contending that Garifuna practice sustainable forms of resource use. In addition to "territory," the organization uses the phrase *habitat funcional* (functional habitat) to refer to historic ("ancestral") spaces of occupation and use and to signal the intimate relation between Garifuna and their environment. OFRANEH thus grounds territorial rights as the necessary guarantee of both environmental and cultural reproduction, eschewing a protected areas model of environmentalism for a model of the co-(re)production of nature and culture under indigenous administration. In its "Profile of the Garifuna People"—produced in response to studies by social scientists contracted by the World Bank and other institutions—OFRANEH asserts: "Territorial recognition of the functional habitat that we have maintained for the past 207 years is key to guaranteeing the cultural survival of our people" (2002a, 7). Although the close association between indigenous peoples and the environment has precedents linking Indians with untamed "nature" in ways that denied Indians' agency, contemporary movements articulate these associations with projects that promote indigenous control and ownership of territory.

In discussing discourses of indigeneity and territoriality, I resist a temptation to analyze them in terms of a cultural "essentialism" either to be attacked as intellectually outmoded and politically dubious nativisms (Kuper 2003) or defended as necessary forms of "strategic essentialism" (Robins 2003). To be sure, projects of indigenous territoriality often draw associations among people, culture, and place that may mirror fantasies of a monocultural nation. However, debates over "essentialism" easily devolve into rigid oppositions between "identity politics" and critiques of capitalism and between ethnic particularism and class universalism, ignoring the variety of different political projects that can articulate with discourses of territoriality. Rather than focusing simply on the forms of cultural representation associated with "territoriality," we should pay attention to the political projects associated with territorial claims.

OFRANEH links the promotion and defense of territoriality to a stance against "neoliberalism" and the dominance of foreign capital, drawing connections between the plight of indigenous and Black peoples and other "popular sectors." In a communiqué protesting violence against activists, the organization asserts:

> OFRANEH believes that we are living in a very important historical period. The ratification of the Free Trade Agreement with the United States will speed up the process of economic globalization and lead to increased poverty, given the enormous gap that exists between our country and the North American Empire. The traditional agricultural economies of our country will be undermined and there will be a huge increase in the number of peasants who are forced to migrate to the North . . . The Empire's attempt at economic globalization is a total failure and the situation will only

get worse with the implementation of projects such as the Free
Trade Agreement with the United States, the Plan Puebla Panama,
the Mesoamerican Biological Corridor and the PATH (Proyecto
de Administración de Tierras de Honduras), all of which directly
impact the future of our people's land.[4] Financial institutions such
as the World Bank and the Inter-American Development Bank
are attempting to implement these projects. At the same time,
wherever possible, they try to sow the seeds of division in popular
movements and buy their leaders. (2005b)

The overall tone and content of this discourse will ring familiar to anyone
with a cursory knowledge of contemporary left politics in Latin America.
The analysis here draws an intimate relationship among U.S. imperialism, multilateral institutions, and the Honduran government, connecting threats to Garifuna territory to a broader political–economic critique
that includes accounts of peasants who are forced to migrate and popular
movements that face the divisionary tactics of multilateral and state
institutions. OFRANEH thus articulates its defense of Garifuna and the
promotion of territoriality with a biting critique of neoliberalism.

Analysis of indigenous and Black activism elsewhere in Latin America
also suggests that efforts to defend territory can represent important challenges to capitalist projects. For example, Sawyer (2004) documents the
ways in which indigenous mobilization in the Ecuadorian Amazon contested foreign oil exploitation backed by neoliberal policies. Similarly,
Escobar (2001) argues that certain projects of territorial autonomy, such
as the Zapatistas in Chiapas or Black movements in the Pacific region of
Colombia, defend noncapitalist socioeconomic relations and epistemolo-
gies while participating in a novel politics of transnational networking
that provide alternative visions to neoliberalism. These works suggest that
movements in the defense of culture and territory actively engage in a
politics of articulation with ecological, human rights, and other activisms
that contest the neoliberal terms of "development."

Nonetheless, we must recognize that institutions promoting neoliberal policies and projects do not necessarily oppose ethnic territoriality
but, in some cases, actively promote it. The World Bank, for example, has
provided economic and political sponsorship of indigenous and Black collective lands and/or territories in a number of Latin American countries.
The most prominent case is Colombia, where the bank provided funding

for titling 1,250 "Black communities," a new legal category established via legislation passed in the first half of the 1990s, which was also endorsed by the bank (Sánchez Gutierrez and Roldán Ortiga 2002; Offen 2003). Offen explains the promotion of the "territorial turn" within the World Bank:

> Simply put, the bank views collective titles as necessary to stabilize property regimes in developing countries, to remove biodiverse lands from the vagaries of market forces (by insuring that collective properties cannot be transferred), to foment direct investment, and to attract appropriate technologies to biodiverse areas. From the bank's point of view, each of these goals is mutually compatible. . . . (2003, 51)

The territorial turn, according to Offen, also involves forms of ethnomanagement that attempt to reduce conflict by establishing local representative bodies that can dialogue with state institutions, participate in conservation, and contract with outside entities in development projects and resource extraction. We can thus characterize the embrace of the territorial turn by institutions such as the World Bank as an emergent effort to suture together market logics, collective rights, conflict management, decentralization, capital investment, environment conservation, and local participation.

However, this is a tall order for even the most powerful of institutions. The various objectives do not readily coalesce, and attempts to reconcile them may conflict with key segments of the state (with whom the World Bank must work), national elite (who may attempt to incorporate biodiverse lands into the market), and social movements (with their own visions of collective rights and ecological conservation that may oppose certain forms of capital investment). In Colombia, the optimism attached to the recognition of Black communities has been attenuated as the process of territorial demarcation produced conflicts between indigenous and Black peoples. More importantly, brutal attacks on Black communities by paramilitary forces displaced thousands of residents of newly recognized territories (Wouters 2002). Following the contours of the territorial turn requires attention to the dynamics of struggle over lands and resources within particular countries and regions, with an eye toward the articulations and disarticulations produced across disparate political projects. Even the agendas of single institutions such as the World Bank vary across space and time, in accordance with the dynamics of competing forces within the institution and in relation to particular conditions within the "beneficiary" country (Fox and Brown 1998).

In Honduras, the territorial turn has met formidable opposition within the state, and recognition of territorial rights falls short of the norms provided by ILO Convention 169. Compared to the government of Colombia, the Honduran state grants limited recognition to the principle of territoriality in both national legislation and property titling, and the aspirations of Garifuna, Miskito, Pech, and Tahwaka activists have largely been frustrated. In the sparsely populated, so-called "undeveloped" areas of the Mosquitia—where territorial claims involve the largest amount of geographic area—the state has provided little in the way of land titling, and petitions from Miskito are sometimes viewed as separatist initiatives (Grünberg, 14). As discussed in chapter 3, the National Agrarian Institute has produced collective titles for Garifuna communities, but community leaders deem most of those titles inadequate. Moreover, the regularization and amplification of community lands remain a largely unfulfilled prom- ise. Overall, the state has sought to delimit small areas of highly valued land on the North Coast to a communal land regime and secure the sur- rounding areas for capital investment and protected areas while at the same time upholding the legitimacy of "third-party" property titles.

The World Bank has shown some interest in promoting a territorial turn in Honduras yet also funded contradictory initiatives by the state. The Bank funded a project in 2002 directed by a U.S.-based research organization, the Caribbean Central American Research Council (CCARC), in which selected Garifuna and Miskito communities produced ethnographic maps of their own land claims (CCARC 2003). Both OFRANEH and ODECO participated in that project. However, according to several state officials with whom I spoke, the government largely ignored the project report. Moreover, within two years, the World Bank provided funding for the land administration project PATH, which, in conjunction with the property law discussed in previous sections, promoted a restricted vision of territorial rights.[5] The mo- dality of "participation" pursued by the PATH program merits analysis, as it produced conflict not only between OFRANEH and a World Bank–funded state project but also among Garifuna.

Participation in Conflict: Land Regulation and Territorial Recognition

In 2004, I conducted an interview with the head of the ethnic component of the PATH project, Rodolfo Álvarez, who provided insights into state efforts to manage ethnic activism and limit territoriality. Álvarez spoke as a loyal member of the ruling National Party and related his strategies for project implementation. In our interview at the PATH offices in a suburb of Tegucigalpa, we began by discussing ethnic organizations. Álvarez outlined a typology of organizations that he characterized as "progovernment," "legal opposition," or "illegal opposition." He said that at the moment none of the federations occupied the category "illegal opposition" and placed OFRANEH and COPINH in the position of "legal opposition," noting that the government was working to establish better relations with them. He thus implied that most federations and ODECO could be categorized as "progovernment," in the sense that they demonstrated a willingness to work with the government to find solutions to problems. I was intrigued by the scheme he outlined, but Álvarez was most interested in detailing his plans for resolving land conflicts. The two were, in fact, related.

At the heart of those plans lay a multitiered process of consultation scaled at the levels of nation, region, and community. These processes would draw together a wide array of representatives from the government and "civil society" such as federations, NGOs, and churches to negotiate land conflicts. At the community level, they would incorporate state and municipal representatives, leaders of federations and town councils, local organizations such as the church, parents' organizations, womens' organizations, as well as teachers and local mestizos. By creating a single table incorporating a wide range of actors, PATH would negotiate conflicts to achieve permanent solutions. Although Álvarez did not mention it, the participation procedures were designed in part to conform with World Bank protocols on the necessity for bank-funded projects to implement consultation procedures on projects affecting indigenous peoples. Given his assessment of the federations, I wondered if his vision of consultation also entailed an effort to marginalize the more "oppositional" actors in negotiations over land conflicts.

Toward the end of our interview, I asked Álvarez if there were ethnic demands that, from the state's perspective, were unattainable. He initially said "no," reiterating the professionalism of organizations and their improved relations with the government. Then he remembered a letter he recently received from a Garifuna organization based in the department of Colón (he could not remember the name) which made a series of demands.[6] They wanted the government to buy the land of impresario Miguel Facussé. They requested a Garifuna-run television station and Garifuna representatives in the Supreme Court and Congress. They demanded autonomy in land and territories. Álvarez stated: "we are not going to divide our territory" and characterized the demands as "nothing serious." When I noted that territorial claims were a common feature of indigenous demands throughout Latin America, he responded that the government needed to work with territorial pretensions but that groups often made excessive claims, citing the case of the Miskito who wanted "practically all the Mosquitia" and Garifuna, who, once they received title to 2,000 hectares, wanted 10,000.

Álvarez's comments on the limits of acceptable demands reveal much about the political parameters of ethnic recognition. Hale, in his assessment of multicultural neoliberalism, argues that multilateral and state institutions acknowledge cultural rights as long as they do not challenge the fundamental tenets of neoliberal development or entail sufficient gathering of political clout to threaten established power holders (2004, 18). The line between acceptable and unacceptable demands is variable, subject to negotiation, and dependent on context. Álvarez, a key player in state land and territorial politics, considered ridiculous the suggestion that the state should return lands held by magnate Miguel Facussé to Garifuna, who claim them as their territorial patrimony. Although one of the missions of PATH involves the resolution of land conflicts, Álvarez prejudged the legitimacy of elite interests, suggesting that only some forms of conflicts could come under consideration. He ultimately presented opposition to the government as a kind of irrational reflex derived from past mistakes, a product of distrust rather than dissent. Given this restricted vision of ethnic rights, it is little wonder that the PATH program became embroiled in controversy.

OFRANEH opposed the project, eventually sending a "Request for Inspection" to the World Bank denouncing the PATH (OFRANEH 2006a). A Request for Inspection initiates a process whereby the World Bank investigates a bank-funded project for contravening bank directives and procedures (Clark, Fox, and Treakle 2003), in this case concerning Indigenous Peoples (OD 4.20), Environmental Assessment (OP/BP 4.01), and Natural Habitats (OP/BP 4.04). OFRANEH's request involved a complex array of arguments. I draw attention only to a few aspects concerning participation, specifically prior consultation procedures and the dissemination of information to peoples potentially affected by the program. OFRANEH essentially charged that PATH officials produced incomplete, faulty, and contradictory information. For example, they argued that the program's conflict resolution procedures outlined in its Indigenous Peoples Development Plan (required for bank-funded projects involving indigenous peoples) differed from the new, defective property law. Whereas the latter adjudicates conflicts via the courts, PATH proposes to settle conflicts through mediation and negotiation between parties. OFRANEH questioned both the legality and efficacy of such mechanisms:

> We are concerned because conflict resolution instances are being proposed that do not correspond to the social and political reality of the members of the communities; you cannot propose to resolve conflicts that date back to several decades by means of Interethnic Boards or Conciliation, Settlement or Mediation Procedures, where the disparities of the interests represented, power elites on the one hand and indigenous peoples on the other, cannot but lead to completely unfavorable decisions for the indigenous peoples. (2006a, 7)

OFRANEH worked for a strong legislative framework recognizing territorial rights, whereas the PATH sought to mediate conflicts between communities and third parties via negotiations. OFRANEH argued that such negotiations would favor the elite, especially since the new property law recognized the rights of third parties with property titles in indigenous lands. The implication here is that under a flawed legal framework, indigenous peoples had little leverage over outsiders. OFRANEH thus interpreted the PATH program not only as deficient but also as damaging to the ongoing process of territorial recognition.

In their defense, World Bank project managers argued that the program counted on the participation of a wide array of Garifuna stakeholders, citing the formation of a Mesa Regional (Regional Board) with representatives of Garifuna communities, NGOs, and the Garifuna Pastoral Diocese Commission (World Bank 2006). Prior to OFRANEH's Request for Inspection, announced in October of 2005, divisions had emerged among Garifuna concerning whether to participate in the PATH program. In April 2005, OFRANEH had condemned PATH and the property law as instruments creating "the juridical conditions that protect the interests of foreigners who will wind up being the owners of key territories for the implementation of a fat land market destined for the globalization of real estate..." (2005c). The organization also charged that "the majority of

Garifuna organizations and leaders have been called to a complicit silence with the state, as the handouts that include the PATH, through its projects, have neutralized them" (2005c). One of those leaders was OFRANEH coordinator Amilcar Colón who worked with the PATH program and had been divested from authority in the organization in March.[7] The admission by OFRANEH that a majority of Garifuna organizations and leaders decided to work with the program suggests that the PATH program had been successful in securing more than just token participation, though some community leaders opted out early on. Interestingly, the eight communities selected for land regularization were chosen in part on the basis "that some communities have more problems and are more difficult than others, and that for this process to continue an effort was made to start with the less conflictive ones or those whose leaders were able to negotiate" (World Bank 2006, Annex 3.1: 184). This suggests that those working with the program saw PATH's "conflict resolution" approach as an opportunity to make limited advances in Garifuna land claims within the existing juridical framework. If they ran the risk of legitimating that flawed framework and faced accusations of selling out, OFRANEH ran the risk of obstructing an opportunity to advance land claims.[8]

One of the stakes in the conflicts incited by PATH was the question of who could claim to legitimately represent Garifuna and their interests, as a people and as communities. In the case of individual communities, the issue is relatively clear: An elected patronato (town council) serves as the governing authority of the community and represents it to the state. At the scale of Garifuna as an entire people, however, the situation is complicated. On the one hand, a wide range of civil society organizations, mostly private NGOs that conduct development projects, hold dialogues with the state in the name of Garifuna. On the other hand, OFRANEH is constituted as a "federation" with the authority to represent the Garifuna people. In its Request for Inspection, the organization underscored that OFRANEH "is not a Non-Governmental Organization but rather a Federation the members of which are elected every three years by an assembly of the Garifuna people who grant them the representation of the people in accordance with the provisions of the organization's bylaws" (2006a, 1). The Honduran state is inconsistent in its recognition of that status. In some programs and functions, the state does take OFRANEH as the principal representative of the Garifuna people and not simply as an NGO; the PAPIN program discussed earlier is only one example. On the other hand, state officials also work with NGOs, as representatives of Garifuna. In the case of the PATH program, the state treated OFRANEH as one of a series of "stakeholders" to participate in the project, granting the organization the same position as an NGO. Thus, PATH policies marginalized OFRANEH from its role as the primary representative of the Garifuna people. PATH did not, by itself, construct a contest of representational legitimacy, but it did set the conditions for division over the program by treating the Garifuna federation as simply one among many stakeholders, whose voice of opposition would be diluted by Garifuna representatives who had chosen to participate in the project.

The PATH's model of expansive yet selective participation thus had the effect of marginalizing dissent and fomenting conflict between potential participants. Nonetheless, OFRANEH turned the question of participation back on the PATH, pointing to problems in the consultation procedures of the program in a formal complaint to the World Bank. In 2006, after leading a protest of more than one hundred Garifuna to the capital, the organization secured concessions from the new Liberal Party government of Mel Zelaya to dismantle the Mesa Regional in PATH and to reform the property law (OFRANEH 2006b). Ultimately, the World Bank Inspection Panel (2007) ruled that the consultation procedures were flawed, specifically citing the absence of OFRANEH and ODECO (which also declined to participate) in the Mesa Regional. If the PATH had used participation to marginalize OFRANEH, OFRANEH used participation to derail the PATH. In this sense, we see that participation is neither merely a set of technical procedures nor a technique of governance; it is also an ideological and procedural weapon that can be taken up by different actors in political struggle.

ODECO and Afro-Visibility

The partial story I have told in this chapter of developments in ethnic politics in the postrecognition era of multiculturalism and participation is incomplete without paying attention to other Garifuna organizations besides OFRANEH. Beginning in the early 1990s, a large number of Garifuna NGOs arrived on the scene. These include development NGOs, organizations focusing on Garifuna women, and NGOs dedicated to cultural preservation. The largest and most politically important of these organizations is the Organización de Desarrollo Étnico Comunitario (ODECO). Established in 1992, ODECO defines itself as an NGO open to all Garifuna who wish to join. The founder and president of the organization, Celio Álvarez Casildo, was a member of OFRANEH in the 1980s. Before founding ODECO, he was also the head of the principal Honduran medical union. Álvarez Casildo presides over an organization that has been highly successful in attracting funds from foreign donors and competes with OFRANEH as the national political representative of Garifuna. Although a rivalry exists between ODECO and OFRANEH, they have worked together on a number of occasions, including the 1996 "March of Drums" that led to an agreement on land titling. Patterns of cooperation and conflict between the organizations change over time, and their more personal intricacies are inaccessible to an outsider such as myself. I focus on their public discourses and politics to highlight distinctive models of ethnic politics in relation to state multiculturalism and the dilemmas and possibilities confronting ethnic activism.

As we saw in chapter 3, in the early days ODECO represented Garifuna in close proximity to the indigenous rights paradigm and as beneficiaries of ILO Convention 169, even if the organization was careful to delineate distinctions between negros and indígenas. However, after Garifuna became officially recognized as an "autochthonous ethnic" people with the same cultural status and rights as indigenous peoples, ODECO increasingly came to emphasize the distinctive condition, history, identity, and culture of Garifuna as negros and by the turn of the millennium, as "*afrodescendientes*" (Afro-descendants). In the mid-1990s, ODECO helped found the Central American Black Organization (CABO), a transnational confederation that brings together organizations representing Garifuna and other Blacks/Afro-descendants in Belize, Guatemala, Honduras, Costa Rica, Nicaragua, and Panama. Celio Álvarez has been the president of CABO since its inception. ODECO and CABO also form part of a continental network of Afro-descendant organizations. Thus, unlike OFRANEH, ODECO emphasizes alliances with other peoples of African descent in the Americas over alliances with indigenous organizations. Although ODECO continued to draw parallels between indigenous and Black peoples as victims of discrimination and marginalization, it highlighted the particularity of Black populations and the need to achieve recognition, visibility, and inclusion within a distinct model of struggle.

In 2004, I conducted an interview with Álvarez Casildo in La Ceiba, and he gave me a tour of the new headquarters of ODECO under construction. It was a three-storey building with room for offices, a health clinic, a cultural center, and even hotel rooms. We had spoken on a number of occasions in previous years in his office, decorated with pictures of African diaspora heroes such as Martin Luther King and Nelson Mandela. I asked him about changes in state politics that had occurred over the past few years, and he listed a number of events in which ODECO had participated, such as regional meetings leading up to the World Conference against Racism, Racial Discrimination, Xenophobia and Related Intolerance held in Durban, South Africa, in 2001. ODECO served as the NGO representing Honduras at the World Conference and participated in a number of regional preparatory meetings. The year after the conference, ODECO hosted a Regional Seminar on Afro-descendants in the Americas organized by the United Nations Working Group on Minorities and Office of High Commissioner for Human Rights framed around "The Prevention of Discrimination."

These events reflected the growing attention to the Afro-descendant as a distinct subject in Latin America at the turn of the millennium.[9] Álvarez asserted that while Afro-descendants have used Convention 169 of the ILO as an instrument in their struggles, he also asserted that important institutions (such as the United Nations and Inter-American Development Bank) were changing their discourses, incorporating new agendas such as reparations and affirmative action. Accordingly, ODECO—though yet to pursue affirmative action or reparation claims—developed a number of initiatives to combat racial discrimination and promote the inclusion of Afro-descendants as a particular racial–cultural subject in the nation. Álvarez noted that ODECO had successfully pushed the government to change the "Day of the Etnia Garifuna" (established in 1996) into a "Month of African Heritage" (like Black History Month in the United States). He said that shift marked an important political step for "increasing the visibility of the Afro-descendant community, as well as for changing the word 'negro' to 'Afro-descendant.'" The latter term came to prominence in the meetings leading up to the World Conference Against Racism and represents an effort to define Garifuna as a people of African descent while displacing the term "negro" from official, and ultimately everyday, discourse.

ODECO devoted increasing attention to attacking racial discrimination as a crime. In 2002, the organization championed the cause of Erika Ramírez, the first Garifuna ever crowned Miss Honduras, who accused her coach of racial and sexual discrimination. Ramírez lost her suit (and a countersuit for defamation), but Álvarez said that her case brought greater attention to racism. ODECO also secured a series of campaign promises from presidential candidates leading up to the election of Ricardo Maduro of the National Party. These included promises to support economic, cultural, and health initiatives; promote the study of Afro-Honduran heritage and traditions; foment tourist development (without reforming Article 107 of the Constitution); complete land titling and regulating; include Afro-Hondurans in the government; and generate mechanisms and actions to combat racism (ODECO 2001). ODECO then pushed the government to ratify the International Convention on the Elimination of all Forms of Discrimination (previously ratified by most Latin American states) and to create a National Commission Against Racial Discrimination, Racism, Xenophobia, and Related Forms of Tolerance. The basic mandate of the National Commission involves promoting politics to eradicate discrimination and punish acts of discrimination. Although the Honduran constitution prohibits racial discrimination and many individuals can cite cases where they have suffered discrimination, citizens almost never bring such cases to justice. For Celio Álvarez, establishing the National Commission was a crucial step in developing a state politics to combat racism.

Whether or not the National Commission becomes an effective institution remains an open question. Nonetheless, its creation represents an unprecedented acknowledgement of racism by the state. Even as ethnic activism challenged nationalist mestizaje in the 1980s and 1990s, state officials tended to pronounce that racism was not a problem in Honduras, enacting a "racial exceptionalism" common elsewhere in Latin America (see Anderson 2001). Although that refrain continues to ring in many quarters, the official recognition of racism represents a departure from past rhetoric and contributes to greater recognition of racism in the public sphere. If Blacks initially became officially "visible" as an ethnic group understood as culturally similar to indigenous peoples, the politics of ODECO has made anti-Black racism increasingly visible within Honduran society.

Antiracism and Indigenism

How might we assess the relationship between the two principal Garifuna organizations and the different modes of ethnorepresentation and politics they pursue? I return to the work of Juliet Hooker (2005a) as a frame for approaching this question, though my conclusions differ from hers. As discussed in chapter 3, Hooker identifies a general pattern of "indigenous inclusion" and "black exclusion" within multicultural citizenship regimes in Latin America. After explaining those disparities in terms of the ambiguous position of Blacks within institutional discourses of culture and ethnicity (where indigenous people are taken as the standard subjects of authentic group identity and cultural difference), she highlights the limitations of collective cultural rights politics relative to a civil rights approach to antiracism. Hooker argues that, given the dependence of cultural rights on the recognition of a collective cultural status by the state, many Blacks (and Indians) may not be able to claim collective rights (2005a, 22–23). Similarly, she notes that states can recognize cultural diversity without addressing structural, racial inequalities. Another danger "is that the need to frame their demands in terms of cultural difference in order to gain collective rights might lead Afro-Latinos (and indigenous populations) to privilege issues of cultural recognition over the struggle against racial discrimination as the basis of political mobilization" (2005a, 23). Hooker thus suggests that a "strong" race-based civil rights politics—for example, affirmative action as pursued recently in Brazil (Htun 2004)—provides an important corrective to a cultural rights approach and its tendency to privilege cultural recognition over racial discrimination and social exclusion.

Following this line of analysis, we can interpret the racial politics developed by ODECO as filling gaps in the collective rights approach pursued by OFRANEH. In a sense, ODECO has brought back an emphasis on combating racial discrimination that OFRANEH once embraced but later subsumed under a discourse of indigeneity. After all, OFRANEH itself emerged in the 1970s out of previous struggles against racial segregation and discrimination in areas such as employment. However, with a turn toward indigeneity as a mode of struggle, the Garifuna community became the focus of attention, and efforts to combat racism concentrated less on everyday acts of discrimination than on the denial of cultural and territorial rights. In the mid- to late 1990s, after the state embraced multiculturalism and recognized Garifuna as an ethnic group, ODECO recuperated and revitalized an antiracist discourse, pushing the state to acknowledge racism and adopt antidiscrimination measures. In this respect, we can interpret the development of contemporary antiracist projects among Garifuna as, in part, a product of (and corrective to) omissions within collective cultural rights politics.

Such an interpretation, though valid, remains incomplete without attention to the full range of political programs and strategies pursued by

OFRANEH and ODECO. In fact, an analysis of the two organizations' politics actually contradicts the suggestion in Hooker's work that civil rights approaches entail a more universalistic, progressive politics than collective rights approaches based on cultural difference. In the conclusion to her article, Hooker asserts that, unlike ethnic rights paradigms that often exclude Blacks, "social exclusion and racial discrimination are rubrics under which both indians and blacks can organize to demand rights" (2005, 26). However, in Honduras the organization that emphasizes collective rights, OFRANEH, actively pursues cross-racial alliances—particularly with indigenous peoples—to a far greater extent than the organization that emphasizes antidiscrimination, ODECO. Rather than treat "antiracist politics" and "cultural/ethnic rights" as abstractions whose political effects can be read in advance, we need to examine their contingent articulations with other aspects of political mobilization such as alliances with other groups. Moreover, just as we should critically interrogate the effects of the state's turn to multiculturalism, we need to critically examine the recent embrace of antidiscrimination measures such as the National Commission on Racial Discrimination, Racism and Related Intolerance by the state. The antidiscrimination initiatives may simply bring Honduras into line with other Latin American states at a moment in which the "prevention of discrimination" has been promoted by both activists and institutions such as the United Nations.[10] They may also reflect the working relationship established between government institutions, including the presidential office, and ODECO.

As I have suggested at several points in the preceding pages, ODECO tends to take a less oppositional stance on many government initiatives than its counterpart and rival OFRANEH. In a recent dissertation, Brondo juxtaposes the self-conscious position of OFRANEH as "part of a broader movement against neoliberalism" with a tendency of ODECO to work "within neoliberalism" (2006, 129). This contrast between the organizations should not be overstated—ODECO critiques policies and programs associated with neoliberalism such as the 1992 Agricultural Modernization Law, whereas OFRANEH has worked with some of the same institutions that it critiques (e.g., The World Bank) in order to defend territorial rights. Nonetheless, Brondo highlights important differences in the way the two organizations imagine development and conduct politics.

While OFRANEH works to secure modes of cultural–territorial autonomy against the further imposition of a failed, destructive economic model dominated by elite and foreign interests, ODECO strives to ensure

Garifuna inclusion and participation in processes of globalization. Whereas OFRANEH routinely condemns free trade agreements, the Plan Puebla Panama, and the Mesoamerican Biological Corridor as imperial projects of dispossession, ODECO has promoted the participation of Afro-descendant communities in those projects as important stakeholders and beneficiaries (129–30). In rhetoric and practice, ODECO works for Garifuna participation in projects that critics condemn as "neoliberal" and remains within the boundaries of legitimate demands and politics delineated by state agencies and multilateral institutions. We can thus see why state officials such as Rodolfo Álvarez consider ODECO a "professional" organization, whereas OFRANEH borders on so-called "illegal opposition."

The point in drawing out these contrasts is not to simply reverse the evaluation of cultural rights and a politics of antiracism suggested by Hooker, to use one case to argue that cultural rights politics necessarily represent the most radical projects of social transformation. Rather, the analysis here complicates the effort to identify and promote one political model for overcoming the oppression, marginalization, and exclusion of indigenous and Black peoples in Latin America. If cultural rights politics typically fail to confront all the dimensions of structural racisms, a politics explicitly directed against racism can demand "inclusion" without challenging the full range of structural inequalities, exploitations, and dispossessions produced within racialized capitalism. In the instance under consideration here, an articulation between territorial rights and anti-imperialism represents a more serious challenge to the development agendas of the state, elite, multilateral organizations and transnational capital than a politics geared toward increasing Garifuna participation as a good in itself. Nonetheless, the work of ODECO in calling attention to everyday racism and promoting Garifuna political inclusion has produced significant changes in state and public discourses concerning racism. Perhaps in the future the National Commission Against Racial Discrimination, Racism and Related Intolerance will become a site of political agitation not just for punishing acts of racism but also for further challenging structures of inequality.

Divergent Responses to a Racist Diatribe

In March 2006, a congressman from the department of Intibucá conducted an interview with an online newspaper where he "confessed his disdain (*desprecio*) for Blacks" (Rodríguez 2006). Miguel Gámez, a self-identified

Lenca affiliated with the National Party, expressed pride in his people as the "first ethnic group" and said:

> Notice that there are more negros in the Congress and that negros are a minority in this country and that more agency has been given to negros, who are not natives of Honduras. These men do not even have 200 years living in this country and are not natives like the Lenca, Chortí, Pech, the true [source of the] particularity of the Honduran Republic. (2006)

With a little prodding, he explained his dislike for Blacks: "Because they came from another country to take over legitimate Honduran lands and because they have invaded the particularity [*idiosincracia*] of the Hondurans and I feel very Indian, very Lenca" (2006). He went on to claim that the Honduran soccer team could not qualify for the World Cup because it had too many Black players, who "are not intelligent" and "do not think" (2006).

Gámez's anti-Black diatribe recuperated the racial exclusions associated with twentieth-century nationalist mestizaje, reproducing the trope of blackness as foreign to the nation. His comments created a momentary scandal in the national press and inspired a wave of critiques from mestizos as well as Garifuna. However, judging by some of the blog commentary that followed, his attacks on Black visibility resonated with some mestizos who, in more measured tones, shared his resentment that a small minority could attract so much attention at home and abroad. Soon after the story broke, Gámez apologized to the National Congress, saying that he never meant to offend negros by asserting that they had achieved more recognition than ethnic groups (indígenas) "original" to the country.[11] He thus reiterated a common sense racial–historical position that negros were not true natives.

ODECO and OFRANEH responded to the incident in distinct ways. ODECO immediately announced that it would initiate a legal case against the congressman for the crime of racial discrimination. Celio Álvarez told the press that he "had some mental disorder, since more than 80 percent of the population has African blood."[12] Álvarez thus reiterated the kind of claim Alfonso Lacayo used to make when a mestizo called him a negro ("shake your genealogical tree and you will see a negro fall") to confront the notion that blackness was foreign to the nation. Álvarez Casildo was careful to assert that the deputy's words did not reflect the thought of the Lenca people as a whole. He also noted that his statements "reaffirm that in the majority of Latin American society, and of course in Honduran society, racism, xenophobia and discrimination prevail."[13] The case thus created an opportunity to publicize racism as a crime and push the state to punish it.

Ironically, a couple of days after the Gámez story broke, another case of discrimination involving a deputy from Intibucá was denounced by Lenca activists. Romualdo Bueso Melgen, a mestizo from the Liberal Party, interrupted a meeting between representatives of the Lenca organization COPINH and health officials in La Esperanza, Intibucá, accompanied by armed men. Bueso Melgen demanded to know why he was not invited to the meeting, roughed up members of COPINH, and threatened to kill one of its leaders, Salvador Zúñiga. In the aftermath, OFRANEH issued a communiqué that linked the appalling actions of both congressmen to a politics of violence cultivated by the Honduran elite.

> Although the two [congressman] represent the two different traditional political parties, they are nothing but *monigotes* [fools] cut from the same cloth. The political panorama of Hibueras [Honduras] is held in the hands of two conservative parties of neoliberal cut, attached to the sphere of empire, with which they have accepted the pact of total surrender (CAFTA), plunging the future of the large majority in this country to eternal misery, with the eternal exception of course of the bosses of the maquiladoras. (2006d)[14]

OFRANEH thus framed the question of racism in terms of a corrupt political system and critiqued "supposed multiculturality" as a farce (2006d). As evidence, the organization noted that Melgen Bueso, who threatened the life of one of the most important indigenous leaders in the country, was vice president of the congressional Commission on Ethnic Groups.

The responses of the two principal Garifuna organizations shared much in common: Each denounced the incident as racism, called attention to underlying conditions of oppression, and expressed solidarity with the Lenca to mitigate potential rifts. Nonetheless, differences in their responses reflected the paradigms of struggle each organization had developed over the previous decade. ODECO focused squarely on the issue of racism, especially anti-Black racism, whereas OFRANEH discussed racism as one facet of a corrupt political system that serves imperialism. Although ODECO immediately sought to bring Gámez to justice, OFRANEH demanded an investigation into the supposed plot to assassinate a Lenca activist, sarcastically suggesting that Gámez be given the "National Prize for Racism and Ignorance" (2006d). Taken together, their responses called attention both to the specificity of anti-Black racism and to the hypocrisies of multicultural neoliberalism.

Conclusion

This chapter has explored a series of ironies and paradoxes in the dynamics of organized Garifuna politics in an era of multicultural recognition and participation. One set of paradoxes concerns institutional politics and ethnic rights framed in terms of indigeneity. The Honduran state, with the support and prodding of multilateral institutions, has developed participatory spaces for ethnic representatives yet has produced at best modest advances in the adjudication of collective rights since the mid-1990s, particularly with regard to land rights and territoriality. In fact, recent legislation and programs such as the 2004 property law and PATH program represent efforts to limit territorial claims in ways that make them compatible with the priorities of capital investment in tourism, without adequately addressing demands to address dispossession of lands and resources traditionally occupied and used by Garifuna communities. Even worse, the state has tried to open a path to the "voluntary" privatization of recently formalized communal land regimes and legitimate the property of third parties within Garifuna communities. Within this climate, spaces of participation created by the state appear designed to diffuse and contain opposition by bringing ethnic activists "closer" to government institutions, foreclosing politics of collective rights that challenge market solutions to social injustice.

These developments will not surprise critics of multicultural neoliberalism, but their effects on ethnic activism require careful analysis. As Hale asserts, a turn toward ethnic inclusion has the potential of diffusing opposition and inciting division, as institutional officials draw distinctions between "authorized" ethnic subjects and radically oppositional actors whose demands and discourses are rendered beyond the pale. In the case of Garifuna activism, ODECO occupies the former position in the eyes of many state agents, whereas OFRANEH teeters on the brink of the latter. However, the principle of "participation" also precludes any easy dismissal of OFRANEH as a representative of the Garifuna people to the state and international organizations. That organization, highly sophisticated in its interpretation of state and international laws and norms concerning indigenous peoples, turns the principle of participation back on the state, at times leveraging the same institutions that it critiques as agents of neoliberal imperialism. Moreover, while state practices can exacerbate, even incite, divisions among organizations in debates over whether to participate in a program such as the PATH, the existence of multiple organizations with different agendas and relations to the state may, ironically, turn out to have positive effects. Although I can only speculate here, the Maduro government may have worked with ODECO to embark on certain antiracist initiatives in part to demonstrate its commitment to Garifuna and other ethnic groups in the face of its intransigence around other demands, particularly territorial claims. That is, antidiscrimination reform may be spurred, indirectly, by the challenge of antineoliberal territorial activism.

Another set of ironies turn on differences in the ethnorepresentations and political projects of the two major Garifuna organizations. Although both organizations represent Garifuna as a distinct ethnic group with its own language, culture, and history, they position Garifuna differently vis-à-vis blackness and indigeneity. ODECO represents Garifuna primarily as Afro-descendants and members of an African diaspora. Although OFRANEH does not negate these affinities, it tends to represent Garifuna as an indigenous people, to make connections and comparisons with (other) indigenous peoples and, increasingly, to highlight Amerindian cultural legacies. For example, in a 2006 public message concerning the "Request for Inspection," Miriam Miranda of OFRANEH refers to Garifuna as an Afro-indigenous people (*pueblo Afroindígena*), noting that "we Garifuna are at present the indigenous people with the largest population of island Carib speakers (*caribe insular*) and the cultural inheritors of the Arawaks as well as of the Caribs" (OFRANEH 2006c).

Differences in the ethnorepresentations produced by organizations—articulated with different political visions and strategies—highlight once again how identity formations do not simply reflect "history" or "culture" but become entangled with interpretations of culture and history within contemporary structures of power and possibility. If, in the mid-1980s to early 1990s, articulating Garifuna struggles within a framework of indigeneity provided a successful route to cultural–political recognition, by the turn of the millennium (Black) indigenism and Afro-visibility jostled with and against each other as models of racial–cultural politics.

The ultimate irony here is that while, taken as a whole, the organized politics of Garifuna in Honduras complicate easy distinctions between blackness and indigeneity, the major organizations each tend to reproduce associations between, on the one hand, blackness with questions of race and racism and, on the other hand, indigeneity with questions of culture and ethnicity. That is, the organization that most forcefully locates Garifuna within the African diaspora focuses considerable attention on the problem of racism, while the organization that situates Garifuna in relation to indigeneity concentrates on questions of culture, territory, and peoplehood. Such differences are, of course, not absolute, as ODECO identifies Garifuna as a distinct cultural group with its own traditions, and OFRANEH acknowledges racism as a social problem. Nonetheless, their politics reflect enduring tendencies to locate indigeneity and blackness within different sets of analytical and political frameworks, even as the relationship between them has come under increasing scrutiny by activists and academics. Thus, the lines between blackness and indigenism are themselves subject to continual negotiation, blurred in forms of activism that claim Black identity and autochthonous status and accentuated in those that insist on the particularity of Black identity and struggle. In the following chapters, we see everyday modes of identity formation that produce yet other manifestations of blackness and indigeneity.

5

This Is the Black Power We Wear: Black America and the Fashioning of Young Garifuna Men

In the fall of 2003, U.S. African American hip-hop entrepreneur Sean Combs, aka Puff Diddy, found himself embroiled in a scandal involving workers in Honduras. Combs is the founder of Sean Jean, a clothing company that produces designer sportswear with "an urban sensibility and style." Lydia Gonzalez, a nineteen-year-old worker at a Honduran factory that produces garments for Sean Jean, denounced the sweatshop working conditions of the plant and accused the management of firing employees for attempting to unionize workers (Greenhouse 2003). Gonzalez's trip was sponsored by the New York-based National Labor Organization, a small outfit of antisweatshop activists that in 1996 fomented a similar scandal by exposing the labor conditions behind the line of Walmart clothing promoted by television personality Kathie Lee Gifford.[1] Unlike Gifford, Combs made no apologies and shed no public tears. After a few days, he announced that inspection teams had found no wrongdoing. The owner of the factory, a gringo who said he moved his operation to Honduras from North Carolina as a result of the North American Free Trade Agreement (NAFTA), denied the accusations and insisted that the workers were fired because of "bad quality" and "uncooperative attitude" (Greenhouse 2003). The president of the Honduran Association of Maquiladoras backed him up with a predictable brand of nationalism, declaring that working conditions were "excellent, better than in any factory in the United States." For good measure, he called the head of the National Labor Organization an "international terrorist" (Cuevas 2003).

Although the affair barely registered in the mainstream media, the alternative press kept it around long enough to ridicule the hypocrisy of Combs. How could Combs rail against the exploitation of Black consumers while outsourcing the production of his clothes? How could he claim to support workers when they earn twenty-four cents for each fifty-dollar sweatshirt? Indeed, Combs invites critique. The Sean Jean website featured a picture of him in a designer sweat jacket, standing with his fist raised and head bowed, in a "Black power" gesture that pays homage to the podium protests of Tommie Smith and John Carlos at the 1968 Olympics. At the time, such symbolism figured as part of internationalist movements that promoted third-world liberation. Combs' appropriation of that symbolism to sell overpriced clothes made by hyperexploited labor in Honduras represents a gross example of how the commodification of Black power can contradict its original political impulses.

The Sean Jean affair could serve as the preamble for an array of different stories about race, commodities, celebrities, and capitalism. We might use it to ponder why targeting celebrities seems like the only way to draw attention to the ghastly relations of globalized commodity production. We might wonder what the relative lack of interest in the Sean Jean scandal compared to the one that followed Kathy Lee Gifford tells us about the contemporary media and gender. The Sean Jean affair might be mobilized to exemplify certain cultural critiques, such as Žižek's assertions that multiculturalism expresses the logic of multinational capitalism (1997) or Gilroy's reflections on the demise of Black cultural politics in the United States and the "final commodification of the extraordinary cultural creativity born from the slave populations of the New World" (2000, 272). For Gilroy, the key position of Black imagery within televisual marketing schemes with planetary reach marks a renewed phase of the aestheticization of politics inherited from fascism. In the process, "blackness as abjection gives way steadily to blackness as vitality, eternal youth and immortal dynamism. The idea of the black male athlete or model now supplies a ubiquitous key signature for this strange theme" (2000, 274). In the 1990s, the notoriously apolitical and entrepreneurial Michael Jordan stood as the icon of this iconization of the Black male body, and he, like Sean Combs, became tied to third-world work scandals yet managed to escape with his image intact.

Departing from these provocations on the relationship between contemporary capitalism and the projection of imagined U.S. Black masculinities, we can add a twist to the story by noting an oft-overlooked irony: the *consumers* of things made in factories of the global South for brands associated with the global North are not just located in the North but also reside in the South.[2] For quite some time, Garifuna youth in Honduras have been heavily invested in acquiring the brand name gear they associate with what they call "Black America." Goods with labels like Sean Jean journey from

Honduras to the United States and back to Honduras, accruing different kinds of value and meaning along the way.

In the summer of 2004, I was talking to my friend Milton about changes in style among Garifuna youth over the past few years, when he mentioned how "Sean Jean" was one of the more desirable brands. His cousin once worked for a maquiladora, one of several hundred factories that sprouted in Honduras after the full-scale implementation of neoliberal reforms in the early 1990s (Robinson, 129). I asked him about the scandal, and he said that he read about it in the papers, noting "even though they are made here, you cannot get them here. You have to have someone send them to you from there [the United States]." Milton has family members who do just that, sending back fashionable goods from New York. I prodded him to reflect further, suggesting that people from town might be working for little money in the factories that make the expensive clothes that relatives in the States send back. He said: "Yes, man. Here, there are a lot of things here that if you analyze them, damn, you will see they are illogical. You will see the illogic. Because in the stores here you won't find [these] clothes. It's hard to find them [Sean Jean] and if you find them they are expensive." Milton went on to speak of many things apart from my concern with relations of production. He talked about the "barbarous competition" between youth over wearing the most fashionable clothes and shoes. He told me about a rich mestizo, the son of a congressman who dresses like a Black and hangs out with Blacks, to the chagrin of his father. Milton owns a Haile Selassie shirt that everyone covets and joked that he could barely wear it out because it attracted so much attention. In a more somber tone, he noted changes since my previous visit four years earlier. With the rapid growth of gangs such as the *Mara Salva Trucha*, wearing certain styles, colors, and brands could get you in trouble, either from the gangs themselves or from the militarized police, newly empowered to murder by the "hard fist" policies of the Maduro administration (modeled in part on the "zero-tolerance" policies of New York City mayor Rudolph Giuliani). Ironies and illogics abound within the transnational encounters, networks, and structures of power that animate them. My friend Tyson once spoke of the Garifuna propensity to borrow the styles of Black America in the following terms: "*Eso es el black power que llevamos nosotros*" (this is the Black power we wear). What kind of Black power might he mean? How different is the Garifuna appropriation of Black style from the crass appropriations of Black power imagery by corporations such as Sean Jean?

This chapter explores one of the modes in which young Garifuna men construct and perform race, culture, class, and masculinity: encounters with signs and commodities associated with the unstable signifier Black America. Although Garifuna also engage images and ideas of blackness associated with other geographies, from Caribbean reggae and dancehall to Africa as the source of traditions, Black America represents a particularly intense site of ambivalent emulation and encounter. During my fieldwork in the late 1990s, numerous Garifuna stressed that youth imitated and coveted the styles of Black America, and some provided complex commentary on how and why. On the basis of such commentary, I analyze modes of practice and identification that differ from representations of Garifuna as a traditional people. Black America provides a diasporic resource for the performance of a Black cosmopolitanism that sits uneasily alongside images of Garifuna tradition commonly produced by the state, the media, and Garifuna organizations. This Black cosmopolitanism, I argue, also maps out distinctive relations to U.S. imperialism, drawing on racial resistance and U.S. hegemony to remake the image of Garifuna in Honduras.

I should stress from the outset that this chapter does not concern the variegated subjectivities and lives of U.S. African Americans or the complexities of Black cultural production in that country. It should in no way be read as an analysis of them. Rather, the focus is on how certain Black-identifying subjects in Honduras engage, interpret, and manufacture a Black America received in typically stereotyped forms via various sources. These include cable television, music and videos sent by relatives living in the Unites States, and the talk of transmigrants recounting their experiences abroad. In using the term "Black America" I refer to an imagined entity constructed by Garifuna from such disparate sources. I should also stress that I focus on the practices of young men, the appeal of Black America to them, and the production of masculinity. This focus stems, in part, from the character of my fieldwork—I established closer relations with more young men than women. In addition, men also seemed more invested in consumption of things Black American than women and were sometimes the objects of social critique for this very reason. When I asked young women about contemporary Garifuna styles, many pointed to the baggy pants and hip-hop styles of young men. Nonetheless, young women also engaged in signs, practices, and goods associated with Black America.[3]

Approaching Consumption and Black America

I approach consumption, power, and identity formation by attempting to engage in an analytical balancing act that involves the following injunctions: take seriously the cultural agency involved in consumption without glorifying it as generalized "resistance"; take seriously imperial relations between North and South, without reading consumption simply as an effect of imperialism or capitalism. Some recent work in Latin America and the Caribbean has explored the ways in which signs and goods associated with blackness in the United States are utilized as "diasporic resources" (Brown 1998) in the making of blackness elsewhere (Sansone 2003; Fernandes 2003; Thomas 2004). For example, Livio Sansone (2003) analyzes the transnational exchange of consumer goods informing productions of blackness in Brazil. His work draws attention to inequities implicated in consumption across the hemisphere, as Brazil exports signs of Black *tradition* and imports signs of Black *modernity* in the racialized hierarchies between North and South. However, Sansone conflates the consumption of goods associated with U.S. African Americans with a servile admiration of African Americans on the part of Afro-Brazilians, claiming: "For black people outside of the United States, the creation of a lifestyle inspired by the mythical 'super blacks' in the United States becomes a way to differentiate themselves from local white people while claiming participation in modern ways and the rituals of mass consumption" (98). Rather than project consumption as a sign of subjective deference, we should inquire into the ambivalence surrounding practices of consumption, identification, and imitation. Although my own analysis also explores relationships between blackness, modernity, and consumption among Garifuna, even cursory attention to their perspectives reveals that they do not view U.S. African Americans as figures of complete emulation. Rather they express multiple attitudes towards U.S. African Americans and the forms of first-world blackness they embody.

In a nuanced study of "modern blackness" in a Jamaican community, Deborah Thomas discusses how her informants offered variable interpretations of "America" as both a land of opportunity and an evil empire (246). Such ambivalence extends to the local talk about U.S. African Americans who "despite the stylistic appeal of African American culture and despite the political appeal of transnational racial solidarity, nonetheless are sometimes suspected of carrying the banner of the United States" (248). Thomas notes a pervasive trend among Jamaican youth to embrace (Black) American styles and goods, but she refuses to take a "dim view" of these processes as capitulation to capitalist domination and U.S. imperialism. Drawing on interviews with young men, she highlights how they view the relationship between Jamaica and America as a process of mutual influence as part of their rejection of middle-class creole nationalism. She argues that her informants

> while coveting American "name brands" ... were also quick to point out the extent to which they defined consumer trends ... within Jamaica and to extend this power to Jamaicans overseas. This is what I am calling "radical consumerism." It is not only an eschewal of middle-class models of progress through moderation and temperance, but also an insistence that consumption is a creative and potentially liberatory process and that the ability to both influence and reflect global style is, in fact, an important public power. (250)

Drawing on traditions of cultural analysis that find agency in consumption, she asserts that what might be taken as crass, individualistic materialism involves a collective dimension, a "racially vindicating capitalist consumerism" that refashions selfhood and stereotypes "through—rather than outside capitalism" (251).

> That is, black Jamaicans are simultaneously critiquing, selectively appropriating, and creatively redefining those aspects of the dominant capitalist ethos that they believe benefit themselves and their communities, both materially and psychologically. By making this argument, I do not mean to discount the effects of a globally hegemonic Americanism whereby the viability of global markets is secured for U.S. consumers and capitalists by any means necessary ... What I am trying to stress is that within this context, individuals do find ways to resignify dominant ideologies and practices in order to resituate themselves as powerful actors within their own transnational spheres. (251)

In this argument, racialized subjects refuse the subordinate position assigned to them in the hierarchies of nation-states and global capitalism, drawing on goods to engage in their own forms of self-making.

Nonetheless, if individuals position themselves as self-fashioning subjects and agents via consumption, we need to examine more closely what it means to do so *through* "global markets," "globally hegemonic Americanism," and the forms of blackness produced within them. The approach taken by Thomas suggests that despite American hegemony and capitalism, social agents find ways to creatively consume, reshape their identities, refigure their status, and contest racial, class, and gender oppression. I would not so much contest these arguments as push them in a different direction, viewing "hegemonic Americanism" not just as the structural context in which social agents maneuver but itself a subject of signifying practice where blackness and U.S. power rub together in various types of personal and collective projects. If, as John Jackson asserts, "race-inflected differences are fundamental organizing principles for global capital" (58),[4] then we should inquire further into how commodified versions of U.S. blackness may acquire some of their power from their dual connotations of racialized resistance and hegemonic Americanism. My account here is one of how the consumption of styles culled from Black America by Garifuna men in Honduras involves mimetic practices that tap into the figure of a similar other across the social and symbolic chasm separating the North and the South. I argue that the Black power Garifuna men embrace via consumption of things and signs they relate to Black America operates not simply despite but because of the dominant material and symbolic position of the United States, not simply despite but via global capitalism. The meaning and use of Black America rest in both signifiers—Black and America.

Imitating, Imagining, and Comparing Black America

In the middle of my major stint of fieldwork, my camera broke. Reluctant to use it in the first place, I had taken only a few photographs, and wanting to document a counterpoint to the postcard images of Garifuna as embodiments of tradition, I hired a photographer from La Ceiba to take pictures in Sambo Creek. I asked Marcos, one of the grandsons in the house where I lived, what he thought, and he was all for it. He said he would get his friends to wear their best gear and tell them we were doing it for a fashion magazine in the United States. I told him I would rather let them know that it was for my research project and that I would give them copies of photographs. He laughed and agreed, though he seemed a little disappointed that I had squashed his idea of having us pose as players in the fashion world. Marcos' love of rock n' roll and trick bikes made him seem a little weird and frivolous to his friends and family, but he had a serious side that blossomed when he became the first of his brothers to migrate to New York. In preparation for that trip, sponsored by his mother living in New York, his grandmother asked me if I could give him money to "take a bath" in a community some four hours away. Luz rarely asked me for money beyond what I paid for room and board, but I could not help but ask why in the world Marcos needed to go halfway up the Coast to take a bath. Luz explained, somewhat sheepishly, that the "bath"—a ritual cleansing and protective process—was to guard Marcos from immigration authorities, and it seems to have worked.

In any case, Marcos, the photographer, and I wandered around Sambo Creek and Corozal, and Marcos had little trouble conscripting friends and acquaintances into my project. Some asked us to wait while they changed into the clothes they wanted to wear, emerging in their nicest pair of Hilfiger jeans or Fila sneakers. Most of the young men posed with a serious look on their face, with their caps pulled down low or boxers showing over their jeans. Many posed with hand gestures, tossing gang signs while lacking gang affiliation. My favorite photograph from this session was of three youth, leaning on a door with the Nike swoosh painted on it, throwing gang signs and laughing. Marcos was not to be outdone in the fashion competition he conspired to instigate. We took his photograph in his room, next to the picture of Bob Marley and characters from the Michael Jordan movie *Space Jam* he had painted on his wall. Marcos wore black Boss jeans, a T-shirt embossed with "Real Playaz" that enveloped his slight frame, and a powder blue New York Yankees cap that covered hair done up, as he said, like Snoop Dogg. I could not locate the photographer to acquire permission to publish the photographs but have included a similar image of a different man that I took some years later.

The photo session provided more of a counterpoint to the postcards than I had imagined. I was searching for a representation of the real to subvert staged images of Garifuna acting "naturally" (and typically in "nature")—of men fishing and women cooking, of manaca houses and dance rituals—where signs of any contaminating transnationalism were miraculously absent from view. My own staging of a representation was, in a sense, upstaged by subjects who posed as if they might grace the pages of a magazine. Such acts of mimicking fashions and postures self-consciously culled from elsewhere became a subject of reflection on the part of a

Young man, Nueva Armenia, 2004. Basketball jerseys are a common component of young men's style. Photograph by the author.

number of young men I interviewed. Their interpretations provide the basis for my own analysis of Garifuna engagements with Black America.

I begin with an interview with Dennis, a twenty-year-old at the time of our interview in 1997. Dennis had recently been expelled from a high school in La Ceiba for fighting a mestizo student over a racist comment. (By 2004, he had returned to school and was completing a course in tourism, the only "career" offered in the local secondary school.) He shared the aesthetic preferences of most young men but lacked the economic resources and transnational connections of some of his peers. He was more active than most in local politics and Garifuna organizations, traveling to the capital to participate in the "March of Drums" concerning land rights. Perhaps for these reasons, he provided particularly detailed and critical comments on consumption, style, and the ways in which young men relate to Black America. His own speech reflected that orientation, peppered with English words and phrases such as "Black Americans," "bad boys," "yeah," "right," and so forth.

MA: Could you say something about Garifuna style? It seems to me that Garifuna have a distinct style in the way they dress and...

DENNIS: Oh Papa. The Garifuna of Honduras ... communicates a lot with the Black American. A lot. Because if one is in the United States and sees a group of Blacks they aren't going to know how to distinguish between a Garifuna and a Black American because they look the same. They dress the same. They listen to the same music. There's just a rhythm that they don't have. It's the punta ... The Black always wants to get ahead. He always wants to go around well dressed, to go around looking good. Many (Garifuna) travel with the excuse that there are better opportunities. Sure, there are better opportunities but one can always find a way to make a living; but the Garifuna travels to the United States not just to excel but to look, to dress like a Black American.

Dennis' comments play on understandings of sameness and difference between Black Americans and Garifuna. He immediately links what I called "Garifuna style" to a relationship with Black Americans, a relationship he characterizes in terms of communication and others rendered as imitation. He begins by imagining a scene, not in Honduras, but in the United States, noting how Garifuna typically blend in with Black Americans. At the same time, he notes cultural differences. He then switches to a description of "the Black" as someone concerned with having the "best" clothes, momentarily suturing the differences between Garifuna and Black Americans. Finally, Dennis turns to the image of Garifuna who migrate from Honduras, claiming that Garifuna go to the United States not just to improve their economic conditions but to "dress like a Black American." He suggests, somewhat cynically, that migration does not just result in diasporic desires (for a homeland) but that diasporic desires (for transnational connections) may also result in migration (see Brown 1998, 314).

Our interview continued, and Dennis critiqued the emphasis some youth living in the United States place on clothes.

DENNIS: The majority [of Garifuna] that come [back to Honduras] from there, come dressed yankee, with Guess jeans, a Boss shirt, a Nike cap, Nike sneakers or Reebok, all that. Brand names. And then what? They are falling for the vanity of the North

American, the negro Americano, that is Black American. . . .
I have a friend, his name is Kesler. I have another friend named
Jonathan. He is Garifuna. But Jonathan dresses better than
Kesler and Kesler is North American. When that brand Tommy
[Hilfiger] started he was one of the first in New York to wear
Tommy, of the Blacks, of the Garifunas. So someone asked him
why he did that and he said that he wanted to dress better than
North Americans. His clothes are expensive. [It's] too much,
[it's] very exaggerated. Some don't do the same. For example,
look at the house we have here in front. It was constructed by
Garifunas (living) in New York. Now they have their house
here. If they are deported they will come back under a roof.
And Jonathan? He doesn't have a house.

MA: Just nice clothes.

DENNIS: Just nice clothes.

MA: Why are people so fascinated with dressing like Black
Americans?

DENNIS: For this. For the simple fact of being Black. Of having
this color. This is their virtue. This is what they believe in their
mind: "He is Black, the same as me. And I can wear what he
wears. Because what he bought, he bought with money and I
can earn the same money he earns in order to dress the same."

Once again, Dennis suggests an ambivalent relationship between Garifuna
and Black Americans. He draws attention to the importance of certain
brand names and their association with notions of dressing well and looking good, key elements in competition over status, not just in New York but
also in Honduras. The scenario he depicts of his friend Jonathan striving
to "look better" than Black Americans calls attention to status differences
between Garifuna and Black Americans, such that Black Americans' style
becomes the object of emulation in the effort to assert one's own standing
in relation to them. A critical perspective comes to the fore, as Jonathan
represents a case of "exaggeration," an overemphasis on the acquisition of
expensive clothes at the cost of neglecting his future and family. Dennis
evokes a negative image of a particular kind of transmigrant, one who
shirks duties to self, kin, and community. As we see in the next chapter,
the trope of the pompous and irresponsible transmigrant can be invoked
in discourses that worry over class distinctions and ruptures of sociality

associated with transmigration. Dennis characterized an interest in things Black American in a deceptively straightforward fashion, "for the simple fact of being Black" (*por el simple hecho de ser negro*). He repeated the phrase in a discussion we had about preferred movies and videos among his peers.

> MA: I've noticed that if there is a movie that has a lot of Blacks in it then everyone watches it.
>
> DENNIS: Ahh papa. That's how it is. The most popular movies in Garifuna communities, the most popular in this community, are of Garifuna, I mean, of bad boys, bad Blacks in the street, American movies of Black Americans like *Boyz n' the Hood*, *New Jack City*. The other most popular movies are [those of Claude] Van Damme, karate movies, yeah. A lot of people saw the death of Tupac [rap and film star Tupac Shakur] and many say that Tupac isn't dead and everybody knows this history like the palm of their hand for the simple fact that Tupac was a Black. If you ask someone if they know of Nelson Mandela, yes, they know, they know his story very well, from the videos. For the simple fact of being Black. But if you ask someone if they saw the message of Pope John Paul they won't know it. If you ask someone "Do you know of Eddie Murphy?," [they will respond] "Oh yes. I know Eddie Murphy. Oh Oh. Eddie Murphy. The number one comic in North America." For the simple fact of being Black.

If Dennis grounds a Garifuna interest in Black America under the sign of racial sameness, I hope that I have presented enough of his discourse to suggest that, for him, being Black is not at all simple but shot through with national, cultural, and economic difference. In fact, his distanced appraisal of a Garifuna attraction to Black America—the use of the third person and reported speech, the critique of consumerism, the parodic juxtaposition of the Pope and Eddie Murphy as subjects of attention and knowledge— complicates simple racial solidarities and hints at the notion that blackness is constructed and performed rather than given and assumed.

Nonetheless, Dennis (and others I know) sometimes elaborated on the Black body as a structure that conditioned the possibilities of its proper signification. In the middle of our interview, I attempted to turn our discussion to the effects Garifuna practices of style and fashion might have on their position within Honduras and their relationship with mestizos.

MA: Is it fair to say that here, well, I have friends here that say that today mestizos are looking at Garifunas like, like something heavy.[5]

DENNIS: Yeah. Not just heavy. They take them as bad boys, *chicos malos*. The Garifunas dress well here in Honduras. Because the blancos are taking our look.

MA: Yes?

DENNIS: We have a hairstyle called high-look that is a little bit of hair here [around the top of the head] and shaved on the bottom [around the ears]. We use a cream called "Wave" for the hair, in order to make little waves. For us it works because our hair is coarse, it's rough. But in the hair of the blanco it's very difficult to make the waves. But they are becoming involved in this, because they like it. So they are imitating us.

MA: It's called "high look"?

DENNIS: "High look." This cut is called high look. They shouldn't become involved in this because, really, their hair doesn't permit it. It's very smooth. Their hair is for using gel, for using something like that, so that their hair keeps growing long. But we can cut it, wear our hair shaved and not look like a bull. When we see a blanco with shaved, shaved hair we call him hedgehog ... So we tell them that they shouldn't do this. They shouldn't try to imitate us too much because, truly, there are things that are for a person, and other things that are not for a person. For me, it wouldn't look good to wear my hair long, very long, and loose, because it's not smooth. For me, I could wear long hair, but with braids, with dreadlocks. How could a blanco wear long hair with dreadlocks? They can't because it's very smooth. And they want to use dreadlocks but their hair is very smooth and it looks really ugly. How can you make dreadlocks from a horse? You can't.

MA: [Laughing: my own hair, long at the time, was often matted].

DENNIS: Yeah. They don't want to understand this. And now, we, [hesitates] the Garifunas Americanos (Garifuna who live in the United States) bring a look to Honduras of wearing the pants a

little bit below the waist and use box [boxers], the underwear of
old people, wear the pants like that, right, and big shirts.

MA: Uh huh, very wide.

DENNIS: This is a matter for Blacks, for their physique. A lot of
times the physique of a Black is stronger than that of a blanco.
The blanco is more thin. The Black no. The majority of Blacks,
you can see if you look, have strong arms, big chests, muscular
backs. Because of this they used us in the conquest of Columbus. They used us as instruments of work and from there, from
that region [the Caribbean], we descend. A blanco that's thin
can't wear a shirt XXL. It's too big but they still do it. It doesn't
make sense. They practically want to imitate one and the Blacks
realize it and we laugh in their face.

Within this discourse, the racial body signifies certain natural differences
between negros and blancos/mestizos. In reality, of course, members of
different groups show considerable variation in their "types" of hair and
body. In discussions of racism, Dennis often liked to say, "we are all flesh
and bone" to highlight the essential equality of different races. In this instance, Dennis conflates identity with phenotype and asserts that negros
and blancos each have distinctive kinds of hair and physiques with qualities that condition the way they should be arranged and dressed. The very
product "Wave" (a hair relaxer that might be understood as a whitening
agent) is interpreted as a product suitable only for Blacks. According to
this logic, since the hair and physique of blancos cannot conform to the
practices developed around the Black body, blanco attempts to imitate
Black practices appear absurd, like a horse trying to grow dreadlocks.

Nonetheless, discourses and practices surrounding the Black body constantly maneuvered between rendering blackness as a physical "fact" and
manipulating its significance. A friend from Sambo Creek once told me
that Blacks had an advantage over gringos because they could wear their
hair in many ways while gringos like me were limited to wearing our hair
short or long, with few options to wear it high or in braids. He, like Dennis, implicitly challenged the notion, common both in the United States
and Honduras, that "good hair" is straight and smooth and that "bad hair"
is coarse and kinky. This takes on particular significance when we consider that in Honduras, some barbers reportedly still refuse to cut a Black
person's hair, claiming either that they do not know how to cut it or that

Blacks have a scalp disease that will contaminate their combs.[6] In general, Garifuna I know rarely exhibited aesthetic preferences for "whiteness" and showed considerable pride in the aesthetic elaboration of blackness.

Many young Garifuna men and women spend considerable energy arranging and rearranging each other's hair in styles largely borrowed from Black Americans. Indeed, hairstyling typically involved extensive forms of sociality among young men and women. Almost every Saturday afternoon small groups of men would gather on the porch of the house where I lived to cut each other's hair with electric shavers and razor blades. Most of the men wore their hair cropped short, but some grew it so that it could be plaited or braided in a variety of ways. In some cases, they would have a friend shave a particular sign on their head, such as their name or the Nike "swoosh." Young women also gathered to arrange their hair in numerous ways. While perhaps a majority of them wore their hair "straight," others preferred cornrows, plaits, and braids, forms of hair arrangement that display a dazzling variety of styles. Practices of hair arrangement highlight the affirmation and manipulation of blackness on the individual and social body.

These comments point to the interplay between discourses of blackness as a "simple fact" and practices that produce blackness in excess of that "fact." They also point to the materiality of blackness as a signifying practice saturating the manipulation and experience of tactile bodies. Blackness, like other products of racialized discourse, is indeed a "construction" but one that links bodily distinctions, social practices, and lived experience. As analysts, we should not simply dismiss notions of blackness as a "simple fact" out of hand. Garifuna sometimes explain (or assume) their interest in Black America and identification as Blacks on the basis of a racial sameness that appears, to some degree, as a given part of the social world. Experiences of racial interpellation, identification, and discrimination have given shape to a sense of racial self, constantly renegotiated in the terrain of social life and articulated in different ways at different moments and places. Nonetheless, it is not inevitable that Garifuna should identify themselves as Black. Rather, Garifuna actively *produce* specific forms of blackness through their own modes of signification and "imitation," especially in fashion. Black America is a site of significant attention here, a site for producing a sameness and difference within the racial category Black and a site for imagining, through comparison and contrast, what it means to be Black in Honduras.

Young woman, Sambo Creek, 1994. Photograph by the author.

Studies of "race" in Latin American countries are often framed, explicitly or implicitly, within a comparative paradigm with the United States (Hanchard 1994; Marx 1998; Twine 1998). Rarely do such studies consider the ways in which social agents who confront racism draw comparisons between different racial formations, racisms, antiracisms, and survival strategies, relying instead upon modes of comparison that distinguish racial formations across societies. There are, to be sure, critiques of the ways in which Latin Americans deny racism through favorably contrasting their own countries to the United States (Dulitzky 2005) but few efforts to seriously consider how transnational encounters invite cross-national comparisons within everyday life.[7]

Garifuna I know frequently made such comparisons and sometimes sought my gringo perspective. Tyson showed a particularly keen interest in Black America, both in the questions he asked me and through his own presentation of self. At the time of my initial fieldwork, he was in his early twenties and living in his mother's home. He had received a year of technical schooling as an electrician and worked construction. Tyson, like many youth, aspired to go to the United States, which he eventually did after purchasing a passport someone had bought from a U.S. African American soldier. When I saw him in Texas, in 1999, he joked that the border patrol agents couldn't tell one Black from another and so he passed over with no problem. When I got to know Tyson in Sambo Creek, he was always improving his English and frequently asked me the meanings of certain words or phrases, particularly from what Craig Watkins (1998) calls "ghetto action films," films like *Boyz n' the Hood* that circulated on videos. Like other young Garifuna men, he greeted others with phrases like "What's up?" "Cuz," and "Chillin."

During one of our conversations, I asked Tyson why Garifuna liked to watch movies about Black Americans. He responded:

> Practically all Garifuna love these kind of films because they show us how they live, the system, how they express themselves, the environment in which they live and we take hold of a piece of the most important parts. But nevertheless in our environment here there are people that take all the bad (he cites local youth gangs, that don't really cause much trouble). So they dress like Black Americans and you know, sometimes they try to take a little bit of the bad. But nonetheless it is a life that, hey, for us it's pleasing to imitate them. It's not for nothing but something more related to racism that makes it more essential. That is what makes us more engaged to watch the actions of them, because they always fight against racism. There, the most important thing is that the people that want to extend racism against us (mestizos) aren't worth anything there. Because there, eh, a lot of guys go around real quiet, they don't mess around because they know that there Blacks have a lot of power.

Tyson provides a layered explanation of why Garifuna, including himself, take an interest in representations of Black America, implicating himself to a greater degree than Dennis did. First, he suggests that the films of inner-city Black youth depict the way Black Americans live. Such representations provide knowledge—stereotyped as it is—of the "environment" where Garifuna in the United States also dwell, an environment that many youth hope to join. However, like Dennis, Tyson offers a critical perspective on U.S. African Americans. Neither he nor anyone else I knew viewed Black Americans as "mythical super blacks." In fact, he and others sometimes circulated familiar stereotypes of U.S. African Americans, particularly men, as dangerous, violent, lazy, and so on.

Tyson then turns to the pleasures and politics of imitating Black America, suggesting that antiracist struggles associated with Black Americans provide inspiration for Garifuna struggles against racism in Honduras. This is not new. As we saw in chapter 3, Garifuna political movements have long drawn from the civil rights and black power movements associated with the United States. Tyson, though aware of these legacies, does not reference a specific political project of Black liberation. Rather, he draws comparisons between race relations in Honduras and the United States. Speaking from a position in Honduras, he focuses not on the question of Black and white, in the sense of negro and gringo, but rather on the opposition between negro and mestizo. It is with this in mind that we should interpret his comment that "Black Americans have a lot of power." As an assessment of the position of African Americans within the racial hierarchies of the United States, such a statement is clearly misguided. But in Tyson's vision, the shift of context from Honduras to the United States involves a kind of reversal of race relations where mestizos have little power over Blacks, where mestizo men go around "real quiet," and where they would not dare hurl racial insults in public. Later on, Tyson related that a cousin had told him that there were parts of New York where only Blacks lived, and they ran things. He said he liked the idea, because "that way one can live in peace." It might seem odd that someone living in a small, beachside town with a reputation of being peaceful could envision New York as a place where one could "live in peace." Tyson's discourse should be viewed in the social context of Sambo Creek, where Garifuna feel pressured by land loss and an increased mestizo presence and where a long social memory of racism endures, bolstered by activist discourses of ancestral belonging and cultural autonomy. In 1980, mestizos composed approximately 10 percent of the town's population. Twenty years later, they were 50 percent. Land prices have risen dramatically as a result of real estate speculation and anticipated tourist booms, and most owners of substantial property do not come from the community. There are few local economic opportunities, and everyone knows that to really get ahead you have to leave. Visions of Black autonomy in the United States, however skewed as depictions of the social realities of Black America, reverberate back as modes of comparison to the lack of autonomy at home, a lack that conditions the dream of going abroad.

At this point, we can take a step back and return to one of the questions motivating this inquiry: what kind of Black power do young Garifuna men imitate, engage, and wear in their encounters with Black America, from afar? The preceding account suggests a series of elements they identify, including the power of self-affirmation as Black (in a context where blackness is denigrated); antiracist consciousness and stances (where the existence of racism is routinely denied); and visions of racial–cultural autonomy (where community appears under siege). Elsewhere, I have analyzed the ways in which young men appropriate and embody stereotyped images of U.S. African American men as "bad boys" in ways that perform defiant masculine postures and contest stereotypes of Garifuna men as peaceful and passive (Anderson 2005). Dennis, the young man who made critical remarks on Garifuna engagements with Black America, told me later in our interview that if he went walking on the streets with baggy clothes, not just any mestizo would mess with him. Black America becomes a terrain through which differences in the racial order may be imagined, compared, and, through affiliation, manipulated.

Black Power and Brand Names

The account I have provided so far is the kind that many anthropologists working on these topics tend to produce: one that emphasizes local agency—often understood as resistance—in global encounters; one that insists we situate practices within specific social situations and relations while remaining suspicious of metanarratives that would reduce social practice and imagination to cultural imperialism or global capitalism. But what can we do with "brand names," those marks that travel under the corporate sign of the same? As Coombe argues, trademarks merit attention not simply as signs of something like cultural invasion but as cultural forms available for signifying practice.

If the trademark figures at all in ethnographic discourse ... it marks the pending *loss* of cultural identity, but is rarely one of its sources. A mere sign of Western hegemony, like the Coke bottle in the Kalahari, it figures more often as a harbinger of homogeneity or irrevocable social transformation than as one cultural resource among others. Intellectual properties are, however, significant cultural forms in contemporary public arenas. Endlessly reproduced and circulated by mass media, they are identified with by subaltern groups who use them to construct identities and communities, to challenge social exclusions, and to assert difference. Their ubiquity in commercial culture makes them particularly available for the signifying activities of others, and the fact that they are everywhere the same seems to invite others to use them to inscribe social difference. (204)

Although I am drawn to this formulation, I would emphasize the inscription and performance of sameness as well as difference implicated in the circulation and appropriation of brands as distinctive kinds of cultural resources. So far, I have tried to argue that many young Garifuna men I know link the branded styles they wear to an ambivalent affiliation with Black America in the affirmation and reconstitution of blackness in Honduras as tied to their efforts to confront racism. Nonetheless, the making of racial–cultural difference at home involves complex productions of sameness, in which not just the "Black" but also the "America" of Black America matters. Exploring what Garifuna make of brand names provides additional insights into what Tyson might mean by "the Black power we wear" and how it might work.

"In style" commodities, and the brand names associated with them, do not just reference blackness but their perceived "excellence," "quality," and expense, the prestige and status associated with the United States, and hip sensibilities with global purchase. They also signify participation in transnational networks, cultural worldliness, and modern modes of living. Tyson responded to a comment I made that Garifuna seem to have their own style in the following manner:

Very distinct. They dress better and more expensive too. This is at a national level. The Black, he that has the least money, the better he dresses. Here the mestizo only wears Levi's. You know, a pair of

> Levi's costs 500 lempiras (almost forty dollars), a pair of Tommy
> jeans costs 700 (fifty-four dollars) or more. You can see that now
> the mestizo is imitating the way Blacks dress.

Here Tyson represents Garifuna practices of style with a kind of status competition with mestizos. Tommy Hilfiger is rendered a Black brand superior in taste and cost to Levi's, another "American" brand. Through transnational networks of extended kin relations, Garifuna tap into the developments of Black style in the United States and, in some cases, have greater access than local mestizos to new consumer goods from the United States. Some brands, such as Hugo Boss in the 1990s or Sean Jean in the early 2000s, are difficult to find in Honduras. Overall, the majority of Hondurans find brand name clothing prohibitively expensive unless they have connections abroad. Much of the clothing worn by the lower classes in Honduras comes secondhand from the United States, leading one critic to dub Hondurans a "citizenry of seconds" (Lombraña 1996). Within this context, wearing a pair of Tommy Hilfiger jeans or Nike shoes lends Honduran Garifuna a degree of social distinction, both as individuals and as a group. As another young man put it, "we feel higher up when we wear brand names."

Clothing offers distinct advantages over other forms of material culture in the display of social identity. Relative to other status symbols, it is easy to acquire and may be readily trafficked across social and physical space. Moreover, because it adheres to the body it permits the individual to carry signs of individual status and collective identity wherever he or she moves in the social world. It also permits a blurring of status categories and, for some, can be used to highlight the artifice of status distinction itself. As Tyson noted, "The Black, he that has the least money, the better he dresses." These same qualities of flexibility and accessibility, however, mean that the symbols and status associated with clothing remain open to manipulation and appropriation by a wide range of persons. As we have seen, young Garifuna men often claim that "their" style is now being imitated by mestizos, who increasingly dress in the same brand names Garifuna prefer and sometimes adopt the look associated with hip-hop style. Mestizos, of course, may not see themselves as imitating Garifuna at all; but it is the Garifuna perception of mestizos imitating Garifuna, themselves imitating Black Americans in their use of a corporate copy, that interests me. Identifying mestizo imitation of Garifuna style confirms the prestige associated with such practices, as when Milton marveled at the son of a congressman embracing blackness. However, imitation by the locally dominant other threatens to undermine the specific association of certain styles with blackness (and thus Garifuna). Those Garifuna who are most concerned with style often monitor the practices of mestizos and are careful to maintain a sense of distinction from them. For example, Tyson berated a younger cousin for wearing a white shirt with horizontal orange and blue stripes that he had purchased in La Ceiba. On his way out one night, Tyson laughed and said: "And this? You look like an indio." His cousin changed the shirt a few minutes later, and I never saw him wear it again beyond his own yard. Tyson himself ceased wearing a Nike baseball cap because he had seen fake versions for sale on the streets of La Ceiba.

The significance of brand name clothing can be linked to a more general sense that Garifuna have improved their economic and social position relative to mestizos in Honduras. Garifuna often discuss improvement in racism as a direct result of their changing socioeconomic position within Honduran society, sometimes framed as becoming more modern. These processes are, in turn, linked to transnational migration, increased enrollment in secondary and university education, and efforts to combat racism. Tyson, noting that "racism" had changed but would always exist, liked to point out how Garifuna have now economically surpassed many local mestizos:

> The mestizo, no matter how poor, considers himself more important than the Black. But now, in communities themselves, this is not reality. Because I can tell you that here [in the community] there are more poor mestizos than negros. Incredible. The system of life of Garifunas here is much more average than [that of] mestizos because a [Garifuna] from almost any family has relatives in the United States and with what they send from there the system of life changes. Like you can see, if you go to (nearby mestizo communities) you will see mestizos that still live in houses of manaca with their entire families ... We won't even talk about the rural areas, where the peasants are.

Tyson's use of the image of the manaca house (a house of mud walls and a thatch roof) as evidence of mestizo poverty also speaks to historical representations of Garifuna as "backward," "primitive," and "inferior" that still weigh on social relations. The manaca house represents a sign of Garifuna tradition yet connotes poverty as well. By associating that house with poor mestizos, Tyson asserts the superiority of a new Garifuna "system of life" enabled by transmigration. Maribel, a young woman who worked for a time in the maquiladora factories of San Pedro Sula, echoed these sentiments, arguing that Garifuna were "surpassing" many mestizos. Noting that "in my view, life is modern," she said that the growing number of Garifuna professionals has meant that mestizos "stop humiliating us. The humiliation is for them now." Although neither Maribel nor Tyson form part of the professional class, they can point to its emergence as evidence of a kind of collective mobility. The humiliations associated with the racism suffered by Garifuna, humiliations also represented by certain aspects of Garifuna tradition, become opposed to new, albeit tenuous, possibilities linked to education and migration. Material goods, particularly those that can be used to represent blackness, can provide visual evidence of the changing position of Garifuna and the will to assert it.

The complexities and contradictions of the circulation of brand names within Honduras can be illustrated through a discussion of one of its more prominent icons, the Nike trademark or "swoosh." In the mid-1990s, the Nike swoosh appeared all over Honduras and was particularly prominent within the Garifuna communities I knew. Nike shoes, caps, shorts, sweats, and other goods were among the most desirable consumer items. New shoe stores that traded almost exclusively in Nike products opened in La Ceiba. At the same time, a counterfeit industry emerged to cash in on the brand. Most interestingly, the swoosh became detached from material commodities and appeared all over the place: painted on the sides of taxis, on the rocks by the river, on the side of houses, and on the backboard of a basketball hoop. For a while, a few Garifuna inscribed it on their very bodies, tattooing the swoosh on their arms or shaving it on the back of their heads. When I asked individuals why they marked their bodies with the Nike symbol, they either gave vague responses such as "se llega la marca" (the brand is hot) or laughed and never answered the question. Their friends occasionally chided them for lacking the "real" product or becoming a "live advertisement." Nevertheless, the sign acquired an obvious, if opaque, importance, perhaps because it distilled in such a compact manner the complex relations between blackness and the United States and between transnational corporations and consumer practices.

The association of the Nike trademark with inner-city blackness has a layered history. The Nike Corporation self-consciously looked to African American playgrounds as both market and inspiration for their products. The first 1985 Air Jordan commercial, with Michael Jordan rising to dunk a basketball on a dilapidated playground, neatly connected images of masculine, athletic prowess with urban authenticity (Anderson and Millman, 167). The Nike Corporation successfully maneuvered within a charged symbolic space that sold images of inner-city blackness while simultaneously attempting to render them palatable to white consumers. The swoosh also signified "resistance." According to one commentator, Nike products "underwent export as a stowaway aboard hip-hop" and "became an icon of hip-hop's resistance to marginalization and oppression" (Flusty, 61). Whether hip-hop hijacked the swoosh or Nike hijacked hip-hop is perhaps beside the point, as the brand took on the symbolic freight of a stereotyped Black America. Among Garifuna in Honduras, the Nike swoosh circulated as a polyphonic icon of youth resistance, racial blackness, economic status, and corporate power. It was omnipresent, in one sense the same everywhere, yet announced the presence of alterity via its

Young Men, Sambo Creek, 2004. Photograph by the author.

symbolic associations with blackness and America. It represented the extension of corporate branding upon bodies and the landscape yet signaled racial difference from the normalized whiteness of U.S. racial hierarchies and the normalized mestizaje of Honduras. For Garifuna, it signified the sameness and difference of blackness but was also appropriated by mestizos. For these reasons, the Nike swoosh might also stand as an icon for the tensions, complexities, and contradictions inherent in Garifuna practices of consumption and engagements with Black America.

Conclusion: Consumption, Black America, and Indigeneity

In this chapter, I have tried to write about certain practices of consumption (and what people have to say about them) to reveal something of the complex sets of relations and identifications that shape the lives and imaginations of young Garifuna men I know, as they strive to redefine their position vis-à-vis each other, other Garifuna, mestizos, and the world at large. Focusing on the consumption of things that Garifuna relate to Black America, we see how Black America marks a racial and cultural particularity within the category "America" and the category "Black." It is a space of contradiction characterized by the material promise of the good life and the vanities of consumerism, by the realities of racism and the possibilities of racial solidarity, by the gap between living in the North and South, and efforts to transverse that gap. It is a space of comparison and ambivalent affiliation. I have focused on consumption, because it is largely via consumption that Black America is known, made, and mimicked and it is via consumption that Garifuna tap into a certain kind of Black power to refashion their position in Honduras, a Black power that invokes the status of America as part of the remaking of blackness at home. I have tried to avoid celebrating or condemning such practices in order to show something of the complicated relations between forms of racial, ethnic, class, and gender differentiation within transnational encounters and neoliberal capitalism and the ways in which social agents navigate and produce them.

The material in this chapter can be located within renewed efforts to understand race, gender, and nationality as "structural features of global capitalism" that we can analyze in chains of commodity production, distribution, and consumption (Tsing 2009). Forms of class and gender differentiation, imbricated with racial and ethnic ascriptions and identifications, are not simply results of capitalism; they are constitutive features of capitalism. The marketing of blackness by clothing companies like Sean Jean and Nike is an integral element of their chains of commodity production, not simply an addition to the way they farm out the making of commodities (itself underpinned by differentiations of labor along lines of class, gender, race, and nationality). The symbolic associations of blackness with "cool" masculinity, bad boy stances, and youthful resistance are integral to their marketing strategies (Ebron 2008). Of course, the production of blackness by Blacks exceeds its commodification; that is one reason why it is commodified. The resourceful self-fashioning and oppositional creativity of Black diasporic subjects thus become subject to renewed cycles of branding and profiteering. The hypocrisy of Sean Jean's use of Black power symbolism to make clothes that exploit third-world labor highlights the contradictions both within and across capitalist chains of production and marketing.

The ironies of the Sean Jean scandal are magnified when we consider the reactions of Honduran Garifuna who might both work in the factories making the brand and desire to consume it. The garment maker in a maquiladora could never, on her or his salary alone, buy a pair of Sean Jean jeans or sweatshirt. The maquiladora industry pays poorly but represents one of the few available opportunities for employment, particularly for women without access to remittances or secondary education (who are shut out of certain economic sectors like construction or fishing and who find subsistence agriculture and vending less viable than in the past). Most Garifuna I know held up migration to the United States as the most promising route to social mobility, and the economic status of families typically hinged on their relatives living abroad. The most likely source for acquiring a brand such as Sean Jean was a transmigrant relative living in the United States. Such goods do not just travel on transnational networks; they signify participation in them and the class status tied to Black America. Taking these processes into consideration helps us understand how Milton, the young man with transnational ties with whom I discussed the Sean Jean scandal, appeared more interested in consumption than production, in the difficulties and pleasures of acquiring branded blackness than in the exploitation of factory labor that is predominately female and feminized. Consumption is a site where his masculinity, class status, and blackness are produced and affirmed. We do not need to celebrate consumption to recognize its importance in identity formations in every struggles over ethnoracial marginality.

Consumption practices involving Black America produce alternative visual representations of Garifuna identity to the typical representations of Garifuna produced by the state, media, anthropologists, multilateral institutions, foreign NGOs, and Garifuna organizations. Whereas Garifuna attract the attention of others on the basis of their ethnic particularity, cultural traditions, and history of Carib-African intermixture, the identity practices discussed in this chapter highlight the participation of Garifuna in modernity, as Blacks. The source of diasporic fascination reflected in these practices is not so much African origins as contemporary relations with first-world blackness. Here, worries over authenticity do not dwell on the integrity of traditional culture but on the circulation of "fake" brands and the appropriation of hip-hop fashion by local mestizos. While most representations locate Garifuna in coastal communities, the consumption of Black America highlights worldly connections produced through circuits of transmigration. Consumer goods do not just travel on those circuits; they index transnational relationships and the class and status implications associated with them.

The contrasts between the modalities of Black power analyzed in this chapter and the forms of Black indigenism radicalized by OFRANEH are particularly striking, both as modes of representation and as forms of struggle. The first mode enacts a self-conscious Black cosmopolitanism that visibly challenges images of Garifuna parochialism and primitivity. The second represents Garifuna as an indigenous people with a traditional culture in projects defending community and territory. The distinction here between cosmopolitanism and indigeneity should not be interpreted literally. In practice, the politics of indigeneity is thoroughly cosmopolitan; it involves transnational networks of activists and institutions, international laws and courts, and models of peoplehood that evolve and travel while taking on local, regional, and national valences. The politics of indigeneity is a global practice, and its leading practitioners are often worldly. Rather, the distinction lies in how different forms of representation produce different images of a collective Garifuna subject for different ends.

Black indigenism represents Garifuna as a distinct people located in their own communities and territories who retain a non-Western culture and cosmovision. This image of peoplehood is a key basis for claims to political and cultural rights. It necessarily emphasizes cultural particularity, located in territory. The transnational connections and consumption practices associated with the performance of a Black cosmopolitanism are irrelevant to the making of political claims within this paradigm of struggle. (As we see in the next chapter, they are also objects of critique by activists.) If Black indigenism downplays the cosmopolitan dimensions of Garifuna lives, forms of Black power that draw on brand names and Black America produce the opposite effect, downplaying the particularity of Garifuna as an ethnic subject with a traditional culture in favor of an image associated with first-world blackness, resistance, and success.

These modes of identity formation also articulate differently with questions of capitalist domination and U.S. imperialism. As we saw in the previous chapters, the forms of Black indigenism produced by OFRANEH are directly linked to a politics of antineoliberalism and anti-imperialism. OFRANEH attacks globalization projects based on ideologies of free market capitalism as the latest modality through which the rich North, particularly the United States Empire, plunders the South with the complicity of the Honduran government and the elite. The result for Garifuna communities is impoverishment, environmental destruction, loss of land, resources, and territory, and the possible dissolution of a whole way of life. The Black cosmopolitanism performed through style and consumption marks out a different relationship with U.S. dominance in Latin America. Its practitioners draw on images of U.S. blackness in everyday struggles over the meaning of race and ethnicity in Honduras, which focus primarily on relations with mestizos and the overcoming of racial–cultural stereotypes. They wed assertions of a diasporic racial identity as Black and antiracist resistance to the elevation of class status associated with the participation in transnationalism and the consumption of U.S. brand names. These practices *rely* on capitalism and the symbolic centrality of U.S. power to refashion Garifuna identity and blackness in Honduras. They do not involve a political project against anti-imperialism but a set of everyday tactics in which the racialized terrain of consumer capitalism provides symbolic resources.

Local engagements with Black America represent only one, albeit prominent, mode of representing blackness among Garifuna in Sambo Creek. The Caribbean, particularly Jamaica, provides another site of diasporic interest and affiliation mediated by consumption. Reggae iconography and the music of Bob Marley remain prominent in the lives of many young men I have known over the years. These images of a Caribbean blackness evince South–South connections, albeit connections mediated by transmigrants in the North who send reggae videos or Haile Selassie T-shirts back home. The use of these resources to represent the self involves a different kind of cosmopolitanism to produce a "roots" image more visually in tune with assertions of Black indigeneity and the ethnic particularity of Garifuna as a rural, coastal people. Moreover, as I have insinuated in this chapter, Garifuna who perform a version of Black cosmopolitanism via engagements with Black America can also engage in self-representations as a traditional people in defense of community. A Black power that taps into Black America via consumption is not the only form of self-representation and struggle in town, even for those who wear it. The following chapter explores the local meanings of indigeneity in Sambo Creek, returning to the tensions between different facets of identity formation as Garifuna navigate structures of power in which "traditional culture" represents a source of pride, a resource, and a stigma.

6

Political Economies of Difference:
Indigeneity, Land, and Culture in Sambo Creek

In 1996, a group of Garifuna (and a few mestizos) from Sambo Creek performed a play as part of an AIDS awareness campaign coordinated by OFRANEH. The actors were mostly young men and women directed by a local OFRANEH representative who I call Mauricio. Mauricio was a painter who I met during my initial visit to Honduras. Back then, he sold me a picture of a Garifuna woman wearing a headscarf, holding her infant son. He was from a community near Trujillo and had aspirations to run for mayor of his municipality. His wife lived in Sambo Creek, and while he worked on the AIDS education project, he lived there too. Mauricio didn't think much of Sambo Creek as a Garifuna community. In contrast to his own town, everybody in Sambo Creek was crowded together in disorder. He hated the pigs that roamed freely and lamented the high price of fish, higher than in La Ceiba. He noted that people spoke less Garifuna in Sambo Creek than in many other communities and that some children barely learned it at all. "There are Garifunas that are not Garifunas," he liked to say, suggesting that there were individuals who had lost touch with their spiritual practices and cultural traditions, who no longer knew who they were.

The play he wrote and directed with input from the actors reflected these concerns. It was performed as part of a competition among several Garifuna communities held in the community of Triunfo de la Cruz, in the Tela Bay area. I watched several rehearsals and traveled with the troupe to the competition concluding the AIDS awareness campaign. By the mid-1990s, Honduras had the highest infection rates of AIDS in Central America, and Garifuna communities were known to have some of the worst indices of infection in Honduras. The play put on by the troupe from Sambo Creek dramatized the dangers of foreign contamination, drawing on disease as a metaphor for the pernicious effects of migration that can be healed only via cultural revitalization and a spiritual return to self and community.

The dramatic action revolves around "José the New Yorker," a transmigrant who returns to Honduras after living in the United States. José enters the stage embodying a Garifuna version of the ugly American. He wears a gaudy orange shirt and Ray-Ban sunglasses and carries a briefcase. He speaks in English to an admiring but confused crowd of women who ask him, "Don't you speak Spanish? Don't you speak Garifuna? Is not your skin still Black?" José laughs nervously and replies, "Umm, there was a lot of sun in Mexico," suggesting that his passage South has begun to transform a whiter self that resides in New York. José now speaks in Spanish but still puts on airs and flaunts his dollars. He wins the affection of one of the women, with whom he exits the stage. The next scene opens with José suffering from a disease. We do not know whether he acquired it in the United States or Honduras. Trembling, he visits a doctor who tells José he has AIDS and that there is no cure. Dejected and humbled, José again encounters the group of women, who convince him to consult a *buyei*, a Garifuna healer/spirit medium. The buyei—played by a young woman dressed as an older woman—decides that he has been afflicted by the spirits of his ancestors, who are angry that he has neglected them. She tells him he must undergo a *dügü*, a ritual ceremony that appeases the ancestors and cures the sick. The play concludes with a brief presentation of the ritual, characterized by extensive food offerings, dancing, and spirit possession. At the end of the dügü, José is cured.

The didactic lesson of the play revolves around the dangers of migration and the need to venerate Garifuna tradition and identity. The New Yorker's cultural arrogance, conspicuous consumption, and denial of his ethnoracial identity all appear linked to the ancestors' anger and the onset of his illness. His cure, therefore, must be social, cultural, and spiritual. The dügü is the most elaborate and venerated of Garifuna healing ceremonies and involves curing an individual through reestablishing relations to the spirits of the ancestors.[1] Women, particularly the elder relatives of the sick, often take leading roles (Kerns 1983). In the play, particular kinship relations are ignored such that the ancestors represent the entire Garifuna people, and the transmigrant's transgressions dramatize the need to respect and retain traditions. Ironically, the play from Sambo Creek could not completely reflect that message; it was delivered mostly in Spanish because too many of the actors spoke insufficient Garifuna. (The judges awarded first prize to a troupe from Triunfo de la Cruz, who performed entirely in Garifuna.) The actor playing "José the New Yorker" was the child of transmigrants and helped run his family's corner store. Like many youth with transmigrant connections, he sported the hip styles associated with diasporic blackness and hoped to migrate to the United States, succeeding a few years later.

The character of the arrogant transmigrant was an established figure in cultural critiques. "José the New Yorker" was borrowed from the play *Loubavagu* ("The Other Side, Far Away"), perhaps the most famous Honduran theatrical work of the late twentieth century. The drama was created in 1979 out of collaborations between mestizo director Rafael Murillo Selva Rendón, Garifuna intellectuals, and members of the Garifuna community of Guadalupe (Selva Rendón 1997).[2] *Loubavagu* tells the Garifuna story from the ethnogenesis on St. Vincent to the contradictions facing contemporary communities. The "New Yorker" appears in the last act. He is prepared to give 1,000 dollars toward the building of a road linking his community to the closest city, but he is also full of vanity. He shows off his presents, speaks English, and pines for American foods. His comeuppance arrives in the form of a flood that washes his new goods out to sea, carrying away a woman who tries to rescue a television set. Ruined, the New Yorker takes back some of his gifts and sells them to a merchant who, having a monopoly on the market, offers a pittance. Meanwhile, community members decide to build the road themselves to gain better access to markets. However, the road brings its own threats as a masked man arrives to buy land, like in the days of the banana companies. In the end, the character of an old woman takes center stage, voicing a refusal to sell land as she calls on the spirits of Garifuna ancestors to help in the struggle.

This drama, like the Sambo Creek play modeled on it, juxtaposes the destructive allure of foreign ways and consumer desires with the protective and healing powers of tradition, embodied by old women. Both plays offer critical perspectives on migration and dramatize conflicts within Garifuna communities between modernity and tradition and cosmopolitanism and indigeneity. They provide a nice reference point for examining how Garifuna navigate tensions between these ideologically loaded oppositions in everyday life. How do critiques of migration and consumerism resonate in Sambo Creek, where transnational consumption plays a key role in struggles over racial and cultural status? How do discourses of indigeneity figure in the lives of community members? How do Garifuna negotiate what it means to be Garifuna in an era characterized by transnational migration, economic insecurity, territorial displacement, social mobility, and ethnic mobilization?

In the chapters on Garifuna activisms, I analyzed indigeneity as a mobile model, a traveling discourse of rights and concepts involving global connections and institutions. Sambeños, typically less fluent than lead activists in the formalized vocabulary of indigeneity, nonetheless produced their own forms of indigeneity in affirmations of culture and place, deep presence and roots in community, and distinct customs and traditions. They rarely used the word "indígena" to denote themselves or these attachments, perhaps because that word also marks a distinct subject, the "Indian." Nonetheless, I find it important to speak of an everyday indigeneity in which Garifuna render themselves a unique people with distinct customs rooted in place as community. The term "Garifuna ancestrality" perhaps best captures this mode of indigeneity, as Sambeños often refer to the ancestors in speaking of their territorial and cultural heritage. These sentiments provide grounds of articulation between community members and Garifuna organizations. On the one hand, organizations shape perspectives in the community, providing a language of rights, models of struggle, and legal support. On the other hand, their production of Garifuna indigeneity does not simply derive from global discourses but is informed by the everyday experiences, memories, and practices of ordinary Garifuna. Whereas organizations paint an overwhelmingly positive picture of Garifuna indigeneity, Sambeños tend to offer a variety of positions on their past and culture, valorizing some traditions while critiquing others, affirming the way of life of their ancestors while hoping to transcend its perceived limitations.

These everyday negotiations are at the heart of this chapter. I argue that they are responses to the problems of making a living and "getting ahead" in the margins of the neoliberal economy that reflect the enduring symbolic oppositions between indigeneity and cosmopolitanism. I explore how current political economies driving transnational migration and tourism shape local evaluations of Garifuna culture and indigeneity. In so doing, I refuse a separation between "material conditions" and "symbolic practice". The political economies at work here are symbolic to their core. I title the chapter "political economies of difference" to highlight the importance of identity differentiations within structures of economic and political power. I am particularly interested in how Garifuna take up "culture" as an object of discourse and evaluation within conditions of neoliberal economic transformations (especially the tourist industry), transmigrant social relations, and reworked racial–cultural marginalization.

In the first part, I compare critiques of migration and consumerism produced by organizations with those I heard in Sambo Creek, arguing that local evaluations of transmigration in the community worry less over the loss of tradition than the fragmentation of social relations and class disparities among Garifuna. The point of this comparison is not to condemn cultural activism but to point to some of the obstacles it confronts in local sensibilities of social mobility and development. I then return to local discourses of culture as custom discussed in chapter 1. I examine how the tourist industry identifies value in Garifuna culture, ultimately appropriating that value in ways that produce frustration among Garifuna themselves. I argue that these dynamics produce contradictory effects, as Garifuna both reaffirm the integrity of their ethnic particularity and, as we saw in chapter 5, find alternative modes of self-assertion in the cosmopolitanism associated with transnationalism and Black America. In the final section, I analyze a local land struggle that mobilized widespread support among community members, particularly women, and articulated directly with OFRANEH and its politics of indigeneity. This struggle reveals that despite their refusal to identify solely as traditional subjects, Garifuna draw on indigeneity as a frame for asserting native claims to place. Ultimately, I discuss tensions between different modes of identity formation among Garifuna as a product of the contradictions and limitations of institutional multiculturalism and everyday racial–cultural discourse.

Activist Critiques of Migration and Consumerism

In chapters 3 and 4, we examined a politics of Black indigenism that positions Garifuna primarily as a people of African descent who bear the cultural–historical status of an indigenous people. We also saw how OFRANEH maintains a politics of indigeneity, whereas ODECO tends to position Garifuna within a transnational network of Afro-descendant organizations and movements. Nonetheless, both organizations represent Garifuna as a culturally unique, traditional people with a special relationship to the land whose existence is threatened by structural forces impinging on communities. Both organizations also critique the negative effects of Garifuna migration and consumerism within those communities. The president of ODECO, Celio Álvarez, argues:

> Remittances should complement the efforts made by the people here. The people should be producing, working, praying, making investments. But it is totally the opposite. Remittances put the people to sleep . . . waiting for the check. And the boys wearing Fubu . . . wearing Nike . . . everything in style. So remittances put the community to sleep, disarm the community, cut the community off from work, especially the most economically active part of the community, the youth. (CCARC, 4: 12–13)

ODECO points to other negative social and cultural consequences of migration, asserting that migration has led to an "increased polarization between those that receive dollars and those that do not" and that "immigrants have unconsciously been converted into dynamic agents of a growing process of acculturation."[3] OFRANEH also identifies the problem of acculturation, attributing it to U.S. imperialism.

> Unfortunately the influence of the massive communication media are leading to the incorporation of people into mass culture schemes that nourish a false concept of Honduranness and attack our spirituality. Our suspicions in the face of spiritual and cultural aggression are based in the poverty derived from imported cultural limits, where local cultures are diluted in a caricature of the dominant culture derived from the United States empire. (2002a, 16)

This perspective, consistent with OFRANEH's critical engagement with neoliberalism, links cultural "dilution" to the subordinate position of Honduras to U.S. mass culture and consumerism. In other accounts, the consumption of goods produced outside of Garifuna communities is taken as a sign of the dissolution of ethnic particularity. Armando Crisanto Meléndez once told a Garifuna audience:

> In various countries they have told us that of all the negros in Latin America only the Garifuna have their own language and that we

are good because we have and maintain our own culture. But I cannot understand why the youth of today does not want to speak Garifuna. . . . Another thing, we should be proud of our hair and not put chemicals in it to make it smooth, because the day will come when someone will ask them why they do that and they will not know how to answer. Do not sell your coconut water to buy Coca-Cola. (López Garcia 1993, 140)

Although these critiques take different forms, they all suggest that trans-national consumerism produces dependent, fractured communities and cultural impoverishment.

Curiously, these accounts take an ambiguous position on the consumption of goods associated with "Black America." Although ODECO's Celio Álvarez critiques the use of brand names such as Fubu and Nike, he does not explicitly associate them with U.S. African Americans. OFRANEH laments a cultural dilution resulting from imperialism yet remains silent on the racialized dimensions of popular engagements with U.S. mass culture. The play performed by Sambeños also avoids engaging these aspects of Garifuna transnationalism, as José the New Yorker does not dress in the hip-hop fashion typical of many male return migrants but as a cari-cature of a semiprofessional on vacation. In the didactic logic of the play, that choice of attire makes sense. Part of José the New Yorker's problem is that he rejects his blackness. Were he to appear dressed in the styles actu-ally recognized as fashionable—linked as they are to "Black America"—his initial rejection of his identity would become muddled. Dressed in the trappings of whiteness, his betrayal of racial and cultural identity is transparent.

If the play renders a stark opposition between community values and foreign contamination, we saw in chapter 5 how such simple opposi-tions cannot capture the complexity of lived engagements with the for-eign, particularly when the foreign is marked as Black. Consumption of things associated with "Black America" produces a visual representa-tion of Garifuna as Black cosmopolitan subjects who do not abandon an identity as Garifuna but draw on diasporic affiliations to assert racial and ethnic resistance and status. Recall that even hair-relaxing agents can be-come interpreted as products for elaborating the Black body rather than as products for whitening. Garifuna produce rather than deny blackness through their consumption practices. Garifuna organizations may avoid directly attacking consumption practices linked to blackness and Black America because those practices cannot easily be reduced to an abandonment of ethnic identity and because blackness and Garifunaness are themselves deeply intertwined in everyday consciousness.

Transmigration, Sociality, and Class in Sambo Creek

Sambeños I know offered their own critiques of transmigrants that differ in subtle but significant ways from those of activists. Most criticism was less concerned with the loss of tradition than with ruptures in sociality. In chapter 5, we saw how young men offered critical accounts of Garifuna who fell for the "vanity of the North American" and neglected their families in their zeal for acquiring the latest brands. Women were particularly critical of men for spending too much money on themselves. We also encountered local critiques of Garifuna who embraced the purported delinquency of the Black American and became involved in drugs and gangs. These figures were often depicted as "lost," severed from community and the mores of virtuous living. Older youth worried over the fate of the next generation, concerned that delinquency would only rise as economic opportunities remained limited and migration abroad became more difficult. They sometimes even echoed concerns expressed by parents and teachers (mestizo and Garifuna) that parental absence would create lost youth given to vice and crime. If these views echoed dominant stereotypes of failing Black families in the United States, they also suggested that "bad" influences from the United States contributed to the problem.

The figure of the arrogant transmigrant represents a different set of concerns. The migrant returning to visit Sambo Creek is esteemed for succeeding abroad and supporting family and community at home, representing a success story of social mobility. Yet he or she can come under critical scrutiny for neglecting to provide material support to relatives or failing to engage residents in everyday sociality. Transmigrants must make choices concerning who among their extended kin they give gifts and financial support; the excluded can interpret their neglect as assertions of superiority and ruptures in social relations.[4] A generalized critical image thus emerges of a type, a Garifuna who won't even acknowledge you when you pass them on the street. One particularly bitter young man, with no relatives abroad to help him, told me he hated the return migrants who wore gold chains and thought they were better than everyone else. The figure of the arrogant return migrant shadows the image of dependent Garifuna often critiqued by transmigrants: unmotivated people who sit at home, waiting for the check, relying on the "Garifuna welfare system" (England 2006, 166–69).

Many Garifuna I know said that Garifuna saw themselves as part of a large family. Out of familiarity and/or respect, they often use kinship terms to hail friends and sometimes strangers. Tyson related how that sense of family could be violated.

> There are some negros, especially those that have their little bit, whose life is more *solvente* (solvent, economically secure) that think they are indios. They will not be seen with negros, only indios. We call them "Black Spanish" because they think they are indios. They don't have any Black friends, just indios.

The subjects of this critique are not just transmigrants who live in the United States but professionals or wealthy Garifuna in Honduras who prefer to socialize among mestizos. They may appear Black but they betray their race. This portrait of inauthentic Garifuna is different from the one voiced by Mauricio, the director of the play who told me: "There are Garifuna that are not Garifuna. They only have the color but they don't speak the language, they don't practice the customs." Under a strict interpretation of those criteria, more than a few Sambeños would qualify as "Garifuna that are not Garifuna." Rather than employ a notion of authenticity based on linguistic and cultural retention, most residents evaluated Garifuna on the basis of their practices of sociality.

However, even the most sociable of return migrants can provoke considerable class anxiety, as I learned at a party thrown by Waldi, a twenty-five-year-old woman who returned home for a month's vacation. Waldi had left Honduras in the mid-1980s (when she was ten years old), joining her mother who had left shortly after her birth in the mid-1970s. She worked in a post office in Manhattan and had managed to get four weeks off to visit home with her two children. She liked Sambo Creek, where everything was relaxed and her kids could play in the yard without her having to worry about traffic. Gregarious with everyone, she hung out with the young men from the house where I lived, who remarked that she was different from many return migrants. Waldi shared the same image of herself:

> Some people when they come back they don't even pay attention to the people that are here. They just walk by ... I can't walk by you without saying "hi." That's just the kind of person I am. If I'm friends with you I want to speak to you wherever I see you. Why can I come here and then not speak to you? So this way everybody likes you because you're not the type of person that thinks she's all that.

A few nights before she left, Waldi held a party and invited everyone from our house. I came home in the evening from La Ceiba, and the boys from the house had already gone to the party. Doña Luz was home drinking a bit of *guifiti*—a concoction of rum and herbs used for medicinal and recreational purposes—that someone had brought from the party. She said she was thinking about dropping by, so I convinced her to come with me.

The party was small but in full swing. Although a few older men and women were present, most of the guests were in their twenties, chatting in small groups or dancing to dancehall reggae. The grandsons had dressed in their best baggy pants and branded T-shirts, as they did whenever they went out at night or made a trip to La Ceiba. Luz arrived barefoot and dressed in the clothes she had worn while washing laundry earlier in the day, a faded green dress once used for rituals such as funerals and wakes. Her grandsons were visibly uncomfortable, shot her disapproving glances, and muttered under their breath. We might have stayed for one drink and Luz decided to leave. We were chatting on the porch when her grandsons returned, and one of them reproached her: How could she come to the party "looking like that" around "people that have money"? I got angry, telling him he should show more respect for his grandmother. He looked chagrined and said more softly: "You know, the reputation of this family isn't so great." From his perspective, his grandmother not only violated codes of respectable public appearance by showing up barefoot, in shabby clothes, and a little tipsy but she also threatened to expose the vulnerable position of the household. The economic situation of the family was always in flux, contingent on the remittances Luz's daughter could send from New York. My presence helped the finances but it was temporary. In the time since my last visit, Luz had been forced to sell part of the sofa section to pay an overdue electric bill. Waldi may have been generous and humble, but she nonetheless lived "there" and "had money." She formed part of an incipient social class that could inspire admiration and envy among the status conscious; and while Waldi (and I) had the privilege of minimizing the meanings of class disparities between the North and South, Luz and her grandsons did not.

The story of Waldi's party exemplifies how transmigration contributes to class polarization. It also reveals an anxious recognition of the social distance between individuals in different parts of the Garifuna diaspora, which a shared consumption of cosmopolitan Black diasporic styles cannot fully close. The critiques I heard in Sambo Creek worry over that distance, but they do not offer the same kinds of structural analysis of immigration produced by activists, focusing instead on the behavior of transmigrants. This likely reflects the importance of transmigration to the political economy of the town and the predominance of the idea that the most likely route to social mobility lies in migration abroad. It is also likely that the hegemony of dominant development discourses, which emphasize greater linkages between the local community and global markets and individual agency over structural constraints, inhibits the embrace of structural critiques offered by organizations.[5] Local perspectives on transmigration nonetheless voice concerns about the fragmentation of communal sociality and solidarity also at the heart of activist critiques. As with the moral lesson generated by the play, critiques of the bad transmigrant admonish community members to not forget kin and community and to remain humble in a world rife with class distinctions overlain by geographical separation. That these critiques tend not to dwell on cultural authenticity may reflect the ambiguous value of Garifuna culture under contemporary structures of ethnoracial recognition and hierarchy.

The Elusive Value of Culture

Since I began research in Honduras in 1994, I have found discourses and images of Garifuna culture everywhere. The term "Garifuna" itself evokes images of a rural, tropical people with their own songs, dances, drums, traditions, foods, spirituality, and so on, no less among Garifuna themselves than among mestizos or foreigners. It is not just that Garifuna are understood as culturally distinct; they are represented as culture full, a people rich in traditions and customs inherited from the past, which endure in the present. State representatives, activists, anthropologists, human rights experts, tourist workers, and ordinary citizens all collude to some degree in representing Garifuna in terms of culture. In many cases, the idea of culture put to work here is not the twentieth-century, professional anthropological one of a (largely unconscious) symbolic system guiding thought and behavior but a notion of culture as a collection of customs and beliefs. Of course, various protagonists hold different understandings of culture, highlight distinct aspects of culture, and fight over its meanings in struggles over ethnoracial rights and hierarchies. However, the association of Garifuna with culture is ubiquitous.

Marked as culturally different and culture full, Garifuna I know often affirmed that difference to distinguish themselves from mestizos. Larissa, a woman in her early twenties, responded to an interview question concerning cultural differences between Mestizos and Garifuna by saying:

> We have culture, customs. They—I don't know if they have them. I don't know. They probably do. Because our culture is, there are customs. It is very different from theirs. We live what our ancestors left us, understand? They have not ceased yet. We still practice culture and customs. In contrast, among them, I'm not sure they practice customs because for them it is strange to see what we do. . . . They want to humiliate us because of what we are but nonetheless I'm proud of what I am.

Customs, traditions, and culture (the words tend to be used synonymously) refer to practices and beliefs viewed as distinctively Garifuna, such as the Garifuna language, musical and dance forms such as punta, certain foods, and productive practices, particularly fishing and the cultivation of yucca. Garifuna residents of Sambo Creek show pride in these customs and promote their preservation for future generations. They enjoy speaking the Garifuna language or attending rituals, deriving pleasure from the self-conscious perpetuation of traditions. They also emphasize the right to control land and resources as an integral component of the community inherited from the ancestors. In all these ways, local evocations of cultural ancestrality resonate with broader discourses of indigeneity.

However, as I argued in chapter 1, certain aspects of tradition and particular customs are also subject to negative evaluations. Sambeños can admire members of other communities for preserving the "purity" of language and traditions, yet they also associate such purity with the lack of economic resources, educational attainment, modern amenities, and consumer goods. The "traditional" productive activities of fishing, cultivation, and vending of fruit and baked goods are all associated with a relative lack of wealth and status compared to office work or wage labor abroad. Few young men and women I knew aspired to make their living through them.

Nevertheless, Garifuna customs acquire certain kinds of value, particularly in relation to tourism. The potential value of Garifuna and their culture for the tourist industry has been recognized for several decades but has taken on particular importance in the current era. The folklorization of Garifuna in the 1970s proceeded, in part, through state efforts to make Garifuna tourist attractions. The state multicultural, multiethnic policies and programs of the 1990s emerged not just at the urging of ethnic activists but of multilateral institutions that view culture as a form of capital, as a resource that can generate profit. In 1999, the president of the World Bank, James Wolfonson, asserted: "There are development dimensions of culture. Physical and expressive culture is an undervalued resource in developing countries. It can earn income, through tourism, crafts, and other cultural enterprises" (Yudice, 13). In practice, such valuations of culture engender contradictory effects for the "producers" of culture.

Local opportunities for earning income through culture were limited in Sambo Creek. A couple of Garifuna dance groups earned small amounts of money performing at town fairs in the region or other special events. During the Sambo Creek fair, which drew large numbers of visitors to the community, some local families sold "typical" food. There was one hotel and a couple of inexpensive restaurants that served locals and visitors alike. One restaurant built as a tourist destination—run by a man who had worked as a cook aboard a cruise ship—failed within a few years. The most popular destination for visitors was a large restaurant that specialized in fish and some Garifuna foods; it was owned by a well-off mestizo nicknamed Nissan (after the brand of car he drove) who developed real estate in the community and had a reputation as a scoundrel. With the exception of a family that made drums and other artisanal products, no one produced artifacts for sale in the tourist industry.[6]

Even in communities with a consistent tourist presence, most Garifuna find few opportunities to cash in on their culture. A study of attitudes toward culture and tourism in the community of Punta Gorda, located on the highly traveled island of Roatan, highlights local frustrations (Kirtsoglou and Theodossopoulos 2004). These Garifuna do not mind tourism; in fact, they want more of it. What they resent is how outsiders make money off them. For example, members of a local company that dances for tour groups argued that they were never paid enough for their efforts (147). More generally, Garifuna complained: "they are taking our culture away." When challenged by foreign social scientists to identify how that process worked, they argued that photographs of Garifuna appear in expensive books in fancy hotel gift shops, yet no Garifuna receive compensation. I heard similar contentions about a book I owned; the cover photograph depicts an old woman wearing a traditional headscarf. People said that she died in poverty and never received any money for the photograph that helped make the book. For a long time, I interpreted such accounts as a combination of justified resentment at the ways outsiders offer little in return for the production of knowledge about Garifuna and inflated expectations of the monetary rewards such knowledge production entails. I now understand them as a product of the gap between the intangible yet potent value of the *image* of Garifuna culture and the devaluation of the producers and performers of Garifuna culture, that is, Garifuna themselves. This is the gap historically produced by national appropriations of racial–cultural difference (Latin American indigenismo is the classic example), now key to tourist development. I illustrate this argument via an extended discussion of the position of Garifuna—as labor, culture, and image—within a new tourist complex located several kilometers from Sambo Creek.

The Palma Real Beach Resort and Casino was constructed in 2001 with capital from wealthy Honduran investors from Tegucigalpa. The tourist complex is designed to attract foreign tourists and Honduran day visitors. It contains a central hotel, bungalows, a swimming pool (with attached bar), snack bar, buffet-style restaurant, nightclub, tennis courts, and water park. In 2004, approximately thirty people from Sambo Creek, mostly Garifuna men in their twenties, worked in the hotel in service positions as porters, bartenders, waiters, cooks, and dishwashers. Several young Garifuna and mestiza women also worked there cleaning rooms. One Garifuna woman worked behind the snack bar, and two others earned small amounts of money braiding the hair of guests on the beach. The salaries earned by employees at the hotel were slightly better than the Honduran minimum wage and ranged from approximately 2,000 to 2,500 lempiras a month (~110–130 dollars), though the porters, waiters, and bartenders—positions given to men—earned tips. Most of the other employees were mestizos from La Ceiba or the nearby town of Jutiapa.

I spent a day at the Palma Real, arriving on the employee shuttle that came from La Ceiba and collected workers from Sambo Creek and Jutiapa.

We turned off at the road built exclusively for the tourist development, and I got off at the security gate to get clearance. After filling out some paperwork, the guards gave me a pass and told me to pay at another station. I walked past a sprawling water park and a series of private homes, realizing that the tourist complex doubled as a gated community. At another checkpoint, I paid 40 dollars for a day pass that allowed me access to most of the facilities and all the food and drink I dared consume. The hotel lobby was large and opulent, leading into the most popular part of the complex, a large pool area with a swim-up bar staffed by Sambeño men serving rum, beer, and piña coladas. The mostly Salvadoran and Honduran guests shuttled between the pool, bar, snack bar, and restaurant.

The "all-inclusive" model of tourism found at the Palma Real has become common in Caribbean tourist enterprises and reinforces the politics of spatial exclusion produced by the security regime and the isolation of the compound. The Palma Real is designed as a self-contained world that strictly regulates who can enter and that inhibits contact with members of any nearby communities who might sell goods and services to tourists.[7] Guests at the hotel have little contact with Sambo Creek, and Sambeños interact with guests as low-level hotel employees. The resort also offers snorkeling tours to the nearby cays (the Cayos Cochinos) that largely bypass local fishermen and inhabitants. It is no wonder that activists from OFRANEH and ODECO join critics questioning trickle-down theories of tourist development and condemn the all-inclusive model as offering little benefit to Garifuna communities.

The overall design of the Palma Real projects a rather generic, luxury beach resort tourism experience, reflected in the slogan "a touch of elegance in the Caribbean." However, some signs of local cultural particularity are present, and, not surprisingly, they call forth the image of Garifuna. The bar/disco is called "Guifiti" after the Garifuna beverage, and a drink is named "Sambo Creek." Every Wednesday—at least when enough guests are present—the Palma Real offers a "Typical (*Típico*) Garifuna Show" put on by a group of nine men and women from Sambo Creek. Two of Tyson's brothers, Wilson and Antonio, were musicians that formed part of the group. The group sang and danced to acoustic instrumentation (drums, conch shell, and maracas). Wilson called this type of group "cultural" to distinguish it from "commercial" groups that use electronic instruments. He and his brother had spent a couple of years in Mexico working for a group that could take both "cultural" and "commercial" forms. I would like to have seen the show, but it was cancelled that week because there weren't enough guests at the hotel.

On the way back to Sambo Creek, I asked several employees I knew how they liked working there. They complained a little about the low wages and labor discipline, noting that a friend had recently been fired for slacking off and pinching food and drink. "You can't screw around there." However, they appreciated the opportunity to interact with foreigners and, most importantly, were glad that they could work near home. A few days later, a different picture emerged when it came to the question of compensation for *cultural* labor.

The night before I left, a group of young men, including several resort employees, gathered around a bottle of rum at the house where Antonio and Wilson lived (their mother's home). As often happened on such occasions, the young men discussed their adventures abroad, sharing accounts of other places and "races." One fellow I did not know, sporting a Los Angeles Dodgers baseball jersey, opined that "Black skin" was the strongest skin, and others chimed in that negros were more physically powerful than other races, pointing to Antonio's thick physique. Elmer, who worked as a porter in the hotel, interrupted this account of the virtues of the Black body. He said that he had respect for other races, that he had mestizo friends in San Pedro Sula who would work eighteen hours straight, and he didn't know any Garifuna who would do that. Antonio countered that he wouldn't work like that unless "they pay me." Carlos, who managed the pool bar at the Palma Real, observed that Antonio and Wilson were not paid enough for their work as musicians in the group that performed at the Palma Real. Everyone, including Elmer, agreed. Wilson asserted: "Two hundred lempiras for six hours of work. It's not enough! They pay much more in Mexico and Belize." They compared wages in different countries for a moment, and the LA Dodger fellow said, "Look. It's not just anybody that can play music like us, with a rhythm so original, or who can dance like this," standing up and briefly demonstrating punta to the laughter of everyone. Somebody offered more soberly, "They don't know the value of this culture."

The value of culture is elusive. The critique voiced by these young men does not simply suggest that the Palma Real resort inadequately compensates the skilled labor of musicians but also that it undervalues the collective cultural knowledge and inheritance of Garifuna. The exploitation of cultural labor thus appears particularly egregious, even to young men who do not ply a trade in culture. Lying beyond that critique, I would suggest, is a sense that the Palma Real, and the Honduran tourism industry as a whole, appropriates the image of Garifuna to attract customers and differentiate Honduras from other possible destinations.

The rather modest, if crude, evocations of Garifuna culture found at a resort casting itself as a luxurious Caribbean destination take on greater significance when placed in the larger symbolic universe of Honduran tourist promotions. Almost any pamphlet or Web site produced by the Honduran Tourism Institute features images of Garifuna communities (emphasizing canoes and thatched houses) or Garifuna engaged in activities such as fishing or dancing. A recent initiative by the Honduran Tourism Institute bore the slogan, "Honduras: Nature's Laboratory, Culture's Library," drawing on a still vibrant equivalence between nature and (indigenous) culture to activate fantasies of enduring life ways in romantic environments. This program, initiated in the presidency of Ricardo Maduro (2002–2006), was called Scientific, Academic, Volunteer, and Educational (SAVE) Tourism. SAVE offers travelers "the opportunity to explore its authentic natural and cultural landscapes, and at the same time collaborate with local communities to *add value* to these natural and human resources (emphasis added)."[8]

The purported benefits for Hondurans include "strengthening of human resources, fostering pride among ethnic communities of their vibrant culture and traditions, more effective conservation of Honduras' rich natural heritage, and the generation of a lasting credibility for Honduras as a destination." The language of value here misdirects. The program posits that tourism "adds value" by ignoring how the tourist industry *extracts* value out of both nature and culture.

What is at stake here is not simply skewed representations of contemporary Garifuna but the appropriation of Garifuna culture and indigeneity to add value to Honduran tourism. Obvious examples include a tourist agency owned by non-Garifuna that calls itself "Garifuna Tours" and a company with a line of T-shirts depicting figures of Garifuna. The problem goes beyond any single enterprise that might be held accountable for violating intellectual property rights. The image of Garifuna as tourist attraction is produced by a host of actors (the state, the media, tourist books, travel Web sites, etc.) and circulates liberally in the public domain. It offers the promise of value for those with the means to capitalize on "nature" and "culture" and who, by and large, are not Garifuna but more powerful actors in the tourist economy. Tourism thus extracts value from Garifuna thrice over: exploiting their labor, undervaluing their culture, and expropriating their image.

This argument extends the critique of dominant models of (neoliberal) multiculturalism beyond a concern with efforts to manage ethnic activism to interrogate the uses and abuses of "culture" in the extraction of value. The effort to render culture as potential value in the market overstates the benefits accruing to the producers of culture while masking, but only partially, the various means through which value is extracted from them. Curious contradictions ensue. The inability of Garifuna to realize the value of their culture in the market produces frustration and reinforces their apprehension of racial and cultural discrimination; at the same time, the promotion of Garifuna as a tourist attraction contributes to a sense of their ethnic distinction in Honduras. Recall the comments of a transmigrant I quoted in the introduction to this book who, engaging me as a tourist, insisted that "Garifuna had the best culture of Honduras." During a more recent visit in 2004, a leading land activist in Sambo Creek expressed similar sentiments, asking rhetorically:

> Why do international organizations want to invest in Honduras? Why does the World Bank want to invest in Honduras? Because of our culture. Yes. Tourists who come here, do they want to go to Tegucigalpa? They come here and prefer to stay in a house of manaca and mud because it's cooler. And the government wants to not even give us one percent of our ancestral land? No.

The activist uses an image of Garifuna culture as tourist attraction to call attention to the injustices of the government's refusal to deliver community lands. In the movement that he helped instigate, notions of Garifuna particularity and indigeneity would play a key role in a struggle over land, which pitted private property against collective ancestrality.

Fighting for Ancestral Territory
How Sambeños and Their Allies Recovered a Plot of Land

During my extended fieldwork in the 1990s, there was little overt political–cultural activism in Sambo Creek. Mauricio from OFRANEH lived there for a while, but he did not organize a political movement, and he left when the AIDS campaign ended. Some community members were involved in struggles over resource and property rights in the Cayos Cochinos, but they were less active in protests than fishermen from other nearby communities. In fact, the head of the fisherman's association was accused of working in concert with the authorities for his own benefit. People I knew generally appreciated the efforts of ODECO and OFRANEH and sympathized with their projects of cultural retention, territorial reclamation, and combating racism. Yet in moments of cynicism, they critiqued activists along the lines they depicted politicians, tourist brokers, and anthropologists: as individuals who profited off the people they represented. Things changed at the turn of the millennium, as a group of Sambeños, working closely with OFRANEH, set out to recover lands in the name of the community, organizing mass land occupations in 2001 and 2002. I was not present during these events. The account I provide here is based on documents concerning the land conflict, the work of Keri Brondo (2006), and interviews with participants and state officials in 2004.

In 2001, Garifuna men and women from Sambo Creek formed a land defense committee led by a man in his early thirties nicknamed "Rasta" for his long dreadlocks. Rasta had spent over a decade in Belize and returned to a community that, despite receiving a communal title in 1997, was experiencing a severe land shortage and dramatic real estate inflation. The community patronato had deemed the land title inadequate when it was delivered, but it took the efforts of Rasta to catalyze a land reclamation project. The committee organized a community-wide effort to recuperate land acquired by outsiders, focusing on a large tract of land owned by the Castillo family from La Ceiba.

The history of this parcel's ownership testifies to the presence of powerful outsiders throughout the twentieth century. According to a report by the INA,[9] the land had passed hands from an independent banana company to a subsidiary of the SFCO in the 1920s. The banana company sold the land to a mestizo, who in the early 1950s turned it over to Habencio Fernandez (the police chief of La Ceiba during the Carías era) as payment for a debt. Sambeños remember this man as a tyrant who violently removed them from their yucca plots. Habencio Fernandez eventually sold the plot of approximately 32.25 manzanas (~55.8 acres) to another mestizo who in turn sold it to Miguel Angel Castillo, a lawyer and businessman, in the 1980s. Castillo acquired a contiguous, smaller plot of 8.53 manzanas (~14.75 acres) in 1988. According to Sambeños, at least some of this land had been acquired earlier from poor Garifuna who were forced to sell the land out of necessity (Brondo, 155).

The land, located in the heart of the community, was largely unused. Nominally a cattle ranch, it had acquired immense potential exchange value as real estate. In August 2001, the land defense committee organized a mass occupation of the territory, erecting living structures. The Castillo family quickly secured a court order against the "invaders" for the crime of "usurpation." A news report stated that 1,000 Garifuna were present (mestizos were also involved) when a large police contingent removed them by blows and tear gas.[10] Several women were injured, and a pregnant woman lost her baby. A number of leaders of the occupation were taken prisoner, and community residents blocked the highway in response. OFRANEH helped secure the freedom of the detained leaders and initiate an investigation of the property title by the INA.

The findings were curious. The Castillo family did have registered ownership of the property, but the plots had been mysteriously expanded to 50 manzanas from the 40.78 manzanas found in the two original titles. In other words, the Castillo family had appropriated almost ten manzanas beyond their titles. Despite these irregularities, the court ruled in favor of the Castillos.

Undeterred, the following year the land committee led an occupation of another, smaller plot of land owned by the Castillos in a rocky area on the southern side of the highway. Approximately eighty Sambeño families occupied this site in October and were evicted in mid-November.[11] The leader of the defense committee was arrested and targeted for prosecution. OFRANEH played a key role in defending his case, providing legal representation and mediation with the state Special Prosecutor for the Ethnic Groups, which also worked on the case. OFRANEH publicly denounced the "racist and arbitrary" execution of local justice and outlined the community's "dramatic history with regard to the loss of its ancestral territory" that had resulted in the current land crisis and reduction of its "functional habitat" (2002b). OFRANEH also worked with the INA to promote the community effort to reclaim ancestral territory. On the day that a judge in La Ceiba ordered the eviction of Sambeños from the disputed land (November 7), OFRANEH declared its intention to file a grievance against the Honduran state with the Inter-American Commission on Human Rights (Brondo, 164–65). A Garifuna organization in Boston with close ties to Sambo Creek also supported the struggle.

Sambeños and their allies leveraged a series of legal arguments in support of their claims. At one level, they located the struggle as an assertion of "ancestral" rights to land and territory historically violated by outsiders. OFRANEH was particularly adept at articulating the struggle within the frame of indigeneity. Activists emphasized the community's right to territory under ILO Convention 169 and previous, unfulfilled agreements that the government would regulate community lands. OFRANEH noted that the area in question fell under the "functional habitat" of Garifuna communities because it provided access to Sambo Creek's water source. Rasta made a similar argument in court, stressing that community members developed a land defense committee in part because they recognized that the ancestral possession of land extended far beyond the title given to the community in 1997.[12] These claims amounted to nearly ten times the land recognized in that title. The language of "ancestral territory" is not only closely affiliated with indigenous rights legal paradigm but also taps into social memories of the historical possession, use, and dispossession of land in Sambo Creek.

At another level, arguments in favor of the community highlighted contradictions in the existing land titles. Strategies for land recuperation did not rely solely on ancestral rights but focused on the irregularities in the documentation of ownership. As in the case of the first land plot the committee tried to recover, the second plot bought by the Castillos had mysteriously expanded from 12 manzanas to 13.34 manzanas. Moreover, the land fell within the same area as a collective "guarantee of possession" that the INA had provided Sambo Creek back in 1979. This fact suggested that the purchase of the land in question by the Castillo family, which occurred in 1987, was invalid. The committee had chosen a good target for reclamation.

Eventually, the INA resolved the dispute by purchasing from the Castillo family the smaller, less valuable plot of land occupied in the second wave of recuperations and delivering a collective property title to Sambo Creek. The government negotiated a resolution not simply because determined Sambeños had a compelling case but because OFRANEH brought that case to the Inter-American Court of Human Rights. Indeed, as Brondo (169) suggests, the land struggle represents an instance of activism coordinating across multiple scales, as local groups connected to the national work of OFRANEH, which in turn tapped into transnational indigenous activism, international human rights courts, and sympathetic state offices. Moreover, the struggle reveals how the language and discourse of indigeneity readily translated into local idioms. The "indigenous rights" model became grafted to Sambeño notions of ancestrality, of attachments to culture, place, and the legacies of ancestors, to produce a notion of "ancestral rights." In 1996 and 1997, I rarely heard people in Sambo Creek use the phrase "ancestral rights," though the sentiments associated with it were present. By 2004, the phrase was ubiquitous.

We should not overestimate the success this story represents as a vindication of collective territorial rights. After all, the struggle resulted in the community's acquisition of a plot of land that was roughly one-third the size of the land originally occupied by community members in 2001. Indeed, the titled land amounted to only a couple of manzanas more than the additional ten manzanas of land illegally appropriated by the Castillo family in the titles to the first plot. In addition, the state implicitly recognized the Castillos' private property rights by paying them for land. I heard reports that the government paid the Castillos the equivalent of 10,000 dollars for the land. The original, documented purchase price in 1987 was 425 lempiras (212.50 dollars).[13] The Castillo family clearly did well on their land investment. In the end, the government had hardly sent a message to the elite warning against land speculation in Garifuna communities. In fact, an INA official told me that the settlement did not set a precedent for future land purchases; even if the political will could be mustered, the state did not have the money to make such purchases, and multilateral institutions—the IDB, the World Bank—had little interest in providing funds toward that end.

I raise these issues not to minimize the efforts of those involved in the land struggle but to highlight the difficulties they confront when state and international institutions that recognize collective property, nonetheless, refuse to challenge private property. The struggle of the Sambeños, articulated in the language of collective, ancestral rights, was ultimately based on the lack of land access resulting from the land privatization of previous decades. In some respects, the struggle replayed the efforts of community members a generation earlier to reclaim land that had resulted in the creation of the neighborhood "Liberty." Their children faced anew an acute land shortage; but in their neoliberal world, property values had exploded beyond anything their parents could have imagined, and the public language of struggle would invoke not just poverty but ethnicity.

Larissa's Perspective

Having provided a bird's eye account of the struggle, I turn now to an account of the struggle by a participant named Larissa. Her perspective allows us to explore in a more personal light the dynamics of struggle for place, including its gendered dimensions. Larissa is a sister of Tyson, Wilson, and Antonio. When I first met her in 1994, she had recently given birth to a son, nicknamed "Gringo" because of his light skin tone. Her relationship with the father ended soon thereafter, and he did not provide much support. Larissa worked for a while in a maquiladora in San Pedro Sula but returned home to live with her parents due to the low pay, poor conditions, and distance from her son. A few years later, she had a second child with a Garifuna man from another community who came to live with his mother in Las Vegas. He sent her remittances, but when I talked to Larissa in 2004, she said that the support was less frequent and she worried he was with someone else. Lacking any family inheritance to set up her own household, her economic situation was tenuous. Larissa said she joined the land struggle in part because participants were allotted small plots, but she described her needs as shared by many others in the community, particularly young mothers.

We taped an interview one day on the porch of her mother's house while her kids played in the yard and her mother listened in the background. I asked her to tell me about the land struggle and her involvement in it, and she began rather formally: "Our struggle was that we who live in a Garifuna community, Sambo Creek, saw how many necessities that there were for us here." She identified Rasta as the catalyst sparking the movement:

> He saw how *gente extraña* (foreigners, outsiders) were profiting
> from our land and without us being able to defend one little piece
> of her. . . . One day he said, "We here are like a post, just watching
> people coming and going. Look how the people here abandon land
> on the beach that still belongs to the Garifuna ethnicity, the
> Garifuna race." So we also got to thinking that so many outsiders
> were profiting from our community because here in Sambo Creek
> tourists and people from other countries come here to know the
> origins of our community. And he said "Well, we have to come and
> fight for our land, to also be beneficiaries." So one night we decided
> to go there, "we're going to invade" no, well, we first said "invade"

but later we began to think that it was to *rescue* our lands. So that
was how he put out his hand and we, as natives of this community
and followers of him, said, "We have to do it because in this town
there are many houses together. If there's a fire over there, the
house next to it will burn too. If you throw water out of your door,
you're throwing water on the other person's house." So we saw that
we needed a piece of land to say: "If I have to throw water there I
won't harm anyone, because I have my little bit of land apart from
other houses." Because in this town, no. So that was how we realized the value of rescuing our lands.

Larissa's discourse reveals multiple layers of motivations behind the land
struggle. The first part of her account narrates how Rasta helped open eyes
to the exploitation of the community and its valuable land by outsiders.
She suggests a subtle shift in perspective in which community members
came to think of land actions not as invasions but as recuperations of
communal patrimony. The last part of her narrative renders the problem
of land shortage not just a question of economy and exploitation but also
an issue of sociality. In the current situation of overcrowding, your neighbor's problems become your problems, and the water you use to wash
your house dirties the house of your neighbor; a small plot of land is thus
required to live decently among fellow community members. From this
angle, the land recuperation struggle did not simply stem from an attachment to place but involved an effort to (re)make place into livable community. Ironically, in a time of land shortage and inflation, aspirations to
a little bit of privacy could only be realized via a struggle for communal
property.

Although she emphasized the importance of Rasta in sparking the
movement, Larissa also asserted that women predominated in the daily
activities of the land occupation, particularly women who, like herself,
were raising their children by themselves. They were willing to confront
the landlord and the police, because they had the greatest need and they
were the ones most concerned about the future of their children. Larissa
thus implicitly critiqued men in the community for not fulfilling their obligations as well as men and women of previous generations for selling
their land. In our conversation, I said that when I was there in the 1990s,
there was a strong memory of land loss to outsiders but no movement
like this one. She responded that at the time there were no men capable

of leading such a movement. She also related how their grandfathers and grandmothers had sold land for next to nothing, albeit often out of the necessity engendered by their poverty. Everything was cheaper in the past and, though everything belonged to the Garifuna, life was difficult, and people did not know the value of the land.

> It is sad to relinquish (*despojarse*) something that has been your life. But right now Mark, for us in the new generation it is not easy that we will sell a piece of land because we know how much the land costs now, what its value is. Before no one knew the value of a piece of land. The life of the ancestors was eating and drinking and they never prepared for a day like today. But us, yes, we think of the future of our children because you know that you as a mother have to leave an inheritance for your children and leave a bit of land where they can plant and eat. How many benefits the land brings us. The land leaves a lot of benefits for us and I think not just for us but for all humans, right?

Larissa, deeply respectful of Garifuna customs inherited from the ancestors, represents a negative side to their way of life, characterizing that life as living for the moment instead of thinking toward the future. However, she does so to highlight the consciousness of her own generation. Her comments echo a refrain I heard in previous visits: While in the past, Garifuna did not stand up to racial oppression, today Garifuna fight against those who would denigrate and exploit them. Although the land struggle was catalyzed by the land recovery committee that embraced an ancestral/indigenous rights framework, it was also grounded in social memories of displacement and forms of racial consciousness among Garifuna with no previous involvement in activism.

A comment on the participation of mestizos in the land struggle is in order here. The public claims to land produced by the land defense committee, OFRANEH, and their allies presented the struggle in terms of the recovery of ancestral land of a Garifuna community. Larissa and other Garifuna involved in the struggle did much the same. However, mestizos also participated in the struggle and were allotted access to plots of the communal land for their own use. Several Garifuna (and a mestizo involved in the struggle) told me that a number of mestizos participated in the first land occupation but did not participate in the second occupation;

Sisters, Sambo Creek, 2008. Photograph by the author.

thus, they did not acquire access to the land eventually recovered. Larissa also told me that the Castillo family had mestizo allies in the community who spied on the movement, singling out "Nissan" as an enemy of the community who saw his own designs for real estate development as potentially threatened by land activism. (During my visit, Nissan had just broken ground on a housing development that abutted the large tract under the control of Castillo.) Some of the racial tensions resulting from the struggle were evident, as several mestizos represented what had happened as an "invasion" of private property by opportunistic Garifuna.

Despite tensions between Garifuna and mestizo residents and the tendency to conflate Sambeño with Garifuna, the antagonists identified in the land struggle were elite mestizos (and foreigners) from outside the community.[14] The committee pursued land controlled by wealthy outsiders to the community rather than by poor mestizo residents of the community who, like Garifuna, had little access to land. At the end of our interview, Larissa insisted that the land struggle was not over, implicitly identifying a class position shared by the poorer Garifuna and mestizos in the community as the basis for future unity: "I don't think the fight will stop here. Every day the inhabitants are becoming more aware in our community. We want a future in which our children have a place to live. Negro or blanco, this is what we want."

Larissa's perspective brings out nuances to the land struggle and local engagements with indigeneity in Sambo Creek. Participants in the struggle embraced their ancestral rights not so much to revive the way of life of the ancestors as to create livable, dignified conditions in an era of remittance dependence and land inflation. Although a number of residents had planted some yucca, most of the rocky area is destined for the construction of homes. Perhaps if the land recuperation movement succeeds in acquiring more communal land, then a process of agricultural revitalization can take place. Any such revitalization project will, however, have to confront and refigure dominant associations of agriculture with some of the negative associations of subsistence production and the life of the ancestors, namely poverty and "backwardness," without falling into a romanticized view of past cultural autonomy that glosses over the subordinate position of Garifuna within ethnoracial hierarchies.

The land struggle also allows us to reflect for a moment on the complexities of indigeneity as politics. Critics of indigenism decry the essentialism of claims to indigenous status and the exclusions in nativist claims to territory. Kuper, for example, argues that "Wherever special land and hunting rights have been extended to so-called indigenous peoples, local ethnic frictions have been exacerbated" (395). The efforts of Sambeños to reclaim land as the patrimony of a Garifuna community certainly have the potential to pit mestizos and Garifuna against one another as distinct groups, a potential feared by some mestizo residents (Brondo 2006). But in practice, these politics have left open the possibility of mestizo participation in the struggle by focusing on wealthy outsiders.[15] That possibility suggests that indigeneity need not practice ethnic exclusivity but can mobilize claims to place and peoplehood that benefit the most marginalized sectors of society across ethnoracial lines. At a broader level, the Black indigenism practiced by OFRANEH involves an anti-imperialist antineoliberal politics that can link to labor, peasant, environmental, feminist, and other projects designed to imagine a new Honduran future. As testimony to these possibilities, I would note that the first person I interviewed about the land struggle had blisters on her face that were the product of her participation in a mass protest called the "March of Life" coordinated by a block of popular organizations protesting environmental destruction and neoliberalism.

Finally, Larissa's perspective also reveals gendered dimensions to the struggle. As Brondo argues, the predominance of women in the efforts to recuperate land reflects how the privatization of land disproportionately affects women, who typically inherit land along matrilineal lines. It also reflects the precarious economic position of young mothers living in Sambo Creek—especially those who cannot count on consistent support from the fathers of their children or other relatives—who face gender discrimination in the labor market. Land provides a means of subsistence and a resource for the future crucial to the well-being of women and the children they are charged with rearing. It is tempting to read the predominance of women in the land struggle as a reflection of their greater attachment to tradition than men, who, after all, provide some of the stronger critiques of custom. Within discourses of cultural preservation, women are often positioned as the ultimate guardians of tradition. However, as England (1998) argues, that responsibility is also a burden that men can leverage to keep women "in place" and that women can reinterpret in critiques of men. Moreover, women such as Larissa may affirm the integrity of customs yet also distance themselves from the lives of the ancestors, viewing agricultural production as a secondary option behind office work or migration abroad. Larissa suggests that women were at the front ranks of the land struggle not simply because of an abstract attachment to tradition but also because of their economic necessities, desire for a dignified home, and commitment to place. Residents recognize that without land there is no possibility of a secure future for Garifuna families or communities. Although the main protagonists in the struggle were young women, virtually every Garifuna I knew in the community supported it.

Conclusion

During the mid- to late 1990s, the most popular musical group in Sambo Creek was a band called "Garifuna Kids." They were one of many contemporary groups across the Garifuna diaspora that fused traditional Garifuna rhythms with electronic instrumentation and musical influences from other styles such as reggae, soca, salsa, and rap.[16] The members of Garifuna Kids lived in New York but hailed from Honduras, Belize, and Guatemala. They combined a wide array of influences into their music and actively promoted pride in Garifuna language and traditions, highlighting the historical connections of Garifuna to Africa. At the same time, they dressed in the latest hip-hop styles from New York and performed a Black masculinity "stylistically similar to the posturing associated with African American Hip-Hop or Jamaican Dancehall" (Perry, 64). Band members themselves view their music as inspiring Garifuna to both "carry tradition" and to keep adapting and advancing with the times (94). The popularity of the band in Sambo Creek across generation and gender stemmed in no small measure from the group's ability to simultaneously perform blackness, tradition, and modernity. Garifuna Kids perhaps represented the ideal that these features of Garifuna identity can coexist together, that Garifuna can embrace their ancestrality and move forward in a changing world.[17]

In some respects, the material presented in this chapter and other parts of the book affirm that ideal by revealing the coexistence of multiple strands of identity formation in a Garifuna community. We have seen how Garifuna embrace an affiliation with the African diaspora, representing their own forms of Black cosmopolitanism via "Black America," *and* how they affirm the value of customs particular to the Garifuna. We have seen how community members view transmigration as a key to economic survival and social mobility *and* how they mobilized a land recuperation initiative articulated in the language of indigeneity and ancestral rights. Garifuna, understanding and representing themselves as Black, connect with the symbolic centers of Black cosmopolitanism *and* figure themselves as authentic natives who, although bearers of an African-derived culture, are firmly rooted in Central America.

Ultimately, however, this chapter highlights significant gaps and tensions between different trajectories of identity formation. Activists critique the consumption of foreign goods—central to practices of self-representation as Black and cosmopolitan—as acculturation. Conversely, the endurance of a distinct, traditional Garifuna culture promoted by activists is a subject of ambivalent evaluation by Garifuna in Sambo Creek. Such tensions do not simply exist between activist projects and ordinary subjects; they exist within the community, even within individuals. Sambeños embrace transmigration as crucial to economic survival and social mobility but express anxieties over the class discriminations it implicates. Discourses of Black indigenism that affirm cultural preservation and ethnic rights resonate widely in the community; yet the way of life of the ancestors can be interpreted as outmoded. Acknowledging these tensions means refusing to picture Garifuna in terms of a seamless cultural hybridity between modernity and tradition and indigeneity and cosmopolitanism.

Tensions and gaps between different modes of Garifuna identity formation reflect political economies of difference inherited from the past, which have only been partially reworked in the contemporary era of multicultural recognition. Throughout this book, I have emphasized the endurance of dominant representations in Honduras that render Garifuna not just as racially other but as culturally inferior to mestizos and other people ideologically identified as modern. At their worst, these representations present Garifuna as primitive and backward. Garifuna challenge such assertions, but the hierarchy between modernity and tradition remains potent in their self-understandings as a people, reflected in common sense notions of class and status that implicate race and culture in efforts to overcome subordination. Widespread preferences for cinderblock houses over manaca homes or for office work over subsistence production implicate more than just desires for material mobility; they involve notions of ethnoracial advancement from the life of the ancestors. Likewise, doubts concerning the utility of learning the Garifuna language or critique of superstition imbricate class and culture. Material mobility cannot easily be divorced from cultural evaluation, despite the promotion of Garifuna culture within activism and the recognition of Garifuna within state multiculturalism.

The new dimensions of political economies of difference that scholars call neoliberal multiculturalism produce diverse, even contradictory, effects. On the one hand, the valorization of Garifuna culture within multiculturalism incites renewed identifications with ethnic particularity and pride in Garifuna customs. Multicultural recognition also opens spaces for political action. As we saw in the case of the land struggle—and more generally in the politics of OFRANEH—Garifuna not only occupy those spaces but also attempt to push their limits by contesting the legitimacy of the private property titles of powerful outsiders. This reminds us that the space between neoliberalism and multiculturalism should be interpreted not as a relation of simple congruence but as a site of contestation.

On the other hand, the valorization of Garifuna culture within neoliberal versions of multiculturalism promises more than it delivers. We see this dynamic at work not only in the recalcitrance of the state in negotiating the scope and implementation of cultural rights but also in development projects, especially tourism, where the extraction of value from Garifuna exceeds the material benefits Garifuna can currently realize. The frustrations that ensue—"they don't know the value of our culture"—highlight the ongoing devaluation of Garifuna culture and subordinate position of Garifuna within structures of power and discrimination. Institutional multicultural recognition remains at a remove from the everyday difficulties of making a living in the neoliberal economy, and the message of cultural valorization continues to value Garifuna primarily as a folkloric attraction. The normalization of the mestizo subject as unmarked "Honduran" remains intact, as does a "harmonious racism" in everyday life that denigrates Garifuna as Blacks with a backward culture. Under these conditions, many Garifuna do not want to be reduced to a folkloric subject of tradition. As a result, the very source of legitimacy in institutional politics—the endurance of a distinctive, traditional Garifuna culture—becomes subject to ambivalent evaluations, and Garifuna turn outward to other dimensions of diasporic blackness to remake their standing at home.

Conclusion

As a subject of anthropological study, Garifuna have always represented a fascinating anomaly within scholarly and popular paradigms for understanding race and culture in the Americas. As the Belizean Garifuna anthropologist Joseph Palacio (2000) puts it:

> Everyone thinks that they are so strange they need to be explained. Here are some reasons. They are not a plantation derived creole culture, although they live in the Caribbean sub-region. They did not originate from slavery but more so in resistance to the slavery of both Africans and Native Americans. They did not originate in Central America but are found there. They have black skins but are mixed both biologically and culturally. So the riddle keeps coming back—what are they? (1)

I began the project resulting in this book from a simple observation. Numerous anthropologists had attempted to answer some version of the question "What (or who) are the Garifuna?" through analysis of their origins, history, and culture. But with a few, partial exceptions, they did not inquire into how different Garifuna understood and represented their own identities, particularly in relation to the nation-states where they lived. I thus undertook a project to explore what Garifuna made of themselves within Honduras, where the largest population lived.

The contingencies of my fieldwork and intellectual training—informed by critical analysis of the racial exclusions of nationalism, an attention to transnationalism and diasporic identifications, and the premise that all identity formations are relational, articulated within fields of power—led me to focus on the politics of Garifuna organizations and everyday struggles over place, identity, and racism in a Garifuna community. I was struck early on by apparent discrepancies between representations of Garifuna as a traditional people and the self-conscious imitation of "Black America" among youth, especially young men. Given that individual Garifuna could engage in both forms of representation, the differences between them could not simply be reduced to camps of distinct subjects—say "traditionalists" vs. "modernists" or "indigenists" vs. "Africanists." Rather, understanding Garifuna identity formation required attending to different trajectories of identity production that culturally–historically constituted subjects might take up in different moments, contexts, and struggles over being and belonging. The central contribution of this book thus lies in its efforts to understand the generation and practice of different modes of identity formation and the relations between them. In the final pages, I highlight a few lessons of this inquiry for analysis of race, culture, and power and for evaluations of struggles articulated through assertions of racial and cultural "difference."

One of the key contributions involves rethinking the dichotomy between indigenous and Black subjects in the Americas. In a review essay on "Afro-Latinos," Peter Wade discusses land struggles in Northeastern Brazil—where communities that seemed to be "generically mestizo and peasant" have asserted identities as Black or indigenous communities—to suggest that emerging practices and movements unsettle simple, permanent distinctions between indigenous, Black, and mestizo identities (2006, 113; see French 2009).[1] He also notes that in Brazil "one community cannot be officially be black and indigenous at the same time—and in that sense the distinction between indigenous and black is maintained" (2006, 113). In the case of Honduras, I have argued that Garifuna are, in a crucial sense, considered Black and indigenous at the same time. As the Special Prosecutor for Ethnic Groups and Cultural Patrimony Eduardo Villanueva once noted, Garifuna should be considered "indigenous" under international norms, particularly ILO Convention 169, because they maintain cultural differences from the majority population and were present in Honduran territory before the consolidation of state boundaries (Anderson and England 2004, 280–81). In so far as indigenous refers to a cultural–historical condition rather than an ethnoracial category (Indian), some people who self-identify as Blacks can also be recognized as "indigenous." Indigenous and Black do not have to describe discrete subjects but can refer to potentially overlapping subject positions.

Garifuna politics does not provide a ready-made model that other groups could easily adopt. Rather, its importance lies in the spaces it opens for questioning the use of blackness to deny subjects a "native" status. Racialized subjects should not be forced to choose between Black and indigenous identities and politics. Of course, structures of recognition and racial distinctions that presume the dichotomy often lead them to do so. At a workshop in 2003, Celio Álvarez of ODECO responded to a question I raised concerning indigenous rights and Garifuna by saying that while ILO Convention 169 was an important political tool, Garifuna would never really be accepted as indigenous, pointing to the skin on his arm. His organization was poised to promote and take advantage of increased attention to the category of "Afro-descendants" by state agencies and multilateral institutions, to pursue political agendas centered around racial discrimination. Indeed, throughout the region Afro-descendants have become visible as distinctive subjects in ways that may allow them to pursue politics beyond the "shadow of the Indian" (Walsh and García, 319), beyond rural communities and the identification of ethnic difference with an indigenous subject. These are important developments that open new possibilities for Black agency in Latin America, but, if Garifuna organizations are at all representative, we should not jump to the conclusion that they will, or should, supersede political projects that engage indigeneity. Garifuna initially achieved recognition as a collective subject via a politics of indigeneity that incorporated blackness and thus interrupted absolute distinctions between them. That politics continues to provide a crucial frame for, among other things, defending Garifuna communities from land and resource expropriation, producing cross-ethnic dialogue and alliances across racial lines, and articulating critiques of neoliberal capitalism, state multiculturalism, and institutional participation that interrupt elite projects. As the Afro-descendant subject receives recognition, indigeneity remains one of the few political resources available for making demands and mobilizing struggles.

Disrupting the Black–indigenous dichotomy does not dismantle the historically constituted distinctions between them that continue to make a difference. But refusing to reify the dichotomy allows us to imagine articulations between them and brings to light dimensions of subject formation that are ignored if we confine studies of blackness to analysis of race or reproduce assumptions that New World Blacks can never be "true" natives. In a broad sense, the concept of indigeneity highlights commitments to place as the site of alternative ways of being in the world, to refusals to accept displacement, and to the reproduction of an ancestral identity. In this book I have shown that not only activists but also "ordinary" Garifuna embrace these commitments, albeit often with ambivalence and in conjunction with other aspirations and affiliations. As a traveling political frame, indigeneity provides a language to render these commitments as claims and rights via notions of peoplehood, territoriality, cosmovisions, customary law, and so on. Elsewhere in Latin America, Blacks have voiced similar concerns and drawn on the conceptual tool kit of indigeneity as a language of political struggle. That most states reproduce a Black–indigenous dichotomy and thereby qualify the recognition of Black collective "difference" and rights suggests that indigeneity may contain progressive possibilities that should not be dismissed or foreclosed.

In addition to opening up the relation between blackness and indigeneity in the Americas, this book also intervenes in discussions of multiculturalism. Critical analysis points to the ways in which multiculturalism involves regimes of governance that arbitrate difference, deciding what types of subjects qualify for "recognition" (Hooker 2005), delineating lines between acceptable and unacceptable forms of politics (Hale 2002, 2005, 2006), and legitimate and repugnant forms of cultural difference (Povinelli 2002). Elizabeth Povinelli argues that multicultural recognition does not simply arbitrate preconstituted difference but incites subjects to embrace and perform particular modes of difference, namely as authentic, traditional, cultural subjects. She draws on research among indigenous Australians to suggest a broad shift between "postcolonial" and "multicultural" modes of power. In the former, regimes of governance incite subjects to identify with the colonizer, producing splits in subjectivity famously diagnosed by Fanon (1967) in *Black Skin/White Masks*.

> . . . multicultural domination seems to work, in contrast, by inspiring subaltern and minority subjects to identify with the impossible object of an authentic self-identity; in the case of indigenous Australians, a domesticated non-conflictual "traditional" form of sociality and inter(subjectivity). As the nation stretches out its hands to ancient Aboriginal laws (as long as they are not "repugnant"), indigenous subjects are called on to perform an authentic difference in exchange for the good feelings of the nation and the reparative legislation of the state. But this call does not simply produce good theater, rather it inspires impossible desires: to be this impossible object and to transport its ancient prenational meanings and practices to the present in *whatever* language and moral framework prevails *at the time of enunciation*. (Povinelli, 6)

In Povinelli's diagnosis of multicultural domination, the subaltern is invited to speak but only in codes of an acceptable, authentic, traditional difference that displace histories of social violence. Moreover, multiculturalism incites the subaltern subject to identify with the "impossible object" of a collective self that must attempt to prove its legitimacy while denying present political or material interests.

Although I sympathize with the spirit of this critique, I also find it important to acknowledge the ways in which social subjects refuse the limits imposed on them by institutional "recognition." Multicultural recognition objectifies and values Garifuna as bearers of a distinctive, non-Western, traditional culture, occluding processes of displacement and discrimination that have informed the making of Garifuna culture and identity in Honduras. Garifuna organizations produce their own versions of authentic cultural difference, selecting from the range of existing discourses and practices of what it means to be Garifuna. Nonetheless, they also attempt to stretch the limits of institutional multiculturalism. On the one hand, ODECO pursues anti-discrimination legislation to confront denials of racism and address a social reality only partially addressed by the rural-dominated paradigm of cultural rights. On the other hand, OFRANEH questions the political limits of institutional multiculturalism by struggling against the neoliberal assumptions and policies that accompany it. Multiculturalism is a site of struggle rather than inevitable defeats.

The stories I have told of everyday Garifuna discourses and practices of identity formation complicate assessments of the subjective incitements and objectifying character of multicultural recognition in a different fashion. Objectified subjects may both embrace their objectification as authentic, traditional subjects yet also refuse that objectification by practicing other modes of identity formation. In chapters 2 and 6, I highlighted how Garifuna express ambivalence about tradition, subsistence production, and the way of life of the ancestors, saturated with the signs of poverty and the stigma of being backward. From the vantage of many Sambeños, the "pure," "authentic" Garifuna subject, the "Garifuna Garifuna," lives elsewhere, out there at the back of beyond, an object of both admiration and pity but not complete emulation or identification. These associations can, of course, be read in terms of (partial) acceptance of dominant standards of prosperity, status, and modernity established long before institutional multiculturalism came into being. The incitements of multiculturalism to identify as a traditional subject thus run up against other codes of class and status differentiation. Moreover, while multicultural recognition provokes identifications with discrete cultural difference, the limited ability of Garifuna to realize the cultural value ascribed to them in local political–economic formations produces frustration and reaffirms a desire to look elsewhere to affirm and perform a distinctive sense of self. Garifuna engage in practices of Black diasporic identification as cosmopolitan "others" in part to subvert an image of the collective Garifuna subject as backward and poor, confined to tradition. In a sense, the failures of multicultural recognition to produce either equal or autonomous subjects ensure that subjects will not be wholly defined by it.

These points lead me to a final set of observations concerning Garifuna activisms and everyday practices. In this book, I have argued that different trajectories of identity formation respond to different facets of racial–cultural oppression. On the one hand, an emphasis on the particular cultural traditions and rooted presence of Garifuna provides a means to respond to land and resource theft, community displacement, and racial–cultural marginalization, attempting to reverse negative evaluations of cultural difference and take advantage of the possibilities opened up by "multicultural recognition." On the other hand, the production and performance of Black cosmopolitanism via engagements with Black America respond to modes of racial discrimination that project poverty, backwardness, and primitivity on to Garifuna as cultural and racial others. Of course, different types of self-representation often come together. But rather than simply revel in the hybridity and multiplicity of identity practices, I have suggested that we examine the tensions between them to understand the ongoing dilemmas of racialized subject formation.

Taking this approach can, I hope, provide those engaged in "identity politics" with more nuanced understandings of the identity practices of people they strive to represent and mobilize. As discussed in chapter 6, Garifuna activists from OFRANEH and ODECO tend to critique the negative effects of consumerism and immigration, without explicitly addressing the racial meanings encoded in transnationalism and consumption. They thus highlight community dependence on remittances, class distinctions produced by differential access to dollars, and the dilution of cultural particularity. What they miss—or at least fail to represent—is the ways in which other Garifuna find racial meanings, including resistance, in transnational consumption. These involve, for example, performances of an aggressive Black masculinity that assert a refusal to submit to everyday racial insults; assertions of the rising class status of Garifuna (vis-à-vis mestizos and others) indexed in the display of goods—"we feel higher up when we wear brand names"; affirmations of participation in modernity; and a refusal to accept the implied constraints of tradition. In these ways, Garifuna engage in diasporic practices to, as Gilroy puts it, "escape the constraints of ethnic or national particularity" (1992, 19).

My point here is not to celebrate a "diasporic subject" or "diasporic consciousness" as antidotes to the politics of ethnic particularity. The diasporic practices here, like most forms of resistance, subvert some elements of power relations while reproducing others. Indeed, Garifuna tap into the power of "Black America" in ways that assert Black cosmopolitanism yet implicitly affirm American hegemony. Conversely, the most direct challenges to U.S. imperialism from Garifuna arise from a politics of particularity. The point, rather, is that Garifuna engage in practices that do not conform readily to the image of a traditional subject yet nonetheless involve forms of racial resistance and consciousness.

Activist projects might broaden their appeal in Garifuna communities by recognizing and confronting the deep associations between racial discrimination, class status, and anxieties over the "backward" connotations of Garifuna ancestrality. Rather than simply condemn consumerism, they might draw on antiracist meanings associated with consumer practices to draw connections between racism and the structural forces impinging on Garifuna at home and abroad, beyond the mestizo–Black dichotomy. They might, say, take the opportunity of the Sean Jean scandal to explore the contradictions between labor exploitation in Honduras and everyday struggles around blackness implicated in the corporate product. Today, as in the past, transnational relations, concerns over social status and mobility, and consumer desires are as much a part of "Garifuna culture" as subsistence production or speaking the Garifuna language. Ultimately, appeals to the authentic, traditional Garifuna subject can only go so far in addressing the contradictions and dilemmas facing Garifuna as they navigate their position as racialized others located both at the geographic margins and centers of global hierarchies. Rather than dismiss mass-mediated cultural forms as threats to cultural integrity, activisms might find in them resources for mobilizing popular consciousness of racial inequality and injustice.

I will end with a final anecdote on ethnoracial consciousness and mass-mediated productions of blackness during a visit to Sambo Creek in 1999, less than a year after Hurricane Mitch and before the emergence of the land recuperation efforts. The house where I stayed had been refurbished by money sent from Luz's daughter, who received an insurance settlement from a car accident. It now had tiled floors, indoor plumbing, and an electric stove, but the household still depended on the ebb and flow of finances from far away. One Saturday night I was out in town with a couple of the grandsons, passing the time playing dominoes. They were anxious we return home by 9:00 P.M. to watch a Brazilian-made and Spanish-dubbed *telenovela* (soap opera) called *Xica de Silva*. Luz was a devoted viewer of telenovelas, but her grandsons rarely took much interest in them; their insistence that we watch this one made me curious.

In the tradition of telenovelas, the plot revolved around a once-poor woman precariously positioned at the upper echelons of the social order. In the case of *Xica de Silva*, the setting is colonial Brazil and the heroine Xica is a light-skinned child of a slave and she has married a white provincial governor. In the episode we watched, Xica is accused of killing a white man through witchcraft. Her husband, the white governor, appears powerless to prevent her conviction and hanging by the white judge and his accomplices, who have obviously prejudged the case. Several generations of Garifuna men and women crowded around the television set, caught up in different ways in the scenes that unfolded. Luz cried out several times to sympathize with Xica's slave mother, locked up in chains as an accomplice to the crime. Outside of the provincial capital where the trial is taking place, there exists a *quilombo*, a fortified community of maroons (escaped slaves and their descendants) fighting against the colonial order. When the scene shifted to the quilombo, a nephew of Luz visiting from another community grabbed the small made-for-tourists drum Luz had bought to display on her shelves. He beat out a quick rhythm and announced approvingly: "These people are heavy man!" When the trial finally arrived, everyone shifted nervously, then cried out in anger and pity when the judge tortured a slave to extract false testimony against Xica. All appeared lost when a white gentleman stepped forward to absolve Xica and identify the real culprit and witch, a crazed white woman. The room erupted in joy, as if the Honduran soccer team had just qualified for the World Cup.

Whatever problematic ideological messages the telenovela contains— for example, its easy contrast between good and bad whites, its uncritical linkage between Xica's relative whiteness and her social mobility, and its idealization of interracial sexual relations and implicit affirmation of racial democracy—the Garifuna in the room found it compelling drama. It spoke to their sense of their past both as a people struggling to remain free from the domination of others and as members of a group subject to subordination. *Xica* told a story of racial suffering and Black redemption. The intensity of the emotions in that room suggests that projects of autonomy and liberation should attempt to engage rather than bemoan the force of mass-mediated culture in the lives of those struggling in their own ways for recognition and dignity.

Acknowledgments

This book has been too long in the making to acknowledge everyone who contributed to it. The greatest thanks goes to the Hondurans—Garifuna and non-Garifuna—who have made my research possible and pleasurable. Their willingness to share their perspectives and pains and their stories and friendship across the vexed borders of race, culture, and nation-states, has created a debt I can never repay. Out of an obligation to maintain their privacy, I will not mention them by name. A particular heartfelt thanks goes out to the extended family anchored by the woman I call Doña Luz. Activists within the Garifuna organizations Organización Fraterna Negra Hondureña (OFRANEH), many of whom have suffered repression, and Organizacíon de Desarollo Étnico Comunitario (ODECO) merit a special thanks for allowing me to follow their struggles; I hope that at least some of their keen insights into racial and cultural politics inform this work.

Other Honduran public figures I would like to thank include Xiomara Cacho, Antonio Canelas, Yani del Cid, Andres Pavón Murillo, Raul Lobo, Livio Martínez Lalin, Carlos Palacio, and Fernando Cruz Sandoval. Historian Darío Euraque has been a consistent source of guidance and resources over the years; his insistence that the complexities of Honduran realities should succumb neither to academic trends nor to ethnographic caricature continues to ring in my ears.

Research for this book was supported by a National Science Foundation Fellowship for Continuing Graduate Research, an Institute of International Education Fulbright Grant for Research Abroad, and a Divisional Research Award, Division of Social Sciences, University of California, Santa Cruz (UCSC). Thanks to Jason Weidemann, Danielle Kasprzak, and Mike Stoffel for guiding the book smoothly through publication. Aisha Khan, Bettina Ng'weno, and Peter Wade provided incisive comments that clarified and refined the arguments in the book. Portions of chapter 3 develop arguments similar to those found in the article "When Afro Becomes (like) Indigenous: Garifuna and Afro-Indigenous Politics in Honduras," published by the *Journal of Latin American and Caribbean Anthropology* (2007, 12.2). I thank Jean Rahier for close readings of this text, which inform my analysis in this book. Over many years, Sarah England has generously shared with me her research on and insights into Garifuna activism and transnationalism. More recently, I have also learned much from Keri Brondo and her work on Garifuna identity formation and land struggles.

This project began its life as my dissertation at the University of Texas (UT) at Austin. My eclectic committee—Edmund T. Gordon, Charles R. Hale, Katie Stewart, James Brow, Pauline Turner Strong, and Darío Euraque—provided unflagging support and challenging visions of what anthropology can be. Postgraduation, Ted and Charlie provided me with the opportunity to return to Honduras to study indigenous and black activism; their practice of activist anthropology remains critical to my scholarship. Other friends and colleagues from UT have supported this work in various ways. I can mention only a few: Robert Adams, Jennifer Goett, Peggy Lott, Rachel Meyer, Jessica Montalvo, Kathleen Murphy, Marc Perry, Brandt Peterson, Ken Price, and Paige Warren. Rachel Chance and Kate Knight were my staunchest critics and best friends.

Colleagues and students at UCSC have helped push my thinking in new directions while sustaining me through the pressures of the academy. I could not ask for a better home than that provided by the faculty, staff, and students of the Anthropology Department. I will not name them all, but Lisa Rofel and Anna Tsing deserve special thanks for their insightful readings of large chunks of the manuscript. I have learned much from the graduate students in the department and give special thanks to Kim Cameron-Domínguez, Roosbelinda Cardenas, and William Girard for research assistance. Juan Mejia made the maps. A faculty reading group—Dean Mathiowetz, Vanita Seth, Megan Thomas, Dan Vukovich—provided detailed feedback on the history chapter. I also give thanks to other colleagues at UCSC—James Clifford, Jonathan Fox, Dana Frank, Kimberly Lau, David Marriott, Lourdes Martínez-Echazábal, Radhika Mongia, and Juan Poblete—for conversations that have helped me articulate the broader significance of my work. Friend and colleague Vanita Seth provided dinner parties, pub nights, intellectual exchange, and unwavering support. My partner Megan Thomas made it all worthwhile, suffering the minutiae of my obsessions while sharing the joys and frustrations of writing. Thanks also to my family, especially my father Kenneth, who made it possible while always encouraging me to find my own way. My mother Dorothy died of cancer while I was in the field. The woman I call Doña Luz died of the same affliction a few years later. I dedicate this work to them.

Notes

Introduction

1. For secondary accounts of Garifuna history on St. Vincent, see: Boucher (1992), Craton (1982, 1997), Gonzalez (1988), Gullick (1976), Johnson (2007), Lafleur (1996), and Taylor (1951). For a fascinating discussion of early French-Carib contacts, see Garraway (2005).

2. See Garraway (65).

3. Some 2,400 Garifuna died during internment, mostly due to disease (Gonzalez 1988, 21).

4. The literature on indigenous movements is vast. Recent collections and overviews include de la Peña (2005), Jackson and Warren (2005), Postero and Zamosc (2004), Sieder (2002), and Warren and Jackson (2002).

5. Herskovits originally tried to send his African American student Hugh Smythe to study Garifuna in Honduras but Smythe was denied entry to the country on the basis of a 1934 immigration law that restricted Black immigration (Anderson 2008; Euraque 2004, 173).

6. See, for example, her essay "West Indian Characteristics of the Black Carib" (Gonzalez 1959).

7. This position emerged out of previous debates on the origins of New World Black culture, particularly family patterns, between approaches that emphasized: (a) the difficult economic position of Blacks and absence of men from households; (b) the historical legacies of slavery; (c) the endurance of an African heritage (Gonzalez 1969, 5). The most famous arguments were between Herskovits (1941) and sociologist E. Franklin Frazier, who argued: "probably never before in history has a people been so nearly stripped of its social heritage as the Negroes who were brought to America" (21). For discussions of these debates in relation to theories of creolization, see Mintz and Price (1992), Khan (2004a), and Yelvington (2006).

8. For an excellent recent ethnography of Garifuna engagements with Africa, especially via religion, see Johnson (2007).

9. In addition to the works cited below, see, for example, Hale (2005), Hooker (2005a), Ng'weno (2007a), and Warren (2001). Precedents include Whitten (1981) and Taussig (1980, 1987).

10. See Wade (1997, 25–30) for a succinct overview.

11. I capitalize the term Black, in part to emphasize parallels between Black and Indian as identity categories. I do not capitalize Spanish racial terms, following standard conventions in that language. This should help the reader visualize when I am using an English word (e.g., Negro, Black) and a Spanish word (negro) in the text.

12. Representative collections include Braziel and Mannur (2003) and Lavie and Swedenburg (1996). Khan (2004b) and Siu (2005) provide insightful ethnographies of the Indian diaspora in Trinidad and the Chinese diaspora in Panama, respectively.

13. Brown (2005) and Edwards (2003) develop particularly nuanced critiques of Gilroy's work.

14. Clifford notes: "when cultural-studies diaspora theorist reject nativism in its racist, little England, Thatcherite forms, they can make all deeply rooted attachments seem illegitimate, bad essentialisms....The native is thrown out with the bathwater of nativism" (2007, 200).

15. *Convention (No. 169) concerning Indigenous and Tribal Peoples in Independent Countries,* Part I, Article 1, 1(b), quoted from Anaya (303).

16. For a polemical critique of indigenous politics along these lines, see Kuper (2003).

17. This dichotomy is analyzed and critiqued in the collection by Harvey and Thompson (2005) as well as by Clifford (1994, 2007). These authors offer a corrective that focuses primarily on the diasporic dimensions of indigenous people's experience, narratives, cultures, and identities. I approach the opposition from a different angle, exploring how people who identify themselves as part of a (Black) diaspora also articulate indigenous subject positions.

18. There are also communities located on the island of Roatan and the Cayos Cochinos located off the North Coast.

19. In the early 1990s, a publication of the Honduran Institute of Anthropology and History and the Confederation of Autochthonous Peoples of Honduras (IHAH and CONPAH 1993) listed the Garifuna populations as 250,000. Rivas estimated 98,000, counting only Garifuna living in communities (257). That the census only names certain "population groups" and identifies everyone else as "other" renders the census figures of dubious value.

20. Another people, Noahas, numbering in the hundreds, are not represented in the census but are recognized by the state.

21. For an insightful analysis of how the category of "ethnicity" is grounded in notions of indigeneity, with specific reference to Colombia, see Ng'weno (2007a).

1. Race, Modernity, and Tradition in a Garifuna Community

1. Khan's work on street vendors in La Ceiba (1987) is an important exception.

2. For an overview, see Warren and Twine (2002).

3. Data derived from the database of the 2001 Honduran census, at the Instituto Nacional de Estadística, http://www.ine-hn.org (accessed August 11, 2008).

4. According to a report from the Caribbean Central American Research Council, Mariano Valerio, from the community of Sangrelaya, was the first Garifuna to settle in Sambo Creek, in 1862 (CCARC, 3: 117).

5. Information taken from *La República*, May 30, 1887, and January 28, 1888.

6. Anthropologists working in other countries with discourses of mestizaje emphasizing indo-hispanic heritage note how the term "indio" can refer to a poor or backward subject without differentiating a distinct cultural-racial group (Freye, 4; Lancaster, 224).

7. Ilsa Diaz Zelaya, "De qué Color es la Piel de Dios," *El Tiempo*, April 12, 1997.

8. For descriptions of racism in La Ceiba during this period, see Centeno García (1997) and Canelas Díaz (76). Coelho describes stereotypes in Trujillo during the late 1940s (49–51).

9. For a comparison to Brazil, see Caldwell (65–69).

10. For a recent overview of racism in Honduras, see the report from the United Nations Rapporteur on racism (Diène 2005).

2. From Moreno to Negro

1. These were fieldnotes Coelho sent to his mentor Melville Herskovits, published posthumously in Portuguese. All quotations are from the English original, available in the papers of Melville Herskovits at the Northwestern University Library, referenced as Northwestern University Archives, Melville J. Herskovits Papers, 1906–1963, African Manuscripts 6, Series 35/6. In subsequent references, I refer only to Box and Folder numbers.

2. Herskovits Papers, Box 105, Folder 2, February 1, 1948.

3. Ibid.

4. Ibid.

5. Ibid.

6. Fifteen years later, Pierre Beaucage and Marcel Samson (1964) would document an "abundant oral tradition" concerning Carib history.

7. Herskovits Papers, Box 104, Folder 4, December 24, 1947.

8. Herskovits Papers, Box 105, Folder 2, February 1, 1948.

9. Herskovits Papers, Box 105, Folder 1, July 22, 1948.

10. During the late 1910s and early 1920s, some Garifuna may have participated in the Universal Negro Improvement Association (UNIA) led by Marcus Garvey, which had branches in the Garifuna communities of San Juan and Travesia (Honduras), Livingston (Guatemala) and Stann Creek (Belize), and in most major Central American ports (Hill, 997–98). Although the UNIA had little impact in Honduras (Euraque, forthcoming; Chambers, 160–65), one man I interviewed said

there were two branches in La Ceiba, one catering to English-speaking Blacks and the other to Garifuna. He said his mother served as secretary of the Garifuna branch but only recalled that Garvey promoted the return of Blacks to Africa. He also mentioned that he and his friends read with great interest news of Italy's war on Haile Selassie and Ethiopia during the 1930s.

11. For an account of the San Juan massacre, see López García (1994).

12. Discourses negating African ancestry had been promulgated in previous decades. For example, in 1908 an article in the "semiofficial" newspaper of the government declared "the intervention of the raza de color negro was so scant that there are barely traces of their ancestry and their meager assistance in the development of the indo-american progeny does not merit importance. By contrast, the mixture of the castellano with the aborigine gave to Central America-like all of the Continent of Colon-a new characteristic face, perhaps superior in physical beauty and improved in intellectual faculties and richness of blood" (Guzmán 1908).

13. For a classic account of the banana industry in the early 20th century, see Kepner and Soothill (1967). The best recent account of the Honduran fruit industry is Soluri (2005).

14. For accounts of mestizaje in Central America and other parts of Latin America during the first decades of the twentieth century, see, for example, de la Cadena (2000); Euraque, Gould, and Hale (2004); Gould (1998); Miller (2004); Stepan (1991); and Wade (1997).

15. "A Diario el Norte," *Diario del Norte*, September 28, 1927.

16. Ibid.

17. Ibid.

18. After careful consideration, a worker's organization with close ties to the Communist Party, the Federación Sindical Hondureña, adopted the policy that negro workers should be organized and disciplined to struggle for their emancipation (Posas, 8).

19. With the exception of "chinos" (Chinese) and "coolies" (East Indians), the other groups were commonly lumped together under the term *"turcos."* The majority of these immigrants were Palestinians and Syrians who began arriving at the end of the nineteenth century. Some families established leading commercial ventures on the North Coast and eventually joined the Honduran economic and political elite (Gonzalez 1992b; Euraque 1996b, 49–68; Amaya 1997).

20. For comparisons to the Creole and West Indian populations of Nicaragua and Costa Rica, see respectively Gordon (1998) and Putnam (2002).

21. John Hepburn to C. Alban Young, December 26, 1916, FO 371/2902, London, Public Records Office.

22. Dispatch 9, "Race Problems," August, 23, 1923, *Records Relating to the Internal Affairs of Honduras, 1910–1929*, microcopy M-647, roll 32, The National Archives and Record Service.

23. Joseph Walter to Dr. Don Jesus Ulloa, April 18, 1929, FO 371/13471, London, Public Records Office.

24. Antonio Canelas, personal communication; interview with Pablo García Nuñez, July 9, 1996.

25. See chapter 1 and Anderson (2005).

26. "De la Ceiba," *El Día*, Septembr 2, 1903.

27. Dispatch 65, April 10, 1905, *Dispatches from United States Consuls in La Ceiba, 1902–1906*, microcopy no. T-545, roll 1, The National Archives and Records Service.

28. "Puerto de la Ceiba," *El Nuevo Tiempo*, January 25, 1915.

29. "Negrura," *Diario del Norte*, July 8, 1933.

30. "Notas de Puerto Castilla," *Diario del Norte*, December 6, 1932.

31. Ibid.

32. Ibid.

33. Manzanares says that the term "folklore" was first used in Honduras in 1927 (26).

34. See Manzanares (25–30) for a discussion of works on Honduran folklore between 1930 and 1955; see also Ortega (1946), Rosa (1952), and Martínez (1963).

35. See Kerns (1983) and Chamberlain (1988) for ethnographic analysis. The phrase "Fiesta de Cupita" was often used by outsiders to describe these rituals. "Cupita" is a corruption of the Garifuna word "Gubida" signifying family ancestors.

36. For an analysis of representations of Garifuna in Honduran literature, see Amaya Banegas (2007).

37. For example, the census recorded the Lenca population of Yamaranguila, Intibucá, as mestizo (Euraque 2004, 80).

38. Efforts to create a state National Indigenous Institute in Honduras similar to that of Mexico never bore fruit. Articles pertinent to indigenismo include Martínez Landero (1942), Lang (1951), and Nuñez Chinchilla (1960).

39. The indígenas he means here are the Tolupanes and peoples of the Mosquitia. The "indios of the interior"–in departments home to people self-identifying as Lenca and Chortí today–"have culturally homogenized themselves with the rest of the country and make common life with the general population that forms the Honduran nation" (1955, 361). Thus, argues Aguilar Paz, they should be considered mestizos.

40. For detailed accounts of the strike, see Argueta (1995) and Barahona (1994).

41. See, for example, "Quejanse los Vecinos de el Triunfo, Distrito de Tela," *Vanguardia Revolucionaria*, May 20, 1950.

42. "En el Puerto de Tela," *Vanguardia Revolucionaria*, April 13, 1950.

43. "Franca Discriminación en el Hospital de la Tela Railroad Company en la Lima," *Vanguardia Revolucionaria*, July 16, 1949.

44. The name also may have paid homage to the Abraham Lincoln Brigade of volunteer communists from the United States (including some eighty African

Americans) who fought against fascism in the Spanish Civil War (Kelley 1994). I would like to thank Dana Frank for suggesting the possible connection. Centeno García says that the name honored the U.S. president who abolished slavery (84).

45. This quote is taken from Oquelí (26). See also Euraque (2004, 223).

46. I would like to thank Professor Martínez for sharing his thesis and other writings.

47. These are titled, "La Auténtica Navidad 'Garifuna'" and "Los Gubidas." According to Professor Martínez, the first was published in *La Prensa* (though he could not recall the date) while the latter was never published.

3. Black Indigenism

1. For overviews see Van Cott (1994), Sieder (2002), Warren and Jackson (2002), Jackson and Warren (2005), and de la Peña (2005).

2. "Ritos y Tradiciones Engloban Legendario Pasado y Presente del Pueblo Garifuna," *La Tribuna*, April 12, 1997.

3. Nonetheless, blackness remained an enigma within the nation. Crisanto Meléndez (1976) complained in the national press that announcements for a performance in the southern department of Choluteca advertised the Afro-Honduran group as Afro-Cuban.

4. "Folklore Garifuna en el Encantador Paisaje del Caribe," *El Tiempo*, Suplemento Turístico, July 15, 1979.

5. Johnson notes that Crisanto Meléndez's emphasis on Yoruba origins–"ciphers of African depth and purity"–implies that Garifuna are "authentically negro and pure" (213).

6. Fernando Cruz has researched the origins and development of ethnic movements in Honduras. I would like to thank Professor Cruz for sharing a draft of his work. This section owes much to his research and conversations with him.

7. Secretaría de Estado en los Despachos de Gobernación y Justicia. 1981. *Expediente No. [illegible] Resolución No. 72, Personalidad Juridica, Organización Fraternal Negra de Honduras.*

8. Ibid.

9. Roy Guevarra Arzú served as president of OFRANEH from 1992 to 1994 and served in other key offices in the 1980s. He earned a degree in economics and, as discussed below, also worked in a state agency during the 1980s.

10. The account that follows is based on news reports: "Honduras: The Dual Effects of CREMS," *Latin American Weekly Report*, August 26, 1983; "Land: U.S. Involved in Compensation Row; 'Illegal' Purchase Could Jeopardize CBI Access," *Latin American Weekly Report*, July 20, 1984.

11. Interview with Roy Guevarra Arzú, July 25, 2004.

12. The taxonomy included a fourth category: "Groups of peasant populations with a strong pre-hispanic indigenous cultural substratum in their contemporary

life." These included the "Indians of El Paraiso and the Indians of Santa Barbara" (SECPLAN, 7). These peasant groups no longer appear as "ethnic groups" in Honduras.

13. The SECPLAN document notes that Creoles did not attend the workshop because they did not have a representative organization (10). During the 1980s, OFRANEH attempted to represent all Afro-Hondurans, including Creoles.

14. Examples include the presidential decree concerning bilingual/intercultural education (República de Honduras 1994) and a 1993 environmental law (República de Honduras 1993).

15. This process was marked by a declaration of federations representing Garifuna, Lenca, Tahwaka, Misquito, and Tolupán after a meeting titled "Fundamentos Histórico—Metodológicos para la Unidad de las Organizaciones Étnicas Autóctonas de Honduras." See "Declaración de los Grupos Étnicos," *Boletín Informativo*, Centro de Documentacíon de Honduras, November 1989. The representatives from OFRANEH were Mateo Martínez, who later came to work for the Fondo Indígena (based in Bolivia) and José Hipolito Centeno, a former member of the Sociedad Cultural Lincoln, who later established an NGO.

16. The term "popular" generally refers to the working classes, but in the transnational activist encounters it also reflected a left political commitment to national unity and transformation that sat uneasily alongside assertions of indigenous autonomy (Hale 1994). The term "negro" was added at the insistence of Afro-descendant delegates (32).

17. In the early 1990s, there were numerous killings of ethnic activists involved in land disputes. The most famous case was of Tolupán leader Vicente Matute, president of the federation FETRIXY and a leading activist in CONPAH. He was killed on September 30, 1992 at the behest of local landowners who were never brought to justice (Stocks 1992).

18. The organization later changed its name to the *Consejo Cívico de Organizaciones Populares e Indígenas de Honduras* (Barahona y Rivas 1998). The original acronym was COPIN. I use the current acronym COPINH throughout this account to avoid confusion.

19. The Sambo Creek title covered 184.23 hectares, similar to the areas of Nueva Armenia (202.60) and Corozal (364) (ODECO 2007). As a point of contrast, the community of Santa Rosa de Aguan, located in relatively remote areas of the department of Colón, received a title for 4,180 hectares in 1994.

20. The petition, titled "Comunicado de Emergencía," was handcopied by the author.

21. Frente Nacional Para la Defensa de la Soberanía Patria, "Pronuncamiento Público," August 26, 1999, public e-mail communication.

22. Information taken from photos in *Honduras Update*, June, 1987.

23. "Los Negros de la Costa Atlántica." *Boletín Informativo*, Centro de Documentacíon de Honduras, February 1991.

4. Paradoxes of Participation

1. See Cooke and Lothari (2001) for an extended critique of "participation" in development.

2. For an important ethnography that interprets indigenous movements in this fashion, see Rappaport's work on "intercultural" (as opposed to "multicultural") experiments in Colombia (2005).

3. For an analysis of indigenous politics and state multiculturalism in Panama, see Horton (2006).

4. The Plan Puebla Panama is a scheme for infrastructure construction in highways, seaports, communication grids, and so on, running from Mexico to Panama, designed to increase export production. The Mesoamerican Biological Corridor is an environment initiative covering extensive parts of Central America and Mexico framed as promoting biodiversity conservation, indigenous and rural economies, and resource extraction for the market. Critics argue that the project represents a form of "green neoliberalism" that entails limited local participation and serves foreign and elite interests (Finley-Brook 2007).

5. Meanwhile, OFRANEH worked on another territorial mapping project in Eastern Honduras directed by CCARC and funded by the Ford Foundation.

6. The organization was likely Iseri Lidawamari, a cooperative operating in the region near Limon, Colón, which, beginning in the early 1990s, occupied disputed lands to revitalize communal agricultural production (England 2006). Iseri Lidawamari has a close relationship with OFRANEH.

7. See World Bank (2006, Appendix 3.1: 167).

8. The rifts between leaders degenerated to the point where OFRANEH refused to meet with representatives of the World Bank and the government in the presence of the Mesa Regional, whereas Mesa Regional members insisted that the government and World Bank could not meet OFRANEH to discuss PATH without the Mesa Regional (World Bank 2006, Annex 2.1: 48).

9. For overviews, see Inter-American Dialogue (2004) and Turner (2005).

10. Latin American states are notorious for refusing to comply with the International Convention on the Elimination of all Forms of Discrimination. For critical analysis of state denials of racism in Latin America, see Banton (1996) and Dulitzky (2005).

11. "Revuelo Causa Diputado Racista," *La Prensa,* March 31, 2006.

12. Ibid.

13. "ODECO Pide Abrir Causa Judicial Contra Diputado Miguel Gámez," *Proceso Digital,* March 30, 2006, http://www.proceso.hn (accessed May 23, 2006).

14. CAFTA is the Central American Free Trade Agreement, modeled on the North American Free Trade Agreement (NAFTA).

5. This Is the Black Power We Wear

1. For a discussion of this incident and a critical analysis of the maquiladora industry in Honduras, see Pine (2008).

2. My use of the terms "North" and "South" refers to metageographical tropes of the hierarchical order of nation-states, also indicated by terms such as "first world" and "third world" or "developed" and "underdeveloped" (or, for that matter, "overdeveloped" and "developing"). For a critique of the languages of geographical differentiation along these binaries, see Lewis and Wigen (1997).

3. Women's fashion styles showed more variation than men's. A few young women adopted a look similar to the "bad boy" look of young men, wearing baggy pants, large shirts, and baseball caps. Other Garifuna women emphasized that their style was more "sexy" than that of mestizos, emphasizing the short skirts, spandex shorts, and tight shirts they sometimes wear when going out at night. Others, typically older young women (in their mid-late twenties), emphasized that they tend to dress more formally than Garifuna men or mestiza women, emphasizing long shirts and "nice" clothes. Almost all of the women with whom I spoke asserted that their different forms of dress, including hairstyles and jewelry, were borrowed from "Black Americans."

4. For an extended discussion of "racial capitalism," see Robinson (1983). The formative work on race and capitalism by Hall (1980, 1986) also provides enduring insights into the need to analyze particular racial formations as they "articulate" with specific forms of capitalism.

5. Among Garifuna youth I know, the term "heavy" (*pesado*) is used to describe something considered cool or in style. The English term "heavy" is also occasionally used with the same connotations or to describe a style of dress characterized by big baggy clothes.

6. I heard these two explanations from two different people, one Garifuna and the other a mestizo. In the first case, an older man in La Ceiba took his son to his barbershop but was refused service on the grounds that the barber was not familiar with the hair of a negro. In the second case, a mestizo teacher told me that he knew of barbers who would not cut the hair of negros because many were said to have a skin disease on the back of their necks.

7. Exceptions include Costa Vargas (2003), England (1999), Hanchard (2003), Matory (2005), and Siegel (2001).

6. Political Economies of Difference

1. For scholarly accounts of dügü, see Johnson (2007) and Kerns (1983).

2. Dr. Alfonso Lacayo, a key figure in promoting awareness of the Black heritage of Honduras and the culture of Garifuna who we met in chapter 2, helped initiate the project resulting in the drama.

3. These quotes are taken from a development plan produced under the auspices of a network of Garifuna organizations (CNOH, 33). The text was mostly written by ODECO.

4. For an excellent account of the personal difficulties of transmigrant relations, especially from the transmigrant point of view, see Glick Schiller and Fouron (2001).

5. England (2006, 149–86), in a nuanced analysis of development discourse in another Garifuna community, notes that dominant narratives tend to focus on individual class mobility and explain community problems such as remittance dependence in individualist/culturalist terms (e.g., highlighting the lack of initiative among community residents). She also identifies a competing narrative that analyzes community problems as a product of structural conditions. This position is associated with a grassroots movement to recuperate land, revitalize agricultural production, and promote local autonomy that has links to OFRANEH. During the mid- to late 1990s, no significant local activist movement along these lines existed in Sambo Creek, and structural critiques of development were not as pronounced as in the community studied by England. England notes that although most people in the community she studied supported efforts toward land recuperation, they did not fully embrace activist critiques of development and alternative projects of cultural-economic autonomy, in part because of the centrality of transmigration to social mobility and earning a living: "Their experiences as migrant workers and consumers make obvious the gaps in the ideal of economic self-sufficiency and cultural autonomy" (185).

6. At one point during my fieldwork in the 1990s, representatives from the government program "Cultural Rescue," funded by the United Nations, toured Garifuna communities, searching for material culture for the tourist market. They were disappointed that Sambeños had no appropriate handicrafts, rejecting the cloth doilies one young woman displayed as an example of her artistry.

7. See Gregory (2007) for an insightful analysis of the spatial politics of tourism in the Dominican Republic. The constructed isolation of the Palma Real ensures that the everyday battles over space and interaction with tourists discussed by Gregory do not occur at the boundaries of this Honduran resort.

8. This quote is cited from http://www.fundacionsave.com/estrategia_eng.html (accessed August 7, 2005).

9. This is an unpublished document I received from a state office.

10. "Garífunas Desalojados a Garrotazos y con Bombas por la Policía por Ocupar un Latifundio del que Tienen Titulos de Propiedad," *Boletín Informativo,* No. 1553, Centro de Información y Documentación Conadeh, Honuras, August 16, 2001.

11. "Desalojan Garífunas de Terrenos en Sambo Creek," *El Tiempo,* November 14, 2002.

12. This part of the account is based in part on documents concerning his case that I was able to review at the courthouse in La Ceiba. See also the CCARC report (3: 113–38).

13. From 1918 until 1990, the Honduran government maintained an exchange rate of two lempiras for one dollar. As part of the neoliberal reform packages initiated in 1990, the government devalued the lempira. At the end of 2003, the exchange rate was nearly 18:1.

14. The land committee also identified land owned by wealthy foreigners as potential targets for recuperation. Brondo provides a nice analysis of varying mestizo attitudes toward the land recuperation effort in relation to class and ethnic distinctions in the community (185–97).

15. For a comparison of similar tensions between Afro-Colombians and mestizos that includes flexibility in the practical application of community membership, see Hoffman (2002).

16. This genre, sometimes called "punta rock," appears to have been created by Belizean Garifuna in the late 1970s (Greene 2002).

17. For an extended discussion of modernity and tradition as associated with "Black music" in Colombia, see Wade (2000).

Conclusion

1. Other works also trouble these distinctions. For example, De la Cadena (2000) provides a nuanced account of intersections between mestizo and indigenous identifications in Peru.

Glossary: Selected Ethnic–Racial Terms and Their Contemporary Uses

Blanco: As a racial term, "blanco" translates in English as "white." In Honduras, the term generally refers to European ancestry, although it can also refer to the majority population of Hondurans (mestizos) as a whole.

Indígena: As a racialized identity category, the term is used to refer to a member of an indigenous group, typically understood to be descendants of the pre-Colombian inhabitants of the Americas (Indians). As an adjective, the term can mean "indigenous" in the sense of native to a particular place, country, or region. It can also mean indigenous as a category of peoplehood in the sense established by state law and international norms. As I argue in chapter 3, in Honduras indígena can refer to a cultural–historical status that is not coterminous with the notion of Indian but includes ethnicities/peoples identified as Black.

Indio: Although the term translates in English as "Indian," it can be used not only to refer to members of an indigenous group (e.g., Miskito) but also, most commonly, to the majority population of Honduras ("mestizos"), often with connotations of lower class or peasant status. The term can be used as an insult implying ignorance, low status, and/or a propensity to violence, although it can also be used as a term of proud self-reference.

Ladino: In general, the term "ladino" today is synonymous with Mestizo. Historically, however, the term referred to a legal category referring to people who spoke Spanish and were considered culturally distinct from Indians but were not considered purely Spanish by blood; the category could include mestizos, mulatos, and negros.

Mestizo: Literally meaning "mixed," as an identity term "mestizo" typically refers to the majority population of Honduras, especially in official discourse. Mestizos are considered distinct from officially recognized ethnic groups such as Garifuna, Miskito, and so on, as well as people of foreign origins such as Chinese. In the colonial era, the term historically referred to the mixed descendants of Spanish and Indians and retains that association, although some people understood as mestizos acknowledge other sources of ancestry, including Black ancestry.

Moreno: A color term that literally means "brown." In Honduras, the term was historically used as a synonym for "Blacks" but over time increasingly came to refer specifically to Garifuna (Gonzalez 1988, 62). Contemporary Garifuna I know often use the term to describe themselves, their language, or their communities (morenales), although they often also state a preference for the term "negro."

Mulato: In the colonial era, the term "mulato" (mulatto in English) referred to the mixed descendants of blancos and negros. In contemporary use, the term can also refer to individuals understood to be the children of negro and mestizo parents.

Negro: As an identity term, it refers to the racial category translated in English as "Black." In Honduras, the ethnic groups Garifuna and Negros ingleses are considered negros. Today, many Garifuna embrace the term as a form of self-reference, although some activists promote the term "afrodescendiente." As in other Latin American contexts, people who do not identify themselves as a part of a distinct Black ethnicity sometimes call lovers or children "negro."

Bibliography

Aguilar Paz, Jesús. 1955. "Problemas de la Población Aborigen de Honduras." *Revista del Archivo y Biblioteca Nacional de Honduras* 33.5–12: 359–63.

_____. 1989. *Tradiciones y Leyendas de Honduras*. Tegucigalpa, Honduras: Museo del Hombre Hondureño.

Altschul, Francisco. 1928. "Informe, Presentado al Señor Presidente de la República Dr. Miguel Paz Baraona, Acerca de la Mosquitia Hondureña." *Revista del Archivo y Biblioteca Nacional de Honduras* 6: 280–82, 298–301, 379–82.

Amaya Banegas, Jorge Alberto. 1997. *Los Árabes y Palestinos en Honduras, 1900–1950*. Tegucigalpa, Honduras: Editorial Guaymuras.

_____. 2007. *Las Imágenes de los Negros Garífunas en la Literatura Hondureña y Extranjera*. Tegucigalpa, Honduras: Secretaría de Cultura, Artes y Deportes.

Anaya, S. James. 2004. *Indigenous Peoples in International Law*. 2nd ed. New York: Oxford University Press.

Anderson, Lars, and Chad Millman. 1998. *Pickup Artists: Street Basketball in America*. New York: Verso.

Anderson, Mark. 1997. "The Significance of Blackness: Representations of Garifuna in St. Vincent and Central America, 1700–1900." *Transforming Anthropology* 6.1–2: 22–35.

_____. 2001. "¿Existe el Racismo en Honduras? Discursos Garífunas Sobre Raza y Racismo." *Mesoamérica* 22.42: 135–63.

_____. 2005. "Bad Boys and Peaceful Garifuna: Transnational Encounters between Racial Stereotypes of Honduras and the United States." *Neither Enemies nor Friends: Latinos, Blacks, Afro-Latinos*. Eds. A. Dzidzienyo and S. Oboler. New York: Palgrave Macmillan. 101–16.

_____. 2007. "When Afro Becomes (like) Indigenous: Garifuna and Afro-Indigenous Politics in Honduras." *Journal of Latin American and Caribbean Anthropology* 12.2: 384–413.

_____. 2008. The Complicated Career of Hugh Smythe . . . Anthropologist and Ambassador: The Early Years, 1940–1950. *Transforming Anthropology* 16.2: 128–46.

Anderson, Mark, and Sarah England. 2004. "¿Auténtica Cultura Africana en Honduras? Los Afro-Centroamericanos Desafian el Mestizaje Indo-Hispánico Hondureño." *Memorias del Mestizaje: Cultural Política en Centroamérica de*

1920 al Presente. Eds. D. Euraque, J. Gould, and C. R. Hale. Antigua, Guatemala: Centro de Investigaciones Regionales de Mesoamérica. 253–93.

Andrews, George Reid. 2004. *Afro-Latin America: 1800–2000.* New York: Oxford University Press.

Argueta, Mario. 1992. *Historia de los Sin Historia, 1900–1948.* Tegucigalpa, Honduras: Editorial Guaymuras.

———. 1995. *La Gran Huelga Bananera: 69 Días que Conmovieron a Honduras.* Tegucigalpa, Honduras: Editorial Universitaria.

Bamrud, Joachim. 2006. "Record Remittances." *Latin Business Chronicle.* 17 April. http://www.latinbusinesschroncile.com (accessed 25 June 2006).

Banton, Michael. 1996. "International Norms and Latin American States' Policies on Indigenous Peoples." *Nations and Nationalism* 2.1: 89–103.

Barahona, Marvin. 1991. *Evolución Histórica de la Identidad Nacional.* Tegucigalpa, Honduras: Editorial Guaymuras.

———. 1994. *El Silencio Quedó Atrás: Testimonios de la Huelga Bananera de 1954.* Tegucigalpa, Honduras: Editorial Guaymuras.

———. 1998. "Imagen y Percepción de los Pueblos Indígenas en Honduras." *Rompiendo el Espejo: Visiones Sobre los Pueblos Indígenas y Negros en Honduras.* Eds. M. Barahona and R. Rivas. Honduras: Editorial Guaymuras. 17–33.

———. 2004. "Del Mestizaje a la Diversidad Étnica y Cultural: la Contribución del Movimiento Indígena y Negro de Honduras." *Memorias del Mestizaje: Cultura Política en Centroamérica de 1920 al Presente.* Eds. D. Euraque, C. R. Hale, and J. Gould. Antigua, Guatemala: CIRMA. 215–51.

Barahona, Marvin, and Ramón D. Rivas. 1998. "¿Existe un Movimiento Indígena en Honduras?" *Rompiendo el Espejo: Visiones sobre los Pueblos Indígenas y Negros en Honduras.* Eds. M. Barahona and R. Rivas. Tegucigalpa, Honduras: Editorial Guaymuras. 81–128.

Beaucage, Pierre, and Marcel Samson. 1964. *Historia del Pueblo Garífuna y su Llegada a Honduras en 1796.* Honduras: Publicaciones del Patronato para el Desarrollo de las Comunidades de los Departamentos de Colon y Gracias a Dios.

Boucher, Philip. 1992. *Cannibal Encounters: Europeans and the Island Caribs, 1492–1763.* Baltimore: Johns Hopkins University Press.

Bourgois, Philippe. 1989. *Ethnicity at Work: Divided Labor on a Central American Banana Plantation.* Baltimore: Johns Hopkins University Press.

Braziel, Jana Evans, and Anita Mannur. 2003. "Nation, Migration, Globalization: Points of Contention in Diaspora Studies." *Theorizing Diaspora.* Eds. J. E. Braziel and A. Mannur. Oxford: Blackwell Publishing. 1–22.

Brondo, Keri. 2006. "Roots, Rights, and Belonging: Garifuna Indigeneity and Land Rights on Honduras' North Coast." Ph.D. Thesis. Michigan State University.

Brondo, Keri, and Laura Woods. 2007. "Garifuna Land Rights and Ecotourism as Economic Development in Honduras' Cayos Cochinos Marine Protected Area." *Ecological and Environmental Anthropology* 3.1: 2–17.

Brown, Jacqueline Nassy. 1998. "Black Liverpool, Black America, and the Gendering of Diasporic Space." *Cultural Anthropology* 13.3: 291–325.

_____. 2005. *Dropping Anchor, Setting Sail: Geographies of Race in Black Liverpool.* Princeton: Princeton University Press.

Browne, Sir Thomas. 1672. *Pseudodoxia Epidemica: or, Enquiries into Very Many Received Tenants and Commonly Performed Truths.* 6th ed. Vol. 6. London: Printed by J. R. for Nath. Ekins.

Brysk, Alison. 2000. *From Tribal Village to Global Village: Indian Rights and International Relations in Latin America.* Palo Alto: Stanford University Press.

Burns, E. Bradford. 1982. *The Poverty of Progress: Latin America in the Nineteenth Century.* Berkeley: University of California Press.

Caceres, Vicente. 1930. "Chancunu: Baile de los Morenos." *En Marcha.* 6 July.

Cacho, Sixto. 1932. "Por la Raza Morena y la Protección de Todos mis Compatriotas." *Diario del Norte.* 14 June.

de la Cadena, Marisol. 2000. *Indigenous Mestizos: The Politics of Race and Culture in Cuzco, Peru, 1910–1991.* Durham: Duke University Press.

Caldwell, Kia Lilly. 2007. *Negras in Brazil: Re-envisioning Black Women, Citizenship, and the Politics of Identity.* New Brunswick: Rutgers University Press.

Canelas Díaz, Antonio. 1999. *La Ceiba, sus Raices y su Historia, 1810–1940.* La Ceiba, Honduras: Tipografía Renacimiento.

CCARC (Caribbean Central American Research Council). 2003. *Diagnóstico del Uso y Tenencia de la Tierra en Comunidades Garífunas y Miskitas de Honduras, 2002–2003.* http://ccarconline.org (accessed 12 August 2008).

Centeno García, Santos. 1997. *Historia del Movimiento Negro Hondureño.* Tegucigalpa, Honduras: Editorial Guaymuras.

Chala Santiago, Valencia. 1986. *El Negro en Centroamérica.* Quito, Ecuador: Centro Cultural Afro-Ecuatoriano, Abya-Yala.

Chamberlain Bianchi, Cynthia. 1988. "Gubida Illness and Religious Ritual among the Garifuna of Santa Fe, Honduras: an Ethnographic Analysis." Ph.D. Thesis. Ohio State University.

Chambers, Glenn A., Jr. 2006. "Foreign Labor and the Struggle for a Honduran Identity: West Indian Workers and Community Formation in the Republic of Honduras, 1876–1954." Ph.D. Thesis. Howard University.

Clark, Dana, Jonathan Fox, and Kay Treakle, eds. 2003. *Demanding Accountability: Civil-Society Claims and the World Bank Inspection Panel.* Oxford: Roman & Littlefield Publishers.

Clifford, James. 1994. "Diasporas." *Cultural Anthropology* 9.3: 302–38.

_____. 1997. *Routes: Travel and Translation in the Late Twentieth Century.* Cambridge: Harvard University Press.

_____. 2007. "Varieties of Indigenous Experience: Diasporas, Homelands, Sovereignties." *Indigenous Experience Today.* Eds. M. de la Cadena and O. Starn. Oxford: Berg Publishers. 197–223.

CNOH (Coordinadora de Organizaciones Negras de Honduras). 1997. *Plan Nacional de Desarrollo para Comunidades AfroHondureñas.* n.p.

Coelho, Ruy Galvão de Andrade. 1955. "The Black Carib of Honduras: A Study in Acculturation." Ph.D. Thesis. Northwestern University.

Collier, George, with Elizabeth Lowery Quaratiello. 1999. *Basta! Land & the Zapatista Rebellion in Chiapas.* Revised Edition. Oakland: Food First Books.

Conzemius, Eduard. 1928, "Ethnographical Notes on the Black Carib." *American Anthropologist* 30: 183–205.

Cooke, Bill, and Uma Lothari. 2001. *Participation: The New Tyranny?* London: Zed Books.

Coombe, Rosemary. 1996. "Embodied Trademarks: Mimesis and Alterity on American Commercial Frontiers." *Cultural Anthropology* 11.2: 20224.

COPINH (Consejo Cívico de Organizaciones Populares e Indígenas de Honduras). 2004. "Historia." http://rds.orgh.hn/copinh (accessed 8 May 2006).

Craton, Michael. 1982. *Testing the Chains: Resistance to British Slavery in the British West Indies.* Ithaca: Cornell University Press.

_____. 1997. *Empire, Enslavement, and Freedom in the Caribbean.* Princeton: Markus Wiener Publishers.

Crisanto Meléndez, Armando. 1972a. "Breve Historia del Negro en Honduras." *La Prensa.* 15 May.

_____. 1972b. "La Cultura Garifuna y el Principio de Nacionalidad." *El Tiempo.* 9 December.

_____. 1976. "Las Danzas Garifunas y su Significado Deben ser Conocidas por los Hondureños." *La Prensa.* 15 May.

_____. 1983. "Ensayo para una Programa Cultural Radial: Escuchad el Tambor en Honduras, Expresión Histórica Garifuna." Tegucigalpa, Honduras: Ballet Folklórico Garifuna. Mimeograph.

_____. 1988. "El Garifuna, su Folklore en Honduras." *Primer Congreso de la Cultura Negra de las Américas.* Cali, Colombia: UNESCO/Fundación Colombiana de Investigaciones Folclóricas. 89–92.

Cruz Sandoval, Fernando. 1984. "La Política Indigenista de Honduras, 1821–1984." *Yaxkin* 6.1–2: 48–55.

Cuevas, Freddy. 2003. "Honduran Businessman Denies Charges of 'Sweatshop' Conditions." The Associated Press. 30 October. http://www.gdsnet.org/classes/SeanJohnSweatshopControversy3.htm (accessed 18 September 2008).

Davidson, William. 1974. *Historical Geography of the Bay Islands, Honduras: Anglo-Hispanic Conflict in the Western Caribbean.* Birmingham: Southern University Press.

Díaz Polanco, Héctor. 1997. *Indigenous Peoples in Latin America: The Quest for Self-Determination.* Trans. L. Rayas. Boulder: Westview Press.

Diène, Doudou. 2005. *Racism, Racial Discrimination, Xenophobia, and all Forms of Discrimination, Addendum, Mission to Honduras.* New York: United Nations Economic and Social Council, Commission on Human Rights.

Dodd, Thomas J. 2005. *Tiburcio Carías: Portrait of a Honduran Political Leader.* Baton Rouge: Louisiana State University Press.

Drake, St. Clair. 1958. "An Approach to the Evaluation of African Societies." *Africa Seen by American Negro Scholars.* Ed. J. Davis. New York: Présence Africaine. 11–34.

Dulitzky, Ariel. 2005. "A Region in Denial: Racial Discrimination and Racism in Latin America." *Neither Enemies nor Friends: Latinos, Blacks, Afro-Latinos.* Eds. A. Dzidzienyo and S. Oboler. New York: Palgrave Macmillan. 39–60.

Ebron, Paulla A. 2008. "Strike a Pose: Capitalism's Black Identity." *Recharting the Black Atlantic.* Eds. A. Oboe and A. Scacchi. New York: Routledge. 319–36.

Edwards, Brent Hayes. 2003. *The Practice of Diaspora: Literature, Translation, and the Rise of Black Internationalism.* Cambridge: Harvard University Press.

England, Sarah. 1998. "Gender Ideologies and Domestic Structures within the Transnational Space of the Garifuna Diaspora." *Diasporic Identity: Selected Papers on Refugees and Immigrants.* Ed. C. A. Moreland. Vol. VI. Arlington: American Anthropological Association. 133–57.

———. 1999. "Negotiating Race and Place in the Garifuna Diaspora: Identity Formation and Transnational Grassroots Politics in New York City and Honduras." *Identities* 6.1: 5–54.

———. 2006. *Afro-Central Americans in New York City: Garifuna Tales of Transnational Movements in Racialized Space.* Gainesville: University Press of Florida.

Escheverri-Gent, Elisavinda. 1993. "Forgotten Workers: British West Indians and the Early Days of the Banana Industry in Costa Rica and Honduras." *Journal of Latin American Studies* 24.2: 275–308.

Escobar, Arturo. 2001. "Culture Sits in Places: Reflections on Globalism and Subaltern Strategies of Localization." *Political Geography* 20.2: 139–74.

Euraque, Darío A. 1996a. *Reinterpreting the Banana Republic: Region and State in Honduras, 1870–1972.* Chapel Hill: University of North Carolina Press.

———.1996b. *Estado, Poder, Nacionalidad y Raza en la Historia de Honduras: Ensayos.* Obispado de Choluteca, Honduras: Ediciones Subirana.

———. 1996c. "La Creación de la Moneda Nacional y el Enclave Bananero en la Costa Caribeña de Honduras: ¿en Busca de una Identidad Étnico-racial?" *Yaxkin* 14.1–2: 138–50.

_____. 1998. "The Banana Enclave, Nationalism and Mestizaje in Honduras, 1910s–1930s." *Identity and Struggle at the Margins of the Nation-State: The Laboring Peoples of Central America and the Hispanic Caribbean.* Eds. A. Chomsky and A. Lauria-Santiago. Durham: Duke University Press. 151–68.

_____. 2003. "The Threat of Blackness to the Mestizo Nation: Race and Ethnicity in the Honduran Banana Economy, 1920s and 1930s." *Banana Wars: Power, Production, and History in the Americas.* Eds. S. Striffler and M. Moberg. Durham: Duke University Press. 229–52.

_____. 2004. *Conversaciones Históricas con el Mestizaje y su Identidad Nacional en Honduras.* San Pedro Sula, Honduras: Litografía López.

_____. Forthcoming. "Honduras." *The Marcus Garvey and Universal Negro Improvement Association Papers. Vol. XI, Caribbean Series.* Ed. R. A. Hill. Los Angeles: UCLA Press.

Euraque, Darío, Jeffrey L. Gould, and Charles R. Hale, eds. 2004. *Memorias del Mestizaje: Cultural Política en Centroamérica de 1920 al Presente.* Antigua, Guatemala: CIRMA.

Fanon, Frantz. 1967. *Black Skin, White Masks.* Trans. Charles Lam Markmann. New York: Grove Press.

Ferguson, James. 2006. *Global Shadows: Africa in the Neoliberal World Order.* Durham: Duke University Press.

Ferguson, James, and Akhil Gupta. 2002. "Spatializing States: Toward an Ethnography of Neoliberal Governmentality." *American Ethnologist* 29.4: 981–1002.

Fernandes, Sujatha. 2003. "Fear of a Black Nation: Local Rappers, Transnational Crossings, and State Power in Contemporary Cuba." *Anthropological Quarterly* 76.4: 575–608.

Fernandez, Selvin. 1997. "Plan Nacional de Desarrollo Garífuna Require Más de 25 Millones de Dólares." *El Tiempo.* 14 April.

Finley-Brook, Mary. 2007. "Green Neoliberal Space: The Mesoamerican Biological Corridor." *Journal of Latin American Geography* 6.1: 101–24.

Flores Andino, Francisco. 1977. "Realidad Indígena Hondureña." Tegucigalpa, Honduras: Institute Hondureño de Antropología e Historia. Mimeograph.

Flores, Luciano. 1950. "Una Raza Oprimida: Enfoque de la Vida del Moreno en la Costa Norte y su Situación Económica." *Vanguardia Revolucionaria.* 18 July.

Flores Lopéz, Oscar. 2000. "Armando Crisanto Meléndez: Baraguatina Nunguai Quei Garifuna." *La Tribuna.* 29 January.

Flusty, Steven. 1997. "Icons in the Stream: On Local Revisions of Global Stuff." *Icons: Magnets of Meaning.* Ed. A. Betsky. San Francisco: Chronicle Books. 52–65.

Fox, Jonathan A., and L. David Brown, eds. 1998. *The Struggle for Accountability: The World Bank, NGOs, and Grassroots Movements.* Cambridge: MIT Press.

Frankenberg, Ruth. 1993. *White Women, Race Matters: The Social Construction of Whiteness.* Minneapolis: University of Minnesota Press.

Franzone, Dorothy Lawrence. 1994. "A Critical and Cultural Analysis of an African People in the Americas: Africanisms in the Garifuna Culture in Belize." Ph.D. Thesis. Temple University.

Frazier, E. Franklin. 1939. *The Negro Family in the United States*. Chicago: University of Chicago Press.

French, Jan Hoffman. 2009. *Legalizing Identities: Becoming Black or Indian in Brazil's Northeast*. Chapel Hill: University of North Carolina Press.

Freye, David. 1996. *Indians into Mexicans: History and Identity in a Mexican Town*. Austin: University of Texas Press.

Garraway, Doris. 2005. *The Libertine Colony: Creolization in the Early French Caribbean*. Durham: Duke University Press.

Gilroy, Paul. 1991. *'There Ain't No Black in the Union Jack': The Cultural Politics of Race and Nation*. Chicago: University of Chicago Press.

———. 1992. *The Black Atlantic: Modernity and Double Consciousness*. Cambridge: Harvard University Press.

———. 2000. *Against Race: Imagining Political Culture beyond the Color Line*. Cambridge: Harvard University Press.

Glick Schiller, Nina, and Georges Fouron. 2001. *Georges Woke Up Laughing: Long-Distance Nationalism and the Search for Home*. Durham: Duke University Press.

Goett, Jennifer. 2006. "Diasporic Identities, Autochthonous Rights: Race, Gender, and the Cultural Politics of Creole Land Rights in Nicaragua." Ph.D. Thesis. University of Texas at Austin.

Gomez Osorio, Justo. 1905. "La Mosquitia, Índole y Costumbres de sus Pobladores." *Revista del Archivo y de la Biblioteca Nacional* 1.10: 279–87.

Gonzalez, Nancie. 1959. "West Indian Characteristics of the Black Caribs." *Southwestern Journal of Anthropology* 15: 300–307.

———. 1969. *Black Carib Household Structure: A Study of Migration and Modernization*. Seattle: University of Washington Press.

———. 1970. "The Neoteric Society." *Comparative Studies in Society and History* 12.1: 1–13.

———. 1983. "New Evidence on the Origins of the Black Carib." *New West Indian Guide* 57: 143–72.

———. 1988. *Sojourners of the Caribbean: Ethnogenesis and Ethnohistory of the Garifuna*. Champaign: University of Illinois Press.

———. 1992a. "Identitidad Étnica y Artificio en los Encuentros Interétnicos del Caribe." *De Palabra y Obra en el Nuevo Mundo, Vol. 2, Encuentros Interétnicos*. Eds. M. Gutiérrez Estévez, M. Leon-Portilla, G. H. Gossen, and J. J. Klor de Alva. Madrid: Siglo Vientiuno Editores. 403–27.

———. 1992b. *Dollar, Dove, and Eagle: One Hundred Years of Palestinian Migration to Honduras*. Ann Arbor: University of Michigan Press.

_____. 1997. "The Garifuna of Central America." *The Indigenous People of the Caribbean.* Ed. S. Wilson. Gainesville: University of Florida Press. 197–205.

Gordon, Edmund T. 1998. *Disparate Diasporas: Identity and Politics in an African Nicaraguan Community.* Austin: University of Texas Press.

Gordon, Edmund T., and Mark Anderson. 1999. "The African Diaspora: Toward an Ethnography of Diasporic Identification." *Journal of American Folklore* 112.445: 282–96.

Gould, Jeffrey. 1998. *To Die in this Way: Nicaraguan Indians and the Myth of Mestizaje, 1880–1965.* Durham: Duke University Press.

Greene, Oliver, Jr. 2002. "Ethnicity, Modernity, and Retention in the Garifuna Punta." *Black Music Research Journal* 22.1: 189–216.

Greene, Shane. 2007a. "Introduction: On Race, Roots/Routes, and Sovereignty in Latin America's Afro-Indigenous Multiculturalisms." *Journal of Latin American and Caribbean Anthropology* 12.2: 329–55.

_____. 2007b. "Entre lo Indio, lo Negro, y lo Incaico: The Spatial Hierarchies of Difference in Multicultural Peru." *Journal of Latin American and Caribbean Anthropology* 12.2: 441–74.

Greenhouse, Steven. 2003. "A Hip-Hop Star's Fashion Line Is Tagged with a Sweatshop Label." *The New York Times.* 28 October. http://www.nytimes.com (accessed 6 June 2004).

Gregory, Stephen. 2007. *The Devil behind the Mirror: Globalization and Politics in the Dominican Republic.* Berkeley: University of California Press.

Gros, Christian. 1997. "Indigenismo e Etnicidad: El Desafío Neoliberal." *Antropología en la Modernidad: Identidades, Etnicidades y Movimientos Sociales en Colombia.* Eds. M. Uribe and E. Restrepo. Bogotá, Colombia: Instituto Colombiano de Antropología. 15–59.

Grueso, Libia, Carlos Rosero, and Arturo Escobar. 1998. "The Process of Black Community Organizing in the Southern Pacific Coast Region of Columbia." *Cultures of Politics/Politics of Cultures: Re-visioning Latin American Social Movements.* Eds. S. Alvarez, E. Dagnino, and A. Escobar. Boulder: Westview Press. 196–219.

Grünberg, Georg. 2003. "Tierras y Territorios Indígenas en Centroamérica." http://www.latautonomy.org (accessed 26 October 2007).

Gullick, C. J. M. R. 1976. *Exiled from St. Vincent: The Development of Black Carib Culture in Central America up to 1945.* Malta: Progress Press.

Gupta, Akhil, and James Ferguson. 1992. "Beyond 'Culture': Space, Identity, and the Politics of Difference." *Cultural Anthropology* 7.1: 6–23.

Guzmán, Ramón. 1908. "Necesidad que Tiene Centro América del Inmigración." *El Monitor.* 2 April.

Hale, Charles R. 1994. "Between Che Guevara and the Pachamama: Mestizos, Indians, and Identity Politics in the Anti-Quincentenary Campaign." *Critique of Anthropology* 14.1: 9–39.

_____. 2002. "Does Multiculturalism Menace? Governance, Cultural Rights and the Politics of Identity in Guatemala." *Journal of Latin American Studies* 34: 485–524.

_____. 2004. "Rethinking Indigenous Politics in the Era of the 'Indio Permitido.'" *NACLA Report on the Americas* 38.2: 16–20.

_____. 2005. "Neoliberal Multiculturalism: The Remaking of Cultural Rights and Racial Dominance in Central America." *PoLAR: Political and Legal Anthropology Review* 28.1: 10–28.

_____. 2006. *Más Que un Indio: Racial Ambivalence and Neoliberal Multiculturalism in Guatemala.* Santa Fe: School of American Research Press.

Hall, Stuart. 1980. "Race, Articulation and Societies Structured in Dominance." *Sociological Theories: Race and Colonialism.* Paris: UNESCO. 305–45.

_____. 1986. "Gramsci's Relevance for the Study of Race and Ethnicity." *Journal of Communication Inquiry* 10.2: 5–27.

_____. 1991. "The Local and the Global: Globalization and Ethnicity." *Culture, Globalization and the World-System: Contemporary Conditions for the Representation of Identity.* Ed. A. King. Binghamton: Department of Art and History, State University of New York at Binghamton. 19–39.

_____. 2003. "Cultural Identity and Diaspora." *Theorizing Diaspora: a Reader.* Eds. J. E. Braziel and A. Mannur. London: Blackwell Publishing. 233–46.

Hanchard, Michael George. 1994. *Orpheus and Power: The Movimiento Negro of Rio de Janeiro and São Paulo, Brazil, 1945–1988.* Princeton: Princeton University Press.

_____. 2003. "Acts of Misrecognition: Transnational Black Politics, Anti-imperialism and the Ethnocentrisms of Pierre Bourdieu and Loïc Wacquant." *Theory, Culture & Society* 20.4: 5–29.

Harrison, Faye V. 1995. "The Persistent Power of 'Race' in the Cultural and Political Economy of Racism." *Annual Review of Anthropology* 24: 47–74.

Harvey, Graham, and Charles Thompson. 2005. "Introduction." *Indigenous Diasporas and Dislocations.* Eds. G. Harvey and C. Thompson. Burlington: Ashgate Publishing Company. 1–14.

Harvey, Neil. 1998. *The Chiapas Rebellion: The Struggle for Land and Democracy.* Durham: Duke University Press.

Hayden, Corey. 2003. *When Nature Goes Public: The Making and Unmaking of Bioprospecting in Mexico.* Princeton: Princeton University Press.

Helms, Mary. 1981. "Black Carib Domestic Organization in Historical Perspective: Traditional Origins of Contemporary Patterns." *Ethnology* 20.1: 77–86.

Herranz, Atanasio. 1996. *Estado, Sociedad y Lenguaje: La Política Lingüística en Honduras.* Tegucigalpa, Honduras: Editorial Guaymuras.

Herskovits, Melville 1990 [1941]. *The Myth of the Negro Past.* Boston: Beacon Press.

Hill, Robert, ed. 1990. *The Marcus Garvey and Universal Negro Improvement Association Papers.* Vol. VII. Berkeley: University of California Press.

Hoetink, Harry. 1967. *The Two Variants in Caribbean Race Relations: A Contribution to the Sociology of Segmented Societies*. London: Oxford University Press.

Hoffmann, Odile. 2002. "Collective Memory and Ethnic Identities in the Colombian Pacific." *Journal of Latin American Anthropology* 7.2: 118–38.

Hooker, Juliet. 2005a. "Indigenous Inclusion/Black Exclusion: Race, Ethnicity and Multicultural Citizenship in Latin America." *Journal of Latin American Studies* 37: 1–26.

———. 2005b. "'Beloved Enemies': Race and Official Mestizo Nationalism in Nicaragua." *Latin American Research Review* 40.3: 14–39.

Horton, Lynn. 2006. "Contesting State Multiculturalisms: Indigenous Land Struggles in Eastern Panama." *Journal of Latin American Studies* 38.4: 829–58.

Htun, Mala. 2004. "From 'Racial Democracy' to Affirmative Action: Changing State Policy on Race in Brazil." *Latin American Research Review* 39.1: 60–89.

Hulme, Peter. 1986. *Colonial Encounters: Europe and the Native Caribbean, 1492–1797*. New York: Routledge.

IHAH (Instituto Hondureño de Antropología e Historia) y CONPAH (Confederación de Pueblos Autóctonos de Honduras). 1993. *Apuntes Sobre los Pueblos Autóctonos de Honduras*. Tegucigalpa, Honduras: IHAH, CONPAH y Programa de las Naciones Unidas para el Desarrollo.

Inter-American Development Bank. n.d. *Program to Support Indigenous and Black Communities (PAPIN) (HO-0193)*. Tegucigalpa, Honduras: Inter-American Development Bank.

Inter-American Dialogue. 2004. *Race Report*. Washington, D.C.: Inter-American Dialogue.

Jackson, Jean E., and Kay B. Warren. 2005. "Indigenous Movements in Latin America, 1992–2004: Controversies, Ironies, New Directions." *Annual Review of Anthropology* 34: 549–73.

Jackson, John L., Jr. 2005. *Real Black: Adventures in Racial Sincerity*. Chicago: University of Chicago Press.

Jackson, Jeffrey. 2005. *The Globalizers: Development Workers in Action*. Baltimore: Johns Hopkins University Press.

Jenkins, Carol. 1983. "Ritual and Resource Flow: The Garifuna 'Dugu'." *American Ethnologist* 10.3: 429–42.

Johnson, Paul Christopher. 2007. *Diaspora Conversions: Black Carib Religion and the Rediscovery of Africa*. Berkeley: University of California Press.

Kelley, Robin. 1994. *Race Rebels: Culture, Politics, and the Black Working Class*. New York: Free Press.

Kepner, Charles, and J. H. Soothill. 1967 [1935]. *The Banana Empire*. New York: Russell and Russell.

Kerns, Virginia. 1983. *Women and the Ancestors: Black Carib Kinship and Ritual*. Champaign: University of Illinois Press.

Khan, Aisha. 1987. "Migration and Life-Cycle among Garifuna (Black Carib) Street Vendors." *Women's Studies* 13.3: 183–98.

_____. 2004a. "Sacred Subversions? Syncretic Creoles, the Indo-Caribbean, and 'Culture's In-between.'" *Radical History Review* 89: 165–84.

_____. 2004b. *Callaloo Nation: Metaphors of Race and Religious Identity among South Asians in Trinidad.* Durham: Duke University Press.

Kirtsoglou, Elisabeth, and Dimitrious Theodossopoulos. 2004. "'They are Taking Our Culture Away': Tourism and Cultural Commodification in the Garifuna Community of Roatan." *Critique of Anthropology* 24.2: 135–57.

Kreimer, Osvaldo. 2003. *Report of the Rapporteur: Meeting of the Working Groups on the Fifth Section of the Draft Declaration with Special Emphasis on 'Traditional Forms of Ownership and Cultural Survival, Right to Land and Territories'.* Washington, D.C.: Permanent Council of the Organization of American States.

Kuper, Adam. 2003. "The Return of the Native." *Current Anthropology* 44.3: 389–95.

Labalenú, Marco. 1903. "La Ceiba." *Diario de Honduras.* 21 October.

Lacayo Sambulá, Gloria Marina. 1998. *Bosquejo de la Vida del Primer Médico Garífuna de Honduras.* New York: La Sociedad Garífuna Prometra, Inc.

Lafleur, Gérard. 1996. "The Passing of a Nation: The Carib Indians of the Lesser Antilles." *Amerindians, Africans, Americans: Three Papers in Caribbean History.* Kingston, Jamaica: Canoe Press. 3–20.

Lancaster, Roger. 1992. *Life Is Hard: Machismo, Danger, and the Intimacy of Power in Nicaragua.* Berkeley: University of California Press.

Lang, Julio. 1951. "Espectro Racial de Honduras." *América Indígena* 11.3: 209–17.

Lavie, Smadar, and Ted Swedenburg, eds. 1996. *Displacement, Diaspora, and Geographies of Identity.* Durham: Duke University Press.

Lewis, Martin W., and Kären E. Wigen. 1997. *The Myth of Continents: A Critique of Metageography.* Berkeley: University of California Press.

Li, Tania. 2007. *The Will to Improve: Governmentality, Development, and the Practice of Politics.* Durham: Duke University Press.

Lipsitz, George. 1998. *The Possessive Investment in Whiteness: How White People Profit from Identity Politics.* Philadelphia: Temple University Press.

Lombraña, Martiniano. 1996. *Realidad Socio-Económica de Honduras.* La Ceiba, Honduras: Talleres Claret.

López García, Víctor Virgilio. 1993. *Lamumehan Garifuna: Clamor Garifuna.* n.p.

_____. 1994. *La Bahía del Puerto del Sol y la Masacre de los Garífunas de San Juan.* Tegucigalpa, Honduras: Editorial Guaymuras.

Lunardi, Federico. 1946. *Honduras Maya.* San Pedro Sula, Honduras: Compañia Editora de Honduras.

Manzanares, Rafael. 1960. *Por las Sendas del Folklore.* Tegucigalpa, Honduras: Imprenta Calderón.

Martínez Lalin, Livio. 1957. "Los Habitantes Morenos de Honduras." Tesis de Grado, Escuela Normal Rural 'El Edén'. Comayagua, Honduras.

Martínez Landero, Francisco. 1942. "Aspectos del Indigenismo en la República de Honduras." *Revista del Archivo y Biblioteca Nacional* 20.11: 706–10.

Martínez, Marquez. 2003. *Marco Conceptual para la Intervención en las Comunidades Indígenas y Negros con el Proyecto 'Facilitación del Comercio e Incremento de la Competitividad'*. Tegucigalpa, Honduras: Banco Mundial Honduras.

Martínez, Sebastian. 1963. *El Folklore en la Tierra de los Pinos*. n.p.

Marx, Anthony W. 1998. *Making Race and Nation: A Comparison of the United States, South Africa, and Brazil*. New York: Cambridge University Press.

Matory, J. Lorand. 2005. *Black Atlantic Religion: Tradition, Transnationalism, and Matriarchy in the Afro-Brazilian Candomblé*. Princeton: Princeton University Press.

McCommon, Carolyn. 1982. "Mating as a Reproductive Strategy: A Black Carib Example." Ph.D. Thesis. Pennsylvania State University.

Medina Bardales, Marel. 1995. *Estudios Sociales, Rendimientos Básicos, Ciclo Común, Primer Curso*. Tegucigalpa, Honduras: Secretaría de Educación Pública.

Mejía, Medardo. 1980. *Froylán Turcios en los Campos de la Estética y el Civismo*. Tegucigalpa, Honduras: Universidad Nacional Autónoma de Honduras.

Miller, Marilyn Grace. 2004. *Rise and Fall of the Cosmic Race: The Cult of Mestizaje in Latin America*. Austin: University of Texas Press.

"Minorías Étnicas." 1976. *Sectante, Revista del Ministerio de Cultura* 1.4: 28–31.

Mintz, Sidney W., and Richard Price. 1992 [1972]. *The Birth of African–American Culture: an Anthropological Perspective*. Boston: Beacon Press.

Miralda, Timoteo. 1904. "Carta de Timoteo Miralda." *Diario del Honduras*. 11 May.

Molina, Vallecillo. 2006. "¿Hasta Cuando?" *El Heraldo*. 4 April. http://www.elheraldo.hn (accessed 23 May 2007).

Muñoz Tabora, Jesús. 1984a. *El Folklore en Honduras*. Tegucigalpa, Honduras: Secretaría de Cultura y Turismo.

_____. 1984b. *Folklore y Educación en Honduras*. Tegucigalpa, Honduras: Secretaría de Cultura y Turismo.

Nash, June C. 2001. *Maya Visions: The Quest for Autonomy in an Age of Globalization*. New York: Routledge.

Ng'weno, Bettina. 2007a. "Can Ethnicity Replace Race? Afro-Colombians, Indigeneity and the Colombian Multicultural State." *Journal of Latin American and Caribbean Anthropology* 12.2: 414–40.

_____. 2007b. *Turf Wars: Territory and Citizenship in the Contemporary State*. Palo Alto: Stanford University Press.

Niezen, Ronald. 2003. *The Origins of Indigenism: Human Rights and the Politics of Identity*. Berkeley: University of California Press.

Nuñez Chinchilla, Jesús. 1960. *El Panorama Indigenista de la República de Honduras, Centro América*. Tegucigalpa, Honduras: Publicaciones de la Secretaría de Educación Pública.

ODECO (Organización de Desarrollo Étnico Comunitario). 1995. "12 de Octubre 1492–12 de Octubre 1995." La Ceiba, Honduras: ODECO. Mimeograph.

———. 2001. "Compromiso de Campaña del Candidato Presidencial del Partido Nacional." La Ceiba, Honduras: ODECO. Mimeograph.

———. 2007. "Problemática Tierra Comunidades Garifunas Paso a Paso." http://www.garinet.com (accessed 12 October 2005).

Offen, Karl. 2003. "The Territorial Turn: Making Black Territories in Pacific Colombia." *Journal of Latin American Geography* 2.1: 43–73.

OFRANEH (Organización Fraternal Negra Hondureña). 1999. *Ley de Demarcacíon y Legalizacíon de las Tierras y Territorios del Pueblo Garífuna.* Unpublished draft.

———. 2002a. *Perfil del Pueblo Garifuna, Primera Versión.* La Ceiba, Honduras: OFRANEH. Mimeograph.

———. 2002b. "Comunicado Público, Sambo Creek." Public e-mail communication. 21 November.

———. 2005a. "Declaración de Unidad de los Pueblos Indígenas y Negros de Honduras." Public e-mail communication. 11 July.

———. 2005b. "Persecution of Garifunas." Public e-mail communication. 28 March.

———. 2005c. "El PATH, la Represión y la Amenaza a las Comunidades." Public e-mail communication. 9 June.

———. 2006a. *Request for Inspection* (Credit No. 3858-HO). http://www.worldbank.org (accessed 1 August 2007).

———. 2006b. "Acta de Entendimiento entre la OFRANEH y Autoridades del Estado de Honduras." Public e-mail communication. 6 October.

———. 2006c. "Petición de Ofraneh al Panel de Inspección del Banco Mundial." Public e-mail communication. 2 February.

———. 2006d. "¡¡La Violencia y el Racismo de los Padres de la Patria¡¡" Public e-mail communication. 3 April.

Oquelí, Ramón. 1977. "Gobiernos Hondureños durante el Presente Siglo." *Economía Política* 13: 5–50.

Ortega, Pompilio. 1946. *Patrios Lares.* Tegucigalpa, Honduras: Imprenta Calderón.

Oxford English Dictionary. 1971. Oxford: Oxford University Press.

Pagden, Anthony. 1982. *The Fall of Natural Man: The American Indian Origins of Comparative Ethnology.* Cambridge: Cambridge University Press.

Palacio, Joseph. 2000. "A Reconsideration of the Native American and African Roots of Garifuna Identity." Professional Agricultural Workers Conference, 58th Session, Tuskegee University, 3–5 December. http://www.kacike.org (accessed 11 May 2003).

Palmié, Stephan. 2002. *Wizards and Scientists: Explorations in Afro-Cuban Modernity and Tradition.* Durham: Duke University Press.

Pastor Fasquelle, Rodolfo. 1997. "Ser Garífuna." *El Tiempo.* 14 April.

Pavón, Victor Hugo. 1997. "Problemas Comunes Comparte la Población Negra en Centroamérica." *El Heraldo.* 12 April.

de la Peña, Guillermo. 2005. "Social and Cultural Politics toward Indigenous Peoples: Perspectives from Latin America." *Annual Review of Anthropology* 34: 717–39.

Perry, Marc. 1999. "Garifuna Youth in New York City: Race, Ethnicity, and the Performance of Diasporic Identities." M.A. Thesis. University of Texas at Austin.

Pine, Adrienne. 2008. *Working Hard, Drinking Hard: On Violence and Survival in Honduras.* Berkeley: University of California Press.

Pineda, Juan Francisco. 1996. "Festival Caribe de Danzas Folklóricas Garifunas." *El Tiempo.* 23 May.

Posas, Mario. 1981. "El Problema Negro: Racismo y Explotación en las Bananeras." *Alcaraván* 9: 6–9.

Postero, Nancy Grey. 2007. *Now We are Citizens: Indigenous Politics in Postmulticultural Bolivia.* Palo Alto: Stanford University Press.

Postero, Nancy Grey, and Leon Zamosc. 2004. *The Struggle for Indigenous Rights in Latin America.* East Sussex, UK: Sussex Academic Press.

Povinelli, Elizabeth. 2002. *The Cunning of Recognition: Indigenous Alterities and the Making of Australian Multiculturalism.* Durham: Duke University Press.

Putnam, Lara. 2002. *The Company They Kept: Migrants and the Politics of Gender in Caribbean Costa Rica, 1870–1960.* Chapel Hill: University of North Carolina Press.

Ramos, Miguel. 1929. "Exploración de Corozo en La Mosquitia y Dpto. de Atlántida." *Revista del Archivo y Biblioteca Nacional* 8.4: 118–23, 180–87, 286–94, 405–8, 430–35.

Rappaport, Joanne. 2005. *Intercultural Utopias: Public Intellectuals, Cultural Experimentation, and Ethnic Pluralism in Colombia.* Durham: Duke University Press.

Reina, Carlos Roberto. 1997. "¡Doscientos Años Después!" *El Heraldo.* 20 April.

República de Ecuador. 1998. *Constitución Política de la República de Ecuador de 1998.* http://www.pdba.georgetown.edu/Constitutions/Ecuador/ecuador98.html (accessed 23 June 2008).

República de Honduras. 1996 [1982]. *Constitución de la República y sus Reformas.* Tegucigalpa, Honduras: Graficentro Editores.

———. 1993. *Ley General Del Ambiente, Decreto No. 104-93.* Tegucigalpa, Honduras: Secretaría de Recursos Naturales y Ambiente.

———. 1994. *Acuerdo de Creación de la Educación Bilingüe Intercultural.* Tegucigalpa, Honduras: Secretaría de Educación Pública.

———. 2001. *Censo de Poblacíon y Vivenda.* Tegucigalpa, Honduras: Instituto Nacional de Estadísticas. http://www.ine-hn.org (accessed 11 August 2008).

———. 2004. *Ley de Propiedad, Decreto Número 82-2004.* Tegucigalpa, Honduras: Secretaría de Estado del Despacho Presidencial.

Restrepo, Eduardo. 2002. "Políticas de la Alteridad: Etnización de 'Comunidad Negra' en el Pacífico Sur Colombiano." *Journal of Latin American Anthropology* 7.2: 34–59.

_____. 2007. "Commentary: El 'Giro al Mutliculturalismo' desde un Encuadre Afro-Indígena." *Journal of Latin American and Caribbean Anthropology* 12.2: 475–86.

Rivas, Ramón D. 1993. *Pueblos Indígenas y Garífuna de Honduras*. Tegucigalpa, Honduras: Editorial Guaymuras.

Robins, Steven. 2003. "Response to Kuper's 'Return of the Native.'" *Current Anthropology* 44.3: 398–99.

Robinson, Cedric. 1983. *Black Marxism: The Making of the Black Radical Tradition*. London: Zed Books.

Robinson, William. 2003. *Transnational Conflicts: Central America, Social Change, and Globalization*. New York: Verso.

Rodríguez, Ivonne. 2006. "Racismo: Parlamentario Confiesa su Desprecio por los Negros." *Proceso Digital*. 29 March. http://www.proceso.hn (accessed 23 May 2006).

Roldán Ortiga, Roque. 2004. *Models for Recognizing Indigenous Land Rights in Latin America, Paper No. 99*. Washington, D.C.: International Bank for Reconstruction and Development/World Bank.

Rosa, Ruben Angel. 1952. *Tradiciones Hondureñas*. n.p.

Sahlins, Marshall. 1999. "What is Anthropological Enlightenment? Some Lessons of the Twentieth Century." *Annual Review of Anthropology* 28: 1–23.

Sanchez Gutierrez, Enrique, and Roque Roldán Ortiga. 2002. *Titulación de los Territorios Comunales Afrocolombianos e Indígenas en la Costa Pacífica de Colombia*. New York: World Bank.

Sansone, Livio. 2003. *Blackness without Ethnicity: Constructing Race in Brazil*. New York: Palgrave Macmillan.

Sawyer, Suzanne. 2004. *Crude Chronicles: Indigenous Politics, Multinational Oil, and Neoliberalism in Ecuador*. Durham: Duke University Press.

Scheper-Hughes, Nancy. 1992. *Death without Weeping: The Violence of Everyday Life in Brazil*. Berkeley: University of California Press.

Scott, David. 1991. "That Event, This Memory: Notes on the Anthropology of African Diasporas in the New World." *Diaspora* 1: 261–83.

_____. 1999. *Refashioning Futures: Criticism after Postcoloniality*. Princeton: Princeton University Press.

SECPLAN (Secretaría de Planificación, Coordinación y Presupuesto). 1987. *Memoria Primer Seminario Taller con los Grupos Étnicos Autóctonos de Honduras, Celebrada en Comayagua del 23 al 24 de Julio de 1987*. Tegucigalpa, Honduras: SECPLAN.

Selva Rendón, Rafael Murillo. 1997. *Loubavagu*. Tegucigalpa, Honduras: Litografía López.

Sieder, Rachel. 1995. "Honduras: The Politics of Exception and Military Reformism (1972–1978)." *Journal of Latin American Studies* 27: 99–127.

Sieder, Rachel, ed. 2002. *Multiculturalism in Latin America: Indigenous Rights, Diversity, and Democracy*. New York: Palgrave Macmillan.

Siegel, Micol. 2001. "The Point of Comparison: Transnational Racial Construction, Brazil and the United States, 1918–1933." Ph.D. Thesis. New York University.

Siu, Lok. 2005. *Memories of a Future Home: Diasporic Citizenship of Chinese in Panama.* Palo Alto: Stanford University Press.

Soluri, John. 1998. "Landscape and Livelihood: An Agroecological History of Export Banana Growing in Honduras, 1870–1975." Ph.D. Thesis. University of Michigan.

_____. 2005. *Banana Cultures: Agriculture, Consumption & Environmental Change in Honduras & the United States.* Austin: University of Texas Press.

Speed, Shannon, and María Teresa Sierra. 2005. "Critical Perspectives on Human Rights and Multiculturalism in Neoliberal Latin America, Introduction." *PoLAR: Political and Legal Anthropology Review* 28.1: 1–9.

Stavenhagen, Rodolfo. 1992. "Challenging the Nation-State in Latin America." *Journal of International Affairs* 34.2: 421–40.

Stepan, Nancy Leys. 1991. *'The Hour of Eugenics': Race, Gender, and Nation in Latin America.* Ithaca: Cornell University Press.

Stocks, Anthony. 1992. "Land War: Land Barons Responded with Murder after Indians in Honduras Organized to Recover their Land." *Cultural Survival Quarterly* 16.4: 16–18.

_____. 2005. "Too Much for Too Few: Problems of Indigenous Land Rights in Latin America." *Annual Review of Anthropology* 34: 85–104.

Stoler, Ann. 2002. *Carnal Knowledge and Imperial Power: Race and the Intimate in Colonial Rule.* Berkeley: University of California Press.

Taussig, Michael. 1980. *The Devil and Commodity Fetishism in South America.* Chapel Hill: University of North Carolina Press.

_____. 1987. *Shamanism, Colonialism, and the Wild Man: A Study in Terror and Healing.* Chicago: University of Chicago Press.

_____. 1996. "The Construction of America: The Anthropologist as Columbus." *Culture/Contexture: Explorations in Anthropology and Literary Studies.* Eds. E. V. Daniel and J. M. Peck. Berkeley: University of California Press. 323–56.

Taylor, Douglas. 1951. *The Black Caribs of British Honduras.* New York: Viking Fund Publications in Anthropology.

Thomas, Deborah. 2004. *Modern Blackness: Nationalism, Globalization, and the Politics of Culture in Jamaica.* Durham: Duke University Press.

Thomas, Deborah, and Kamari Maxine Clarke. 2006. "Introduction: Globalization and the Transformations of Race." *Globalization and Race: Transformations in the Cultural Production of Blackness.* Eds. K. M. Clarke and D. A. Thomas. Durham: Duke University Press. 1–34.

de la Torre, Carlos. 2005. "Afro-Ecuadorian Responses to Racism: Between Citizenship and Corporatism." *Neither Enemies nor Friends: Latinos, Blacks, Afro-Latinos.* Eds. A. Dzidzienyo and S. Oboler. New York: Palgrave Macmillan. 61–74.

Tsing, Anna. 2002. "Conclusion: The Global Situation." *The Anthropology of Globaliza-tion: A Reader.* Eds. J. X. Inda and R. Rosaldo. Malden: Blackwell Publishing. 453–85.

_____. 2007. "Indigenous Voice." *Indigenous Experiençe Today.* Eds. M. de la Cadena and O. Starn. Oxford: Berg Publishers. 33–67.

_____. 2009. "Supply Chains and the Human Condition" *Rethinking Marxim* 21.2: 148–76.

Turcios, Froylán. 1980 [1924]. *Boletín de la Defensa Nacional.* Tegucigalpa, Hondu-ras: Editorial Guaymuras.

Turner, J. Michael. 2005. "Unfinished Business in the Western Hemisphere: Afro Latinos and Compensatory Programs for Social Inclusion." First International Conference of the Affirmative Action Studies Network, Rio de Janeiro, Brazil, 3–7 Jan. 2005.

Twine, France Winddance. 1998. *Racism in a Racial Democracy: The Maintenance of White Supremacy in Brazil.* New Brunswick: Rutgers University Press.

United Nations Development Program. 2005. *Human Development Report: Inter-national Cooperation at a Crossroads: Aid, Trade, and Security in an Unequal World.* New York: United Nations Development Program.

Urbina, Nicolas. 1950. "Discriminación Racial." *Vanguardia Revolucionaria.* 1 April.

Van Cott, Donna Lee. 1994. "Indigenous Peoples and Democracy: Issues for Policy Makers." *Indigenous Peoples and Democracy in Latin America.* Ed. D. L. Van Cott. New York: St. Martin's Press. 1–27.

_____. 2000. *The Friendly Liquidation of the Past: The Politics of Diversity in Latin America.* Pittsburgh: University of Pittsburgh Press.

Vargas, João. 2003. "The Inner City and the Favela: Transnational Black Politics." *Race & Class* 44.4: 19–40.

Wade, Peter. 1993. *Blackness and Race Mixture: The Dynamics of Racial Identity in Columbia.* Baltimore: Johns Hopkins University Press.

_____. 1995. "The Cultural Politics of Blackness in Colombia." *American Ethnologist* 22.2: 341–57.

_____. 1997. *Race and Ethnicity in Latin America.* London: Pluto Press.

_____. 2000. *Music, Race, & Nation: Música Tropical in Colombia.* Chicago: University of Chicago Press.

_____. 2002. "Introduction: The Columbian Pacific in Perspective." *Journal of Latin American Anthropology* 7.2: 2–33.

_____. 2006. "Afro-Latin Studies: Reflections on the Field." *Latin American and Caribbean Ethnic Studies* 1.1: 105–24.

Walsh, Catherine, and Juan García. 2002. "El Pensar del Emergente Movimiento Afroecuatoriano: Reflexiones (des)de un Processo." *Estudio y Otras Prácticas Int-electuales Latinoamericanas en Cultura y Poder.* Ed. D. Mato. Caracas, Venezuela: Consejo Latinoamericano de Ciencias Sociales y CEAP, FACES, Universidad Central de Venezuela. 317–26.

Warren, Kay. 1998. *Indigenous Movements and their Critics*. Princeton: Princeton University Press.

Warren, Kay, and Jean Jackson, eds. 2002. *Indigenous Movements, Self-Representation, and the State in Latin America*. Austin: University of Texas Press.

Warren, Jonathan. 2001. *Racial Revolutions: Antiracism and Indian Resurgence in Brazil*. Durham: Duke University Press.

Warren, Jonathan, and France Winddance Twine. 2002. "Critical Race Studies in Latin America: Recent Advances, Recurrent Weaknesses." *A Companion to Racial and Ethnic Studies*. Eds. D. T. Goldberg and J. Solomos. Oxford: Blackwell Publishing. 538–60.

Watkins, S. Craig. 1998. *Representing: Hip Hop Culture and the Production of Black Cinema*. Chicago: University of Chicago Press.

Whitten, Norman. 1981. "Introduction." *Cultural Transformations and Ethnicity in Modern Ecuador*. Ed. N. Whitten. Champaign: University of Illinois Press. 1–44.

_____. 2007. "The Longue Durée of Racial Fixity and the Transformative Conjunctures of Racial Blending." *Journal of Latin American and Caribbean Anthropology* 12.2: 356–83.

Whitten, Norman, and Arlene Torres. 1992. "The Black Americas, 1492–1992." *NACLA Report on the Americas* 26.4: 16–22.

Williams, Brackette. 1989. "A Class Act: Anthropology and the Race to Nation Across Ethnic Terrain." *Annual Review of Anthropology* 18: 401–44.

Winant, Howard. 2001. *The World Is a Ghetto: Race and Democracy since World War II*. New York: Basic Books.

Wolf, Otto Martin. 1998. "Mientras Tanto, Aquí en la Dulce Honduras." *La Prensa*. 4 June. http://www.laprensahn.com (accessed 11 December 1999).

World Bank. 2006. *Bank Management Response to Request for Inspection Panel Review of the Honduran Land Administration Project* (Credit No. 3858-HO). http://www.worldbank.org (accessed 1 August 2007).

World Bank Inspection Panel. 2007. *Investigation Report: Honduras: Land Administration Project, Report No. 39933-HN*. http://www.worldbank.org (accessed 22 August 2008).

Wouters, Mieke. 2002. "Comunidades Negras, Derechos Étnicos y Desplazamiento Forzado en el Atrato Medio: Respuestas Organizativas en Medio de la Guerra." *Afrodescendientes en las Américas: Trayectorias Sociales e Identitarias*. Eds. C. Mosquera, M. Pardo, and O. Hoffmann. Bogotá, Colombia: Universidad Nacional de Colombia, ICANH, IRD, ILSA. 369–97.

Wright, Richard. 1953. "Introduction." *In the Castle of My Skin*, by George Lamming. New York: McGraw-Hill Book Company. v–viii.

Yashar, Deborah. 1999. "Democracy, Indigenous Movements, and the Postliberal Challenge in Latin America." *World Politics* 52.1: 76–104.

Yelvington, Kevin. 2006. "The Invention of Africa in Latin America and the Caribbean: Political Discourse and Anthropological Praxis, 1920–1940." *Afro-Atlantic Dialogues: Anthropology in the Diaspora*. Ed. K. Yelvington. Santa Fe: School of American Research Press. 35–82.

Yudice, George. 2003. *The Expediency of Culture: Uses of Culture in the Global Era*. Durham: Duke University Press.

Žižek, Slavoj. 1997. "Multiculturalism, or, the Cultural Logic of Multinational Capitalism." *New Left Review* 225: 28–51.

Index

17; ethnic value of, 80–81; Garifuna and, 16–17, 24, 72, 182, 198; indigenous peoples and, 109, 135, 136, 143, 145, 147; mestizos and, 193, 239; New World, 1, 10, 11, 16, 17, 235, 243n7; violence against, 82; blancos, 56–61, 184, 185, 227, 255

Boas, Franz, 10

Boyz II Men, 6

Boyz n' the Hood (film), 183, 188

brand names, 181, 192, 190–96

Brondo, Keri, 165, 219, 221, 228, 253n14

Brown, Jacqueline, 19

Browne, Sir Thomas, 1

Bueso Melgen, Romualdo, 168

Caceres, Vicente, 91, 92, 93

Cacho, Sixto, 89–90, 91, 92, 101, 102

Cacho Gil, Omar, 143, 144

CADEAH. *See* Honduran Advisory Council for the Development of Autochthonous Ethnic Groups

CAFTA. *See* Central American Free Trade Agreement

Callejas, Rafael, 26, 126, 127

capital investment, 150, 154, 169

capitalism, 139, 173, 176, 199; global, 177, 178, 190, 196; neoliberal, 235; racialized, 28, 197, 251n4

Carías Andino, Tiburcio, 51, 77, 78, 86, 91, 101, 219; racism and, 63

Carib language, 115

Caribs, 3, 61, 73, 75, 76, 84, 86, 89, 90, 103, 114, 115, 170; British and, 4; French and, 243n1; Honduran, 87; morenos and, 88, 100; negros and, 85; origins of, 5, 74

Carlos, John, 173

Castillo, Miguel Angel, 219

Castillo family, 219, 220, 226; property rights of, 56, 222

Catholic Church, 93, 119, 124

Cayos Cochinos, 42, 128, 215, 219

CCARC. *See* Central American and Caribbean Research Council

Centeno García, Santos, 97, 100, 248n44

Central American and Caribbean Research Council (CCARC), 155, 250n5

Central American Bank Organization (CABO), 161

Central American Free Trade Agreement (CAFTA), 168, 250n14

Central Intelligence Agency, 4

Chancunu, 91, 92

Chiapas, 127, 128, 153

Chortí, 24, 122, 167

civil rights, 99, 117, 118, 142, 165, 189; cultural rights and, 143; racism and, 164

civil society, 61, 62, 124, 140, 156, 159

civilization, 94, 95, 113

class, 208–11; culture and, 230

class differentiation, 30, 41, 42, 44, 196, 205, 211

class status, 44–49

Coelho, Ruy, 9, 10, 77, 78, 95, 100, 245n1, 245n8; fieldwork by, 73; on Garifuna/mestizo, 74–75

Colindres, Mejia, 81

collective rights, 31, 154, 164, 165, 169

Colón, 83, 92, 130, 156

Colón, Amilcar, 145, 146, 159

Colonia Libertad, 51, 52; map of, 53

Colonia Suazo, 51, 52

colonialism, 15, 32, 58, 95, 129

Columbus, 1, 15, 90, 128, 129, 185

Columbus Day, 2, 125, 128, 133

Combs, Sean (Puff Diddy), 31–32, 172–73

National Development Plan, 150
National Indigenous Institute (IIH), 119, 120, 121
National Institute of Statistics, 57
National Labor Organization, 172
National Party, 78, 86, 112, 138, 156, 163, 167
nationalism, 17, 32, 172; Black, 7, 117; British, 18; Honduran, 7, 25, 33, 61, 73, 87; Indo-Hispanic, 78–82, 88, 90, 92, 100; Jamaican Creole, 177; mestizo, 26, 30
nativism, 17, 19, 21, 244n14
negro, 1, 4, 5, 15, 28, 56–61, 67, 76, 77, 86, 87, 88, 101, 102, 124, 136, 193, 207, 209, 227; blancos and, 185; Caribs and, 85; Communist Party and, 81; cultural origins of, 9–13; defined, 14, 70, 256; Garifuna and, 59; gringo and, 189; hair/physique of, 185; image of, 65; public self-affirmation of, 60; as race, 14; self-evaluation of, 68
neoimperialism, 132, 150
neoliberal economy, 204, 205, 231
neoliberal multiculturalism, 28, 32, 139–40, 157, 169, 230
neoliberal reforms, 28, 41, 107, 126, 174
neoliberalism, 21, 26, 138, 139, 140, 142, 150, 157, 170, 206, 218, 228, 230; Garifuna and, 27; Garifuna organizations and, 31, 165; green, 250n4; ODECO and, 165; OFRANEH and, 152–53; social welfare and, 107; territoriality and, 152
New Jack City (movie), 183
New World Blacks, 1, 10, 11, 16, 17, 235, 243n7
NGOs. *See* nongovernmental organizations
Nike, 192, 193, 194, 195, 196, 197, 206, 207

nongovernmental organizations (NGOs), 27, 67, 129, 134, 145, 156, 158, 159, 160, 198
North American Free Trade Agreement (NAFTA), 152, 153, 166, 172
North Coast, 93, 97, 98, 112, 155; banana trade and, 79, 80 (map); black population on, 83; Caribs on, 90; enclave economy of, 26, 95; ethnoracial differentiation on, 30, 82; land speculation on, 27; politics on, 82; progress on, 85, 79

October Revolution, PDRH and, 97
ODECO. *See* Organización de Desarrollo Étnico Comunitario
Office of High Commissioner for Human Rights, 162
Office of Tourism, 111
OFRANEH. *See* Black Fraternal Organization of Honduras
ONILH, 144, 147
Organización de Desarrollo Étnico Comunitario (ODECO), 2, 31, 59, 104, 129, 167, 168, 206, 207, 215, 219, 235, 238; Afro-visibility and, 142, 160–63; anti-discrimination legislation and, 237; anti-racism and, 170; Garifuna and, 165–66, 169–70, 171; indigeneity and, 2, 126; Maduro and, 163; neoliberalism and, 165; OFRANEH and, 161; political programs/strategies by, 164–65; as progovernment organization, 156; protest by, 125, 131; racial discrimination and, 162; World Conference and, 162

Palacio, Joseph, 233
Palacios, Carlos, 143
Palma Real Beach Resort and Casino, 214–15, 216, 217

Red Caribs, 3
Regional Seminar on Afro-
descendants in the Americas, 162
Reina, Carlos Roberto, 104, 126, 127,
134, 137, 138, 150; ethnic discourse
of, 113; national prosperity and,
105–6
rituals, 84, 93, 179; photo of, 114
Roots (TV miniseries), 117
Rosenthal, Jaime, 150

St. Vincent, 12, 71, 75, 84, 93, 102, 115,
203; deportation from, 2; Garifuna
on, 3, 4; Island Carib on, 5
Sambeños, 204, 207, 208, 209, 212, 215;
ancestrality and, 222; land recovery
by, 218–22, 227
Sambo Creek, 5, 8, 28, 32, 35, 36, 46,
49, 67, 83, 113, 129; ancestral rights
in, 222; cemetery in, 50; class in,
41–45, 208–11; community in,
37, 39; construction work in, 43;
dispossession of, 221; economic
opportunities in, 42–43; fieldwork
in, 4, 37–42; Garifuna in, 51, 55;
INA and, 221; indigeneity in, 200,
227; map of, 53; mestizos in, 66;
photo of, 38, 52; play from, 202–3;
racism in, 64; residential patterns
in, 52; sociality in, 40, 208–11;
transmigration from, 42, 208–11;
work in, 44, 45, 213
San Juan, 83, 150, 245n10, 246n11
San Pedro Sula, 4, 22, 216; maquiladoras of, 44, 194, 223; working in, 47,
66–67
Sansone, Livio, 176
Scientific-Academic-Volunteer-
Educational (SAVE) Tourism, 217
Scott, David, 10, 16
Sean Jean, 173–74, 192, 197, 239

Secretaría de Planificación, Coordinación y Presupuesto (SECPLAN),
121, 122, 133, 249n13
segregation, 36, 70, 97, 100, 164
Selassie, Haile, 174, 199–200, 246n10
self-representation, 13, 20, 30, 31, 72,
78, 103, 200, 238; Garifuna, 68, 100;
multiple forms of, 7
Selva Rendón, Rafael Murillo, 203
SFCO. *See* Standard Fruit Company
slavery, 10, 13, 15, 76, 101, 102, 233;
Garifuna and, 73, 115, 116; history
of, 78, 117
Smith, Tommie, 173
social exclusion, 164, 165
social hierarchy, 55, 58, 67
social justice, 140, 150
social mobility, 28, 47, 63, 197, 204,
205, 211
social relations, 17, 36, 63, 68, 73,
205, 208
sociality, 208–11
Sociedad de Artesanos el Progresso, 80
Society of Geography and History of
Honduras, 91
Soluri, John, 87
Space Jam (movie), 179
Special Prosecutor for the Ethnic
Groups, 143, 220
spirituality, 40, 46, 93, 202, 206, 211
Standard Fruit Company (SFCO), 51,
70, 79, 219; employees of, 42, 86;
strike and, 96
stereotypes, 5, 32, 48, 106, 110, 133, 175,
177; Black, 32, 71, 195, 208; Creole,
71; Garifuna, 62, 65–66, 67, 134,
190; mestizo, 62, 65; racial-cultural,
199; significance of, 65–66
Stoler, Ann, 25
strike (1954), 96, 97, 99, 100
Suazo, Felipe, 51

MARK ANDERSON is an assistant professor of anthropology at the University of California, Santa Cruz.